The Minnesota Beautician and Photographer Who Went to War: Monnie Palmatier and Al Payton

WOMEN

There's work to be done and a war to be won... **NOW!**

SEE YOUR U. S. EMPLOYMENT SERVICE

The Minnesota Beautician and Photographer Who Went to War:
Monnie Palmatier and Al Payton

A Detailed Reference and Guidebook for Genealogy Research

Kathleen M. Cargill

BEEKEEPERS PRESS

DULUTH, MINNESOTA

The Minnesota Beautician and Photographer Who Went to War: Monnie Palmatier and Al Payton

A Detailed Reference and Guidebook for Genealogy Research

Copyright © 2020 Kathleen M. Cargill

All rights reserved. No part of this book may be reproduced in any form, except short excerpts for review and educational purposes, without the written permission of the publisher.

ISBN 978-0-9890478-8-3

Printed and bound in the United States of America
Book layout and design by Marlene Wisuri, Dovetailed Press LLC

Cover photo and interior photographs are from the collection of Kathleen M. Cargill except where credited. Interior and cover graphics and posters – public domain. Cover texture from http://www.textures4photoshop.com.

BEEKEEPERS PRESS
DULUTH, MINNESOTA

Table of contents

- 7   Dedication
- 7   Research Paths
- 11   Preface
- 12   Minnesota's Contributions to the Homefront
- 17   The Palmatier Family of Osakis, Minnesota
  - 18   Abraham Palmatier and Henrietta McKeel
  - 18   Horace Palmatier and Mary Ann Asper
  - 21   Claude J. Palmatier and Emma Wharton
  - 22   The Palmatier Siblings
    - 22   Manuella Joyce Palmatier
    - 26   Claudette Louise Palmatier
    - 27   Wharton Horace Palmatier
    - 30   Winston Erret Palmatier
  - 33   The Palmatier Family in the 1930s
  - 34   The Palmatier Family in the 1940s
- 37   The Government Clerk at Erie Proving Ground: Manuella "Monnie" Palmatier
  - 37   Starting the Job
  - 46   An Undiagnosed Medical Condition
  - 48   Work at the U.S. Army Ordnance Department
  - 54   Resignation as a Government Clerk
- 58   Chief Petty Officer Aerographer Mate: Alfred James "A.J." Payton
  - 58   Civilian Tour of Duty: Civilian Conservation Corps
  - 61   U.S. Navy Tour of Duty: Interwar Years
  - 62   U.S. Navy Tour of Duty: World War II
  - 70   Marriage in a Time of War
  - 71   U.S. Navy: Navy Reserve
  - 72   Life After the War
- 74   Employee Newsletters: Glimpsing Life in Defense Plants
  - 77   Establishing the Culture: Work in a Time of War
  - 82   Becoming "Soldiers of Production"
  - 89   American Red Cross Blood Services and Homefront Workers
  - 92   War Bond Campaigns and the Pressure to Give
  - 98   Conception Data Sheets/ Suggestion Awards to Workers
  - 100   Cafeteria Troubles
  - 107   Victory Gardens: Essential to Improved Nutrition
  - 109   Campaigns for Cigarettes to Servicemen
  - 111   Transportation to Work: Gas and Tire Rationing
- 114   Employee Newsletters: Depicting Women at EPG and in Defense Plants
  - 116   1941 through 1942: When the "Girls" Were "Unique" to Production
  - 118   1943: Midway Through the War When the "Girls" Applied Their Skills
  - 125   1944: When The "Girls" Became Women Essential to Production
  - 137   1945: Bringing the War to a Close
  - 139   Another Way for Women to Serve
- 142   Employee Newsletters: Especially for Women
  - 142   Safety Garb and Office Attire
  - 144   Apparent Competition Among Women
  - 146   Women Production Workers and Child Care

148 Employee Newsletters: Especially for Men
    148 Women in Beauty Contests as Morale-Builders
    150 Reports from War Zones
    152 Recreation for Employees

154 Employee Newsletters: Diversity within the Workforce
    154 Veteran Production Workers
    156 African-American Production Workers
    162 American Indian Production Workers
    164 Sightless Production Workers
    165 "Deaf-Mute" Production Workers
    167 Midget Production Workers

167 Employee Newsletters: Belittling the Enemy
    167 War Department Communicates with Production Workers
    169 Anti-Japanese Rhetoric
    174 Anti-Nazi/ Anti-German Rhetoric

175 Employee Newsletters: Oddities
176 Ending the Research

List of Photographs
    11 Monnie Payton and Kathleen Cargill. Backyard picnic. 1948. Author's collection.
    31 Winston Erret Palmatier, Osakis High School graduation. 1936. Osakis Area Historical Society.
    39 Manuella "Monnie" Palmatier. Employee identification photograph. Erie Proving Ground. 1941. National Personnel Records Center, National Archives and Records Administration, St. Louis, Missouri.
    60 Civilian Conservation Corps Camp members. Company 1721, Camp Isabella F-17, Ely, Minnesota. December 1933. Discovery Center, Chisholm, Minnesota.
    64 Alfred J. Payton looking through a movie camera. 1942. Al Payton's collection.
    64 Alfred J. Payton boarding a North American T-6. Pensacola, Florida. 1942. Al Payton's collection.
    65 News crew interviewing U.S, Army officer, EPG, Port Clinton, Ohio.
    71 Wedding photograph of Chief Petty Officer Alfred Payton and Manuella Palmatier. June 15, 1945. Port Clinton, Ohio. Author's collection.
    73 Alfred J. Payton portrait. Undated. Al Payton's collection.
    73 Alfred J. Payton portrait. Undated. Sally Seward Pesta's collection.
    194 U.S. Navy F4U *Corsairs*.
    195 B29 *Superfortress*, Doc Tour, 2019.

177 Appendices
    177 Ancestry Kinship Diagram for the Palmatier Family
    177 Timeline for Manuella Joyce Palmatier from June 1933 to June 1945
    179 Photograph of CCC Company 1721, F-17, Camp Isabella, or Dunnigan, Ely, Minnesota
    180 Timeline of Service to the United States by Alfred James Payton
    185 Photography Class Training Manual, Table of Contents, World War II, Pensacola, Florida
    186 U.S. Navy Abbreviations Relevant to Alfred Payton's Service

187 Research Resources
196 Acknowledgements
198 About the Author

Dedication

To Manuella Joyce Palmatier, my Aunt Monnie Payton, and to the women across America who believed in their country, and who stepped up to become "soldiers of production" for the duration of World War II. Your contributions were vital.

To Alfred James Payton, and to his brothers-in-arms, who volunteered to serve their country in a time of war.

Research Paths

This book is designed as a guide for genealogists and historians of World War II who are hungry for the details about individuals who fought that war. The smallest of details can be just what a researcher needs to keep looking, to connect events, or to connect people. This book is filled with detail along with the sources of those details.

The most intriguing parts of my writing were the twists, turns, and full stops that I took on several research paths to create a memoir about my Aunt Monnie Palmatier Payton. She is not a "blood relative," but a Minnesota woman who became my aunt when she married one of my mother's younger brothers, Alfred James Payton.

Research is a voyage of discovery to recreate the past to learn about an aunt and an uncle whom I last saw when I was twelve years old. I started with the usual repositories of data used by most genealogists: libraries, on-line genealogy and history sites, and family documents obtained previously for a broader study of the Payton family, especially the role of Payton family members during World War II. With this basis, I created a rough outline for the memoir; and "to-do" lists are part and parcel of any research project. I typed what I had and looked for the holes in my research.

I needed detailed information on what Aunt Monnie did at Erie Proving Ground (EPG), Port Clinton, Ohio, during World War II. I wrote to the National Archives for her Official Personnel Folder (OPF). In December 2018, I received a two-inch stack of documents that detailed Monnie's work life from September 1941 to June 1945. I did not even have my coat off before I paged through this treasure. NARA sent along a CD with her employee photo as well! These documents form the greater portion of her personal story on the home front.

I needed to know about her life as a child growing up in Osakis, Minnesota. I telephoned the Osakis Chamber of Commerce which stated their basement contained all issues of the town's newspaper, the *Osakis Review,* in hard copy archived in large books. The Chamber referred me to the Osakis Area Heritage Center (OAHC) and to the woman with whom I had corresponded just weeks before. She assured me that the archived newspapers belonged to the OAHC and she searched through the issues from the 1933 to 1940 to glean any information about the Palmatier family. Ultimately, she provided dozens of news articles about their lives.

Osakis remains a very small community. Everyone knows all the families. I wanted the news from the 1930s editions of the *Osakis Review* to learn what life was like for the child Manuella and her family. I already knew that her father, Claude, was the town barber, and her mother, Emma Belle, played organ for the church, accompanied the performances of many local organizations, and taught music. Were they well-known enough to have articles written about them? Were their family's comings and goings of interest to others? Did they attend or host social events? Did they travel? Were there any disagreeable pieces of information about the family?

I had used the digitized newspaper, *Bermuda Gazette*, to research the life of Monnie's mother-in-law, my maternal grandmother. It provided decades of family-specific social, cultural, and economic life information. From that experience, I believed the *Osakis Review* would be a fount of information about everyday life in a rural Minnesota town during the Depression. Later, the Minnesota Historical Society provided, through inter-library loan, microfiche of the *Osakis Review* from January 1941 through August 1945. From there, I pulled valuable information about the Palmatier family which had been scattered across the country during World War II and was able to corroborate what was sent by OAHC. The local newspaper did not disappoint. It was filled with details about the Palmatier family.

OAHC let me know that my call to Osakis High School would not provide a copy of yearbooks from the 1930s. The first issue was in 1922, but the next two did not appear until 1939 and 1941. World War II intervened, and the yearbook was not revived until 1946. Aunt Monnie graduated in 1933, so the door to learning about her high school activities appeared to be closed. I called the school district office and asked if they had school records from the 1930s (*e.g.*, grades, teachers'/advisors' notes) that they could share with me. They confirmed her date of high school graduation as June 1933. In addition they sent a printed record of her academics, first through eighth grade, along with the records of Monnie's elder sister and elder brother. Monnie carried an A-/B+ average from fifth through eighth grade.

I learned that Monnie had been a Camp Fire Girl. An email to Camp Fire USA yielded nothing as they had no records "going that far back." This seemed to be a full stop. However The Osakis Area Heritage Center located an elderly woman – age 104 - still living in Osakis, who was a childhood friend and also a Camp Fire Girl. She recalled clearly her young neighbor and provided information about a childhood that she said seemed to be from a simpler time. The two lost contact after high school graduation. In addition, the *Osakis Review* confirmed there were three Camp Fire Girl groups in the area. With this, I confirmed Aunt Monnie's assertion that she was a Camp Fire Girl.

With the above resources, I fleshed out Aunt Monnie's girlhood. Her life as a young woman who trained and worked as a beautician was informed by myriad articles in her home town newspaper. I next wondered what life had been like for Monnie living near and working at Erie Proving Ground (EPG), so far from her home in Minnesota (just under 700 miles). To set my aunt in context during World War II, and to learn about the culture of war production, I used several library and museum archives.

Her father and her elder brother worked at Goodyear Aircraft in Akron, Ohio, and her sister-in-law worked for Bell Aircraft in Marietta, Georgia. I wanted to know if their experiences were different from what Aunt Monnie lived through.

As I read through the *Bell Aircraft News*, I realized that the Erie Proving Ground must have had a similar publication. I found Issue 7, July 15, 1943 of the *EPG Echo* digitized and offered through the Clyde Public Library, Clyde, Ohio. The publication was part of the Ohio Memory Project. In this one issue were articles from the War Department, news about civilian clubs, a push for the purchase of War Bonds, interviews with employees, news about local women who enlisted in the military, events at the local USO, war news, pin-up girl contests, articles about solders related to EPG employees, child care, insurance, housing, and articles about proof testing ordnance manufactured at EPG.

I contacted the Ida Rupp Public Library, Port Clinton, Ohio, to obtain issues of the *EPG Echo*. They had none, and referred me to the Ottawa County Museum (OCM) in Port Clinton. The museum Curator, U.S. Navy Captain Margaret "Peggy" Debien (Ret.) asked for Aunt Monnie's full name and said she would look through the other issues of the *EPG Echo* that they had on file. She mailed six publications, issues 3-8, for 1943 only because the War Department stopped the publication that July. I used the data to flesh out the culture at EPG, and found a single reference to Winston Palmatier, Monnie's younger brother, who was a civilian employee during part of the time Monnie was at EPG.

That her sister-in-law, Hilda Isabelle Chapman Palmatier, was a Rosie the Riveter at Bell Aircraft, led me to that company's history. Specifically, I contacted the University of Georgia Libraries, and a doctoral student completing her internship in history, mailed a year's worth of the *Bell Aircraft News*, an employee-based publication, from May 1943 to May 1944. These issues were the only ones they had in their collection. They were filled with war news, tributes to fallen soldiers, awards given to employees for their inventions, engagements/marriages/births, news about employee sports teams, beauty contests, and repeated appeals to employees to purchase War Bonds, donate blood to the Red Cross, as well as admonitions to work harder and more safely. This resource was extremely important as it was a key communication method used by the company to inform its employees.

I sought copies of the newsletter from the Steven F. Udvar-Hazy Center, part of the Smithsonian National Air and Space Museum's annex; it had no issues, but referred me to the Jack R. Hunt Library at Embry-Riddle Aeronautical University, Daytona Beach, Florida. Sadly, their librarian reported the school had a flood and the archived newsletters had been lost. She referred me to Emory University, a private research university in Atlanta, Georgia. I requested copies of the *Bell Aircraft News* from their Woodruff Library in the James Vinson Carmichael Collection which contained copies of the *Bell Aircraft Newsletter*, issues June 1944 through August 1945. I now had a complete set with more than enough information to discover what the work culture was like.

Then I accessed four years of *The Wingfoot Clan*, the employee wartime newsletter for Goodyear Aircraft, Akron, Ohio, to get an idea of what life was like for Claude J. Palmatier, Monnie's father, who worked there from at least January 1943 to his death in September 1945, and about Wharton Horace Palmatier, her elder brother, who also worked at Goodyear. I was unable to discern the actual dates of his employment, however. These newsletters were digitized and could be researched by name or topic.

All three sets of newsletters became essential research tools. The information each contained was much more than I could possibly address fully in this book. I chose a few topics for discussion just to give readers a sense of what life was like at these locations noting the differences in culture that existed within the military installation and within the two defense production plants. I used maybe one percent of the available data realizing that any researcher could complete a master's thesis or a doctoral dissertation by just using data from these period newsletters.

The Rosie the Riveter Association provided vital historical information and insight into the valuable role played by those home front heroes and heroines. However, they did not have an oral history for Monnie's sister-in-law. Related to that was on-line information about Women Ordnance Workers (WOW) which gave historic insight to the home front workers specific to my research needs.

My use of the information provided by the National Archives & Records Administration, St. Louis, Missouri, cannot be over-stated. The material stored in NARA archives is astonishing and provided much needed military records, civilian records for those working in military facilities, and coverage for individuals who worked in the Civilian Conservation Corps during the Depression.

The purchase of War Bonds was a singular focus throughout the nation during both World War I and World War II. Workers were encouraged to use payroll deduction to purchase them. I used online resources as a basis for discussion and, in particular, used the articles about War Bonds that appeared in the *Bell Aircraft News*, the *EPG Echo*, and some articles from *The Wingfoot Clan*. The newsletters spoke directly to the employees about the need for each worker to support the war effort. War Bonds were part of everyday life.

Late in my research, I recalled that my mother, Florence Isabelle "Dolly" Payton Cargill, worked as a tool crib attendant for Minneapolis-Honeywell Regulator Company for a time during World War II. She quit after my birth in January 1945. Although Honeywell records did not confirm her employment, the data on my birth certificate was clear. My mother and Monnie became sisters-in-law in 1945.

The book's bibliography contains the reference materials I used for this project. I am an avid reader of World War II history – on all fronts – but focused on those books and articles needed to write this story.

A final note about my writing style: I italicized direct quotes from forms, letters, books, and newsletter articles throughout the book. I underlined the titles of military forms to differentiate those used to hire, evaluate, and retire my aunt from her service, and to follow the navy career of my Uncle Al. I bolded and italicized the titles of newsletter articles for ease of reading.

Ever the teacher, I hope that my readers enjoy the story, and use the book as a primer to do their own research.

Photo at left: Aunt Monnie and the author at a backyard picnic in Wayzata, Minnesota. Summer 1948.
Author's personal collection.

Preface

This is the second in a series of books about my aunts, Minnesota women whose lives were drastically changed as a result of their activities before and during World War II. This story is about Manuella "Monnie" Joyce Palmatier, an Osakis, Minnesota, resident, who somehow met and married my maternal uncle, Alfred James Payton, a Wayzata, Minnesota, resident and U.S. Navy reconnaissance photographer during World War II.

My book is not a military account of the war's battles or directly about the servicemen and women who fought on the front lines. Those stories, ably told by other historians and genealogists, provide a rich back drop for my story of one woman and one man who served their country on the home front and in battle. The beautician who went to war stepped out of a conventional role and into a military-industrial culture only newly opened for women to enter.

The personal information I collected about Aunt Monnie stems from the research I completed on one maternal aunt, Lucia S. Payton, and her pre-World War II trip in late spring 1939 to England. I wanted to know more about the activities of my aunts. With this perspective in mind, when Manuella Joyce Palmatier listed her job as a *government clerk* on her Ohio marriage certificate, it seemed too general a term to be a complete description for what she was asked to do for nearly five years. Puzzling was that she had been a licensed beautician living in Minnesota for the previous six years and I questioned why this young Minnesota woman was in Ohio. Was she part of the "defense migration"? Did her younger brother assist her in getting the job? How did she meet her future husband? I needed to tease out this jumble of facts to learn what Aunt Monnie's contribution was to World War II.

When my parents, John and Florence "Dolly" Cargill lived in a home with three children in City View Acres, Wayzata, on Highway 101, their self-built house stood next door to mother's younger brother, Alfred James Payton and his wife Monnie. This was in 1950. As detailed in the chapter on him, Uncle Al was a United States Navy veteran reconnaissance aerial photographer in the Pacific Theater during World War II. He was born June 18, 1915, to Eugenie Ann Hollis Payton and Herbert Edwin Payton in Wayzata, Hennepin County, Minnesota. Al was the second of five sons. He served for five years during World War II, his second stint in the navy, and was mustered out in California on September 8, 1945. His rank was Chief Petty Officer/ Aerial Photographer's Mate. He married Manuella Joyce Palmatier on June 18, 1945, in Port Clinton, Ottawa County, Ohio, and they eventually returned to their home state of Minnesota for a few years.

Aunt Monnie, a woman of slight build at 5'2", stood in contrast to her husband, who was a strapping 6'4" who became a painter/ wall paper hanger after the war. A kind woman, with a great sense of humor, seemed frail even to me when I was between the ages of five and seven as I compared her to my tall mother and other aunts. She did, in fact, suffer from a congenital heart condition which took her life at an early age. What I found was a capable woman who honorably served her country in a civilian capacity at Erie Proving Ground, Port Clinton, Ottawa County, Ohio, during World War II. Primarily, this story is another about an independent woman in the Payton family, albeit one who married into the clan. I hope readers agree.

The Story Begins with Minnesota's Contributions

This story is inspired by my growing awareness about the contributions American women made during World War II, either on the home front or in the military. Increasing numbers of books and articles have been published in the last fifteen years addressing the subject of American women during that time – and that not all served as the iconic "Rosie the Riveter." Research on this subject likely will continue as greater numbers of documents from that period are declassified. Many women did work in defense plants assembling aircraft, and ordnance, while others worked in offices as typists, clerks, and filers, and others served as coders/decoders in secret departments, or were journalists on the front lines, or ferried aircraft needed for combat. Initially, unmarried women were recruited, but as the war continued, married women also were hired.

The home front in Minnesota offered civilian opportunities to serve because many industries were put on a war footing as soon as January 1942. One third of adult females in Minnesota were employed during the war years; others operated family farms while their husbands and brothers went to war. For example, sixty percent of Twin Cities Ordnance Plant (which produced munitions for United States Navy and United States Army Air Force) workers were female; the Twin Cities Rapid Transit Company employed women; Cargill Incorporated built refueling ships and towboats; Honeywell built airplane control systems and periscope sights for submarines; and Minneapolis was a railroad center for the northern line for Chicago to the coast. Women worked in the shipyards in Duluth and Superior, Wisconsin, and on Lake Superior.

Cargill's contribution to the war effort did not yield the company huge profits, but the corporation's executives were patriotic and believed their contribution was important. They were rewarded in January 1945 with their first Army-Navy 'E' Award – for excellence in the production of war equipment. That summer, the company was awarded its second 'E' Award. They were given a navy contract to build tankers and oil barges; Cargill was experienced in building grain barges. The site, Port Cargill, they chose for construction was in Savage, Minnesota, just above St. Paul on the Minnesota River. This was the largest of the World War II ship yards in Minnesota and was the only Emergency Ship Builder. At Savage, Cargill had three-hundred thirty-nine employees in 1940, and two-thousand sixty-seven in 1944, including many women; the wartime high for the whole company was three-thousand eight-hundred twenty-two employees. The company built twenty-two ships by the end of the war—eighteen *Patapsco*-class Auxiliary Oil and Gas (AOG) carriers, launching the first one on May 6, 1943. Five AOGs served in the Atlantic, while the remainder were in the Pacific. They also built four towboats. Savage had five more yards and together the six yards produced more than two-hundred-thirty ships. They were: Marine Iron and Shipbuilding, Inland Waterways, Zenith Dredge Company, Scott-Graff Lumber Company, Industrial Construction Company, and Cargill. I refer interested readers to Broehl's detailed and incisive history of Cargill and to on-line resources.

Camp Savage, US Army, was the site for the Military Intelligence Service Language School (MISLS). About eleven-hundred military service people were taught Japanese by American-born Japanese.

The United States Army Air Force, built airfields to train pilots and aircrews of fighters and bombers. These were located in Minneapolis, St. Paul, Lake Elmo, Monticello, and Rochester. In addition, Northwest Airlines, Inc. (NWA), begun in 1934, operated the Bomber Modification Center located on Holman Field, St. Paul, during World War II. *The Army wanted to know if NWA could create a huge bomber modification plant in St. Paul to update these planes for combat so the assembly lines could keep going at optimum speed. Northwest agreed, and the "Mod" was born* (*Reflections*, v.9, no. 3, fall 2011). The facility modified B-24 *Liberators* to add photo reconnaissance equipment and top-secret radar systems. There were thirty-six hundred employees by fall 1942, and the company included Asian workers. Significantly, President Franklin Roosevelt issued an executive order on June 25, 1941, which prohibited discrimination in hiring on the basis of race, by companies that had been awarded military contracts.

NWA flew cargo missions for the military to Canada, Alaska, and to the strategically important Aleutian Islands. Cargo included military personnel and equipment. The Army Air Force flew its transport aircraft C-46s (Curtis *Commando*), C-47s (Douglas *Skytrain*), its medium bombers B-25s (North American *Mitchell*), B-26s (Martin *Marauder*), and a heavy bomber B-24 (Consolidated *Liberator*). The aircraft were flown from production facilities to Northwest in Minneapolis and in Vandalia, Ohio, to be modified for cold weather and long distance flights. Other modifications included radar, a top secret piece of technology, and triple-lensed cameras ("super eye") which… *gave Allied fliers the most advanced photo reconnaissance equipment of the war…including the Japanese sea and air fortress at Truk Island* (*Reflections*, Fall 2011, p. 4).

Women who worked at the Bomber Modification Center were called "Gussie the Gun Moll"…*because so many of them were gunsmiths* (*Reflections*, Fall 2011, p. 4). Northwest has been lauded for this significant contribution to the Allies, especially in the fight against the Japanese in the Pacific. Blind employees were hired to sort small machine parts as well as nuts, washers, rivets, and screws. The company won an Army-Navy "E" award.

The newsletter went on to discuss another Minnesota company that contributed to the dozens of modifications made to these aircraft: Minneapolis-Honeywell Regulator Company. It secured defense contracts to produce tank periscopes, gunners' quadrants, mortars, the C-1 automatic pilot, and the Norden bombsight stabilizer. The C-1 regulated the flight of a bomber and was approved by the military in October 1941. Thirty-five thousand C-1s were assembled before the end of the war. The company won the Army-Navy "E" Award. The company added a military products division and remains as a major defense contractor and is an integral part of the United States' space exploration program.

Northwestern Aeronautical Corporation, St. Paul, assembled troop/cargo gliders, the Northwestern PG-1 and the powered Waco CG-13. Northern Pump Company made naval guns at its Naval Ordnance Plant, Minneapolis.

For the U.S. Cavalry Reconnaissance Troops, Ford Motor Company, in its facility in St. Paul, manufactured the M8, an armored command and communication combat vehicle. Six-thousand three-hundred ninety-seven rolled off the assembly line. The M-8 was used by British and American armies from March 1943 to June 1945. The British called the vehicle the "Greyhound" and it was used for reconnaissance because of its speed and agility. The company was awarded the Army-Navy "E" Award for excellence in production.

One of the country's largest arsenals was located in New Brighton. The Twin Cities Ordnance Plant was built in July 1941. The arsenal started production on February 5, 1942, and eventually had thirty-five production lines. It was considered a model plant because of its company-driven focus on employee diversity; it hired women (sixty percent of employees were women) and one-thousand two-hundred African Americans, unusual for the time. President Franklin Roosevelt visited the plant on October 9, 1942, and had great praise for its work. The facility earned four Army-Navy "E" Awards for quality and production. Sadly, forty-five families were dislocated and their property confiscated to build the ordnance plant.

Gopher Ordnance Works (GOW), Rosemount, was an ammunition factory with six production lines between 1943 and 1945. GOW manufactured smokeless gun powder and related products, and assisted the Allies by producing a propellant for American military ordnance.

In an on-line Minnesota Public Radio spot, MPR reported that 3M was enlisted to make "wet or dry adhesive strips." Sticky on one side, they were used on the edges of plane wings and ambulance runners so that people could stand on them without fear of slipping.

Hormel was enlisted to produce food which was in high demand globally. The United States had a responsibility to feed its citizens and those of allied countries whose domestic agriculture had been disrupted. Hormel had been manufacturing Spam since 1937. In the 1930s, Hormel employed nearly four-thousand five-hundred workers, including about one-thousand four-hundred women. Eighteen percent of Americans ate canned food in 1937 and by 1940, seventy percent were doing so. In 1941, the company became an important part of the Lend-Lease Program (H.R. 1776, signed March 11, 1941), which sent food and supplies to allied countries, initially to the United Kingdom. Spam was part of the K-rations issued to American military personnel.

Northern Minnesota ports and companies also contributed to the war effort. The USS *Robert L. Barnes* (AO-14), was a steel tanker built by McDougall Duluth Shipbuilding Company for the Robert Barnes Steam Ship Company. The company also built larger cargo ships and tankers. The *Barnes* fell into Japanese hands on December 10, 1941, while it was serving in Guam. The Office of Defense Administration appropriated most Great Lakes shipping for the exclusive transport of iron ore needed for war armaments.

The Mesabi and Vermillion Iron Range mines in northern St. Louis County were the single largest suppliers of raw material to the Allies. Ore was shipped by rail to Duluth and by boat to large steel mills in the eastern states. Women were employed as miners, replacing those men called to military service.

Greyhound Bus Line began in Hibbing, Minnesota, and advertised itself as serving more military camps and bases during World War II than any other transport system. Terminals across the nation were busy throughout the war, and more than five-thousand employees served in the military.

From 1940 to 1945, warships, cargo haulers, Coast Guard tenders, and fleet service auxiliaries of many types were launched from Duluth, Minnesota, and Superior, Wisconsin. During the war, shipyards in Duluth-Superior produced in excess of two-hundred vessels of ten main types, all having to sail a two-thousand four-hundred mile journey to the ocean. From nearly nothing in 1939, the shipyards became industries employing thousands of men and women by 1945. They were a major contributor to America's success during World War II.

General Mills and Pillsbury grew and processed food and helped teach households how to survive on rations. Also General Mills used its Mechanical Division to make precision tools such as gun sights.

A final example is from the University of Minnesota. In 1941, Professor Ancel Keys, a psychologist, was commissioned to develop the K-Ration, a prepackaged set of meals. They had to provide energy without being too heavy so that soldiers could carry them. To achieve this, each one had a candy bar. Many soldiers developed a liking for sweets, which was not a standard part of most diets before the war. Sugar was suddenly in high demand, proving to be a boon to Minnesota's sugar beet farmers.

There are probably many more large and small Minnesota companies that contributed to the war effort. The above are just representative samples. At least sixty-two Minnesota companies earned the Army-Navy "E" Award, also known as the Army-Navy Production Award.

The Palmatier Family of Osakis, Minnesota

Osakis is a small farming community in west central Minnesota, not far from Alexandria. The *Osakis Review*, the town newspaper which has been in print since 1901, provided a written view of the culture that influenced my aunt's upbringing. Osakis is a practical community populated by farmers, mechanics, and small retail businessmen. Articles about high school sports were often on the first page, especially if the local teams went to state tournaments. Farmers needed information about the weather, problems with crops, what livestock was for sale, where the best farm equipment could be purchased, and, most importantly to my research, who was doing what, and when did they do it? What was important to the people seemed to be published for all to read before, during and after the war. In this way, the newspaper was a link between events in the war and those who were impacted by them.

As I read the weekly Local News column in the *Osakis Review* covering eighteen years, I got a sense of the "position" held by the Palmatier family in Osakis. In fact, I realized that 21st Century Facebook has nothing on the Local News column of the *Osakis Review*! Since Osakis was a small community with a busy town, the same family names appeared repeatedly in the Local News, as well as in business news, obituaries, and so forth. Quick news about individual travel was covered in a line or two. More exciting or serious topics were covered in three or four lines. News about the lives of local business owners and doctors were in virtually every column. The connection between the editor of the newspaper and the Palmatier family became apparent: the two families socialized and Aunt Monnie worked for the *Osakis Review* for a short time after she graduated high school. These relationships may have contributed to the large numbers of articles printed about the Palmatier family.

The Palmatiers seem to have done well economically and socially. The family together or individually traveled a good bit in the 1930s and the 1940s, which surprised me as I assumed the cost and availability of gasoline would have been prohibitive. The Palmatier children were expected to excel in school and to work after graduation from high school. All four siblings received a post-secondary education: Claudette went to St. Cloud Teachers College, Wharton attended Dunwoody Institute in Minneapolis, Aunt Monnie trained at Paul's School of Hairdressing and Cosmetology in Minneapolis, and Winston went to the West Central School of Agricultural in Morris, Minnesota.

The National Center for Education Statistics indicated that by 1930, only 1.5 million people were enrolled in college nationwide, so the Palmatier children's ability to attend colleges was unusual. Of those enrolled in college, forty percent were women. Technical school training was chosen by Wharton and Monnie, leading to hands-on occupations.

The Palmatier family "motored" (*i.e.*, traveled by car) regularly during the Great Depression as they either went to college or trade school, and returned home at least monthly to visit friends and family, or received family from distances as great as Iowa and Ohio. The family was close-knit and monthly visits throughout the 1930s was common. Roads in Minnesota were paved to a large extent, but ease of travel was not like it became in the 1950s with the development of a nation-wide highway system. Instate distances that family members traveled regularly from Osakis included: 56 miles to St. Cloud; 10.6 miles to Alexandria; 120 miles to Minneapolis; 19.4 miles to Long Prairie; 134 miles to Minneota; 68 miles to Clearwater; and 57 miles to Morris.

~ Abraham Palmatier

Monnie's paternal great-grandfather, Abraham Palmatier, was born in December 19, 1817, in New York, the son of John D. and Elizabeth Weaver Palmatier. One of many families with that surname, they are likely descendants of the original settlers in the Colony of New York. The surname is derived from Old French meaning someone who made a pilgrimage to the Holy Land and carried a palm frond. I found no direct line of Palmatiers to France, only to England in the 18th Century. Perhaps the Palmatier family is descended from those who emigrated from France to England in the 11th Century. What the family believed about their heritage, and what others believed about it, came into play when the War Department conducted a background check on Monnie before her work on the home front.

I was unable to determine if Abraham served in the U.S. Civil War. In December 1842, he married Henrietta McKeel, who gave birth to Horace Palmatier in 1847. Henrietta had three daughters and three sons (1860 *U.S. Census*); Findagrave biography states they had nine children. They lived in Polo, Illinois. By 1891, the Palmatiers had moved to Greene, Butler County, Iowa (*Staples World*, October 19, 1891). Abraham passed October 26, 1900, with Henrietta following him almost to the day two years later. His Findagrave biography reflects the regard his neighbors had for him: *Politically, he is a sound-headed, and life-long Jackson Democrat. Is morally opposed to all secret societies…he is known to be a man of solid worth and substantial principles; has broad and clear views upon all live issues of the day, and is not afraid to advance and defend them.* Clearly, Abraham Palmatier was a force to be reckoned with.

~ Horace Palmatier

Monnie's paternal grandfather, Horace "Hod" Palmatier, was born on November 4, 1847 (1900 *U.S. Census*). He and his parents moved to Illinois just before the Civil War; Horace was one of three sons. He married Mary Ann Asper in 1870. By the 1900 *U.S. Census*, Horace was living in Staples, Todd County, Minnesota. He and his wife, Mary, had four children born, but only one was still living, their son Claude, who was eighteen. Hod was a barber, and two of his brothers lived nearby.

By 1901, Hod Palmatier had moved his barber shop to the Columbia Hotel in Staples. He published the following notice: *Notice! After 1 December 1902, the price of a shave will be $.15, 8 shaves for $1. The hours of closing will be 9 o-clock every evening except Saturday. Wolf and McMahan – Palmateer and Underhill* (*Staples World,* November 1902). The *Staples World* (April 1908) stated: *Hod Palmateer, who was the first barber to open a shop in Staples some twenty years ago and who has conducted it continuously ever since, has sold out to J. D. Linehan, a young man from Fall River, Wisconsin. Mr. Linehan comes highly recommended as a barber and as an all-around 'good fellow'. In addition to these qualifications, he is a fine musician, possesses a fine horse, and is said to be an excellent ball player.*

After a brief stay (about 1908 to 1914) in Mandan, Morton County, North Dakota, the Palmateer extended family, including Hod's son Claude and his wife Emma Palmateer and their son Horace Wharton, moved to Osakis.

The column, *Twenty Years Ago This Week 1914*, revealed how the Palmatier family came to live in Osakis. *Mr. H. Palmatier of Minneapolis this week bought the E. F. Antone barber shop, including the building and the Antone residence property in Osakis, and took possession of the shop Sept. 1. The consideration was $2650 cash. Mr. Palmatier has been in the barber business for 35 years and recently sold his shop in Minneapolis and decided to locate in a country town. He spent several weeks and traveled 1200 miles through Minnesota and Iowa before he reached Osakis, and says that he has struck just the place he has been looking for, and comes here to make his home as long as he lives. His family consists of a wife, married son and two grand-children who will join him in about two weeks* (*Osakis Review,* September 6, 1934).

In *Memory Refresheners from This Week in 1920*, it stated: *Friends of H. Palmateir are pleased to know that he has so far recovered from his late illness as to be able to resume work at his barber shop* (*Osakis Review,* July 11, 1940). In 1940, the town remembered what happened to him in 1920.

Hod eventually moved to Iowa in 1924, but returned to Osakis in October 1929 for a visit: *C. J. Palmatier is enjoying a visit this week from his father, Mr. H. Palmatier, and his wife* (This was Alice, his second wife whom he married in 1926; in 1924, Hod's first wife, Mary Ann Asper, died on May 11, and is buried in Greene, Iowa) *from Greene, Iowa. They came by train last Thursday and the old gentleman is being given the "glad hand" by his many old Osakis friends. Mr. Palmatier says his section of Iowa was the dry belt this summer and crops outside of corn are light. The corn crop, he says is a bumper* (*Osakis Review,* October 2, 1929).

Later on the same page, it reads…*Mr. and Mrs. H. Palmatier of Green, {sic} Iowa, who have been spending this week at the home of their son, Claude J. Palmatier, in Osakis, were guests of honor at a picnic lunch given by a number of their old Osakis friends in the City Park, yesterday afternoon.*

In 1934, the Local News reported: *Mr. and Mrs. Horace Palmatier are visiting from Greene, Iowa, at the home of their son, Claude J. Palmatier* (*Osakis Review,* September 13, 1934). He spent two weeks visiting and his return to Iowa was noted (*Osakis Review,* September 27, 1934). The elder Palmatiers remained a vital part of the Osakis community, even though they lived in Iowa.

The grandchildren visited Hod regularly, with Local News reporting Winston's trip to Greene in August 1936 (*Osakis Review*, August 13, 1936). In June 1938, *Claude Palmatier, wife and daughters "motored" to Greene, Iowa, last weekend and visited Mr. Palmatier's father, H. Palmatier* (*Osakis Review*, June 1, 1938). In early September 1939 the elder Palmatiers and Winston…*went to Greene, Iowa, last weekend to visit Mr. Palmatier's father* (*Osakis Review*, September 7, 1939). Claudette visited her grandparents during a two week vacation to Greene, Iowa, and to visit relatives in Davenport, Iowa, and Springfield and Chicago, Illinois (*Osakis Review,* August 21, 1941). As indicated by the Local News items, the Palmatier family was a close one.

Horace Palmatier was a prominent citizen in both Osakis and in his beloved Greene. His detailed obituary in the *Iowa Reporter* in Greene, a second briefer one in the *Osakis Review,* and a third printed in the *Mason City Gazette*, Mason City, Iowa (April 23, 1943), are telling.

Obituary of Horace Palmatier

Horace Palmatier, age 95, oldest resident of Greene, died at his home here last Wednesday following an illness of complications of advanced age…

Mr. Palmatier was born in Delaware, New York, November 4, 1847. He came westward and lived in Kansas before coming to Greene in 1859.

He entered the barber business at Staples, Minnesota, in 1889, and 20 years later, in 1909, he returned to Greene and engaged in farming. He moved to Minneapolis, Minnesota, four years later. In 1916 he engaged in the barber business at Osakis, Minnesota, where he remained until 1924, when he returned to Greene.

Mr. Palmatier was married to Mary Asper in 1872 at Marble Rock (Iowa). She preceded him in death in 1924. Mr. Palmatier was married a second time, 17 years ago in August (1926) to Mrs. Alice Yerrick.

Besides Mrs. Palmatier, there are living one son, Claude Palmatier of Akron, Ohio, four grandchildren and two great grandchildren. Two sisters and one brother preceded him in death.

Mr. Palmatier was a member of the Flour City Odd Fellows lodge of Minneapolis, Minn.

Iowa Reporter, Greene, Iowa, printed in the *Osakis Review,* May 20, 1943

The man's life, career, and family travails are summarized: he was a barber much of his life, met his first wife in Iowa, married there, and is buried next to her in the cemetery in Marble Rock. It is not known if his son and grandchildren attended his funeral. The war was at a mid-point, gas was rationed, and the press on his grandchildren to stay at their posts on the home front or in the army may have prevented their attending.

~ Claude J. Palmatier

Claude J. Palmatier, born on January 3, 1882, in Downs, Osborne County, Kansas, was the only living child of Horace "Hod" Palmatier and Mary Ann Asper. Emma Belle Warton, his wife, was born May 21, 1880, and died on June 17, 1952. Claude and Emma married on October 31, 1907 {some sources say October 30} and lived next door to the elder Palmatiers until 1924 when Claude's father moved back to Iowa.

In an effort to use the full given name of each of the Palmatiers, I searched in vain for weeks to find Claude's middle name. Finally, on his World War II Draft Registration Card (the Old Man's Draft), signed on April 27, 1942, it is noted that his middle name was simply the letter "J." My search did not have to go further.

Though Claude and his father were barbers, something happened because in November 1917, Claude...*left Friday morning for Granite Falls, Minn., where he has accepted a position in a barber shop. Claude is a practical workman of many years' experience and his friends join in wishing him well in his new location. Should he decide to make Granite Falls his home the family will join him in the spring* (Memory Refreshners from the Week 1917, *Osakis Review,* November 25, 1937).

At thirty-six, Claude registered for the World War I draft on September 12, 1918, but he did not serve in the war. In November 1918, Claude signed up for evening classes three times a week through the Osakis Commercial Department in either shorthand, typewriting, bookkeeping, or business letters (Memory Refresheners from This Week 1918, *Osakis Review,* November 17, 1938). The article did not specify for which classes he registered. According to the 1920 *U.S. Census,* Emma was a stay-at-home mother of four children.

As a barber, Claude paid close attention to his business. He attended a district meeting of the Master Barber's Association in Glenwood, Minnesota, about twenty-five miles away (*Osakis Review,* May 10, 1928). According to advertisements in the local newspaper, Claude charged twenty-five cents for a haircut.

Claude Palmatier maintained ties to friends in Staples throughout his life, where his father had been a barber. The Local News reported: *Mr. and Mrs. Claude J. Palmatier and Winston attended the 50th anniversary celebration at Staples Wednesday afternoon and evening. Mr. Palmatier is a former resident of Staples and enjoyed seeing his old friends* (*Osakis Review,* July 6, 1939).

The barber business met near tragedy in 1939. *Fire Damages Barber Shop* described a structural fire that destroyed the store room of the Palmatier and Brundage barbershop. The barber chairs and supplies were removed before the fire got too far along, and…*the interior will have to be redecorated…Messrs. Brundage and Palmateir resumed their duties in the old location the first of the week* (*Osakis Review*, April 27, 1939).

The Hendricks Insurance Agency Building is on Central Avenue, Osakis. It has changed hands several times in its long history. *Claude Palmatier rented the south section of the building for his barber shop. In 1925 Fred Gelle bought an interest in the barber shop. He stayed until 1928 when he opened his own shop in the building…In 1936 the building was sold to George Herberger. It was sold again in 1940 to Emma Palmatier….Claudette Nordell, a daughter of Emma Palmatier, sold the building and business to Lee Kallgren in 1948…*(*Our Osakis Heritage*, 1940). It seems as though the Palmatier family had a substantial investment in local business.

The lives of Claude J. and Emma Palmatier are explored further in the discussion of the family as a whole in the 1930s and 1940s (p. 33/34).

The Palmatier Siblings

~ Manuella "Monnie" Joyce Palmatier

There was confusion about my aunt's birth certificate. The State of Minnesota Record of Birth 1908-28953 states: *Manuella Palmatier, female, 1 child, born September 13, 1908. Father: Claude J. Palmatier; mother: Emma Wharton, both of Staples, Minnesota. Father born in Kansas; mother born in Illinois. He was a barber; she a housewife. He was age 27; she was age 28.*

The certificate said this was Emma's first and only child to date. This piece of information on the birth certificate was my clue that the certificate was not correct. Monnie was actually Emma's third child, so this was not her birth certificate, but that of her elder sister Claudette Louise Palmatier. This discrepancy in the birth record may be because the family decided not to call their first child Manuella after all, and simply changed the name without formally/ legally changing the birth certificate. Later, on January 12, 1916, they decided to name their second daughter Manuella Palmatier. However, I found no birth record specific to Aunt Monnie, nor any baptismal record.

Monnie's social life was part of the fabric of the town. When she was fifteen, *she… was host on Wednesday evening of last week to eight of her girlfriends at a Halloween party. On Friday, Wharton Palmatier had nine of his schoolboy friends in for an afternoon party where games were played that are enjoyed by young folks. Fine luncheons were served by Mrs. Palmatier* (*Osakis Review*, November 6, 1930). The reporting of social life in the *Osakis Review* netted at least ninety instances of Monnie's activities being mentioned from 1928 to1945. She received the most press among the four siblings.

As a child in rural Minnesota, Monnie was in Camp Fire Girls, an organization formed officially on March 17, 1912, as a corollary to the Boy Scouts of America. She was in the local group for ten years as reported later on her application to work at Erie Proving Ground in 1941.

The first official Camp Fire Girls handbook was published in 1914. The organization's initial thrust was to get girls into the wilderness by attending summer camps, learn the lore of American Indians, and learn skills to improve their self-esteem. During World War I, Camp Fire Girls sold Liberty Bonds (war bonds) to support the Allied effort in Europe. Boy and Girls Scouts also sold Liberty Bonds. There were four issues of Liberty Bonds, two in 1917 and two in 1918. Camp Fire Girls helped to sell over one million dollars in Liberty Bonds.

Thrift Stamps, issued by the United States Treasury Department, cost twenty-five cents. They were designed so that people who could not initially purchase a Liberty Bond, could accumulate Thrift Stamps and trade them in for a War Savings Certificate. The buying and selling of bonds and stamps was a symbol of patriotic duty. This revenue measure often targeted school children. Camp Fire Girls helped sell $900,000 in Thrift Stamps.

Monnie was born just before the United States entered World War I and the proud history of the Camp Fire Girls activities during the Great War was taught to succeeding generations. During World War II, Monnie regularly purchased War Bonds through payroll deduction, and increased the amount of purchase when she received promotions and pay raises.

I contacted Camp Fire USA, headquartered in Kansas City, Missouri, and Camp Fire Minnesota, Minneapolis, for information about the Osakis organization. Neither place had records reaching back into the 1930s and stated the organization was more interested in the present and the future than in the past. Initial verification of Monnie's participation came from an elderly Osakis resident. She and Monnie were in the same Camp Fire Girls chapter.

The *Osakis Review* provided the lion's share of information about Monnie's participation in Campfire in the Local News from 1928 to 1933. There were at least three Campfire groups in the area: Galilena Campfire, Tetapochan (also spelled Tatapochen, or Ta-Ta-Pochan), and, disturbingly, one group called Swastika Campfire Girls. I was relieved to learn that Monnie, as a member, and her sister Claudette, as a Guardian, were associated with the Galilina group and the Tatapochan group respectively. The groups met frequently at the Palmatier home (*Osakis Review*, March 19, 1931; October 5, 1933; February 1, 1934; February 15, 1934; June 7, 1934; and July 19, 1934). I forwarded this information to the offices of Campfire Minnesota for their records.

The term "Swastika" continued to bother me and, in further on-line research by a Boy Scout badge historian, I learned that the symbol was used world-wide on various medals/badges by the Boy Scouts from 1908-1935. It was a "Thanks Badge." The symbol was used in Eurasian cultures, and can be found in the design work of the Navajo

(*Dine*) and Hopi Indians of the southwestern United States. Since the Camp Fire Girls movement was to emulate some of the cultural teaching of American Indians, and it was a corollary group to the Boy Scouts, it is not unreasonable that Camp Fire would have used the name for one of its groups. There is a great deal of information on-line about this topic. I refer readers to those resources.

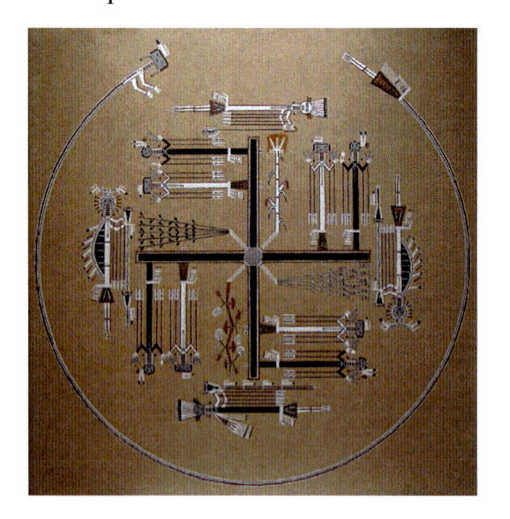

While in high school, Monnie tied her Campfire activities to her duties as school newspaper writer *cum* editor-in-chief. She was the Society reporter during her junior year, and was also elected as the Galilena Campfire Secretary (*Sikaso Hylite* In: *Osakis Review,* October 8, 1931). The Galilena group assembled boxes of dolls, games, and other toys to donate to a local orphans' home at Christmas (*Osakis Review,* November 11, 1931, and December 10, 1931)

One clever idea from the Galilina group seemed to be a nod to Monnie's future career as a beautician. They did a short presentation during a school assembly hour. *The main feature was a beauty parlor scene…some girls were 'beauty specialists' and the others were 'customers'…All the parts were taken well* (*Sikaso Hylite* In: *Osakis Review,* December 17, 1931).

Monnie did not participate in sports, at least no such activity was reported in the local newspaper or the high school newspaper. She was the daughter of a musician and singer, however, and was in the High School Girls Glee Club (*Osakis Review,* May 4, 1933). After her high school graduation she was a singer in a chorus of an operetta given to benefit the Legion Auxiliary (*Osakis Review,* November 30, 1933).

During her senior year in high school, Aunt Monnie became the editor of the school newspaper, the *Sikaso Hylite,* which was printed in the *Osakis Review,* the town's newspaper (*Sikaso Hylite* In: *Osakis Review* September 22, 1932). The high school newspaper varied in length and did not always have the same titled columns. I assume the variations had to do with the amount of space available in the town's newspaper.

She presented the history of the high school class will during the senior students' presentation during its class night exercises (*Osakis Review,* May 25, 1933). **Class Will of This Year's Graduates** headlined an article in which senior students "will" their jobs to a successor. The eighth paragraph reads: *To Sarah Henigers, Manuella Palmatier leaves her position as editor-in-chief of Sikaso Hylite. Start your work now! It's a big job* (*Osakis Review,* May 28, 1933). Aunt Monnie's experience as a high school reporter and editor prepared her for her brief job as a secretary and later as a government clerk at Erie Proving Ground.

When she graduated, Monnie was one of thirty-nine seniors awarded diplomas. This was the largest class in the history of Osakis High School. *Miss Manuella Palmatier…won fifth place (in scholarship)…with a "B" average.* She earned a certificate for the four letters (subjects were not specified) with 112.5 *Total Achievement Points* (*Osakis Review*, June 8, 1933).

From 1933 to 1945, Monnie came into her own by working while still living with her parents, obtaining technical school training, and living on her own in Minnesota and in Ohio. The timeline in Appendix 2 summarizes her life in those years. (p. 177)

Several times in 1938, Monnie brought Ray Ostrowski to her parents' home on Sunday or over the Thanksgiving or Christmas holidays. He lived in Long Prairie, Minnesota, as did she. In 1939, Ray lived in Minneapolis and Monnie moved to that city in September. He was a Christmas holiday guest at the C. J. Palmatier home in December (*Osakis Review,* December 28, 1939). I found no other information leading me to believe that Monnie and Ray were engaged to be married, but they did socialize for at least two years. There were other references as late as September 1940 to *Monnie… and guests of Minneapolis spent the weekend at the C. J. Palmatier home* (*Osakis Review*, September 5, 1940). The guests' names were not given in the article.

The 1940 *U.S. Census* indicated that Monnie, now using that nickname, was a twenty-five year old beautician earning $750 annually at a Minneapolis beauty parlor. She had completed high school and one year of beauty school.

In July 1940, Claudette visited Monnie at…*Bal Moral Apts in Minneapolis* (*Osakis Review*, July 25, 1940). I wondered at the specific reference to the Balmoral apartment building. It was constructed on Portland Avenue in 1917, and was a lovely building. Revitalized in the 1990s, it was honored by the Minneapolis Heritage Preservation Commission with the Historic Rehab Award.

As a close-knit family, it was not uncommon for the children to return to Osakis on Sundays, vacations, and holidays. The parents seemed to watch out for their children even after they left their parent's home and the elder Palmatiers were certainly involved in their children's lives. Between 1938 and September 1941, Aunt Monnie visited in person with her mother, her siblings, or with both her parents either at her home or theirs at least thirty-two times. These visits occurred while she was at the beauty school and when she worked in Alexandria, Long Prairie, and Minneapolis. I do not know if Aunt Monnie had a residential telephone, but presumably she had access to one to coordinate her visits to and from Osakis. There is no record of written correspondence, but letters and post cards were a common form of communication.

One of the most emotional visits the family shared must have been when the elder Palmatiers, Monnie, and Winston took Claudette to Princeton, Minnesota, to resume her teaching duties (*Osakis Review*, September 4, 1941). That same month, Monnie headed to her wartime job in upstate Ohio (Port Clinton) as did Winston.

By October 1941, Monnie had been working in Ohio for five weeks, and this was announced formally in the newspaper: *Miss Manuella Palmatier has a stenographic position at Port Clinton, Ohio, working for the War Department* (*Osakis Review*, October 16, 1941). Monnie's wartime experiences are explored more fully in the section on her job as a government clerk. (pp. 37-58)

~Claudette Louise Palmatier

Aunt Monnie's eldest sibling, Claudette Louise Palmatier, was born in Staples, Todd County, Minnesota, on September 13, 1908. She married Roy William Nordell, born February 14, 1909, and who died November 13, 1987, in Benton County, Minnesota. According to the announcement on-line from the Daniel Funeral Home, Claudette…*taught school in rural towns and city schools for 31 years. She and Roy Nordell lived on a farm on the Clearwater River near South Haven until retirement.*

Of the four siblings, Claudette also received a great deal of press in the local newspaper. Her three childhood surgeries were chronicled, but later surgeries were not listed (*Osakis Review*, June 6, 1928). She was a teacher and her graduation from St. Cloud Teachers College was important news because she was the first in her family to attend college (*Osakis Review*, June 6, 1929). St. Cloud was a two year college at the time, and graduation allowed people to teach, but to earn a Bachelor's Degree, Claudette had to attend summer school. Noteworthy were each time she attended summer school, and each place she taught (Degraff in 1929, Orange Township in 1933, Chicago in 1934, Clearwater in 1934 to 1940, and Princeton, Minnesota, from 1940 to at least 1945). She received her Bachelor's degree in July 1941…*after having completed the last of several summer sessions* (*Osakis Review*, July 24, 1941).

Each time she visited friends in St. Cloud, it was reported in Local News, as were the times she entertained friends at her parent's home, participated in a Campfire group, or when she came home for vacations from her job teaching. Between January 1928 and December 1945 - seventeen years between her ages of twenty and thirty-seven - Claudette is mentioned at least seventy times. At thirty-eight, she married Roy Nordell in 1946/1947 (records differ). When he was thirty-six, he joined the United States Army and served from April 7, 1945 to May 14, 1946. They had no children.

There is an on-line photo attached to her obituary and one of her graduating from St. Cloud Teacher's College in 1929. Claudette died on September 21, 2005, at ninety-seven. She lived the longest of the four Palmatier children outliving her sister by thirty-six years, her brothers each by fifteen years, and her husband by eighteen years.

~Wharton Horace "Paul" Palmatier

Wharton Horace "Paul" Palmatier (sometimes listed as Horace Wharton, and in high school known as "Spike"), born in Mandan, Morton County, North Dakota, on November 30, 1910, was Monnie's elder brother, and the family's second child. He died on June 14, 1990, in Madisonville, Monroe County, Tennessee, at age eighty from complications from heart failure. Heart failure eventually caused the death of at least four members of the family: Claude and his children Wharton, Monnie, and Winston.

Wharton graduated from Osakis High School in 1927. He enrolled at Dunwoody but his attendance could not be confirmed by the college Registrar. This may mean their records were not retained or that his were lost. In fact, the Local News column reported that: *Wharton Palmatier is another graduate of the Osakis High School who has entered the Dunwoody Vocational School in Minneapolis. "Spike" will take up printing and linotype work. He left Osakis Monday noon accompanied by his father, C. J. Palmatier, who is spending a few days in the city* (Osakis Review, January 5, 1928).

By June 1928, Spike was working in Fergus Falls and was visited by his parents one Sunday (*Osakis Review*, June 28, 1928). By December Spike was reported to be working for the Jap Olson Printing Company in Minneapolis. He traveled home to spend Christmas with his parents (*Osakis Review*, December 27, 1928). The following summer, Wharton spent his two-week vacation in Osakis (*Osakis Review*, August 8, 1929). By February 1930, Spike came home for a short visit from his new job in Chicago at the John Haungarth Printing Company, which was planning to relocate company operations to South Bend, Indiana (*Osakis Review*, February 27, 1930).

On his way back to Chicago in late March, Spike stopped to see his grandfather, Horace "Hod" Palmatier in Greene, Iowa (*Osakis Review*, March 20, 1930). This is another example of the close family ties in that Wharton took this side trip on his way back to Chicago. He was home for Christmas from Minneapolis, so he did not move to Indiana (*Osakis Review*, December 25, 1930). His traffic accident, a hit-and-run, in Minneapolis placed him in that city in August 1931 (*Osakis Review*, August 20, 1931). The accident garnered quite a write-up in Local News. His travels back and forth from Osakis were chronicled in the newspaper for the remainder of 1931.

In April 1932…*Wharton Palmatier motored to the Cities Monday to attend a Federal Inspection of the National Guard* (*Osakis Review*, April 21, 1932). I am not sure what the entry means, but assume this twenty-three year old man gave some thought to enlisting. He tried in April to get employment in Chicago, but was back in Minneapolis until the end of August 1932. By November, he was employed in North Dakota and Montana (*Osakis Review*, November 3, 1932). In 1933, he was back in Minneapolis.

In July 1934, Wharton lived in Chicago but had visited his parents just a few days prior (*Osakis Review*, July 26, 1934). By October 5, 1934, Wharton had enlisted in the Civilian Conservation Corps (CCC), and indicated on his induction form that his last job was in December 1933. He worked in CCC Camp F-1, Ely, Minnesota, during the

Depression from October 3, 1934 to March 31, 1935. The stint with the Civilian Conservation Corps confirmed that he had two year's training at Dunwoody in maintaining and installing printing equipment. He was twenty-four, and his previous occupation was printing. At his induction in Morris, Minnesota, Wharton was given three doses of typhoid fever vaccine over a period of fifteen days and he was vaccinated for smallpox. His monthly allotment was assigned to his mother.

He was assigned to Camp F-1 in Ely, just forty miles from Camp Isabella, where Uncle Al, Wharton's future brother-in-law, was stationed. I hoped they might have known each other which could have explained how Uncle Al and Aunt Monnie met. However, the time overlap was only sixty days - October to December 1934 - and the two camps were far apart. There was limited access to vehicles available to the workers. I found no mention that men from the two camps socialized.

Wharton stayed for only six months doing forestry work and was given a clean bill of health when he left the CCC. However, his CCC medical record shows two instances of frostbite – one "moderately severe," the second "severe." The first instance occurred on December 5, 1934, and the second, requiring hospitalization and treatment, was on January 12, 1935. He had been on Fernberg Lookout (a fire tower) when he got frostbitten. In early March 1935, he went to visit his parents, and returned to the CCC camp after several days (*Osakis Review*, March 14, 1935). He did not re-enroll in the CCC after working six months. Wharton did not serve in the military because of his diabetes, which was not life-threatening, according to his CCC physical.

In April 1935, Wharton…*left Tuesday for Chicago where he will be employed* (*Osakis Review*, April 11, 1935). He did not stay in Chicago for long but made his way to Berea, Ohio. On December 26, 1936, he married Hilda Isabelle Chapman and lived with his in-laws, Edwin B. and Nellie Chapman. Wharton worked as a printer for Printer File Works, having completed classes in the printing field at Dunwoody Institute in Minneapolis, Minnesota (Obituary, *Osakis Review*, May 15, 1990).

In October 1938, the well-to-do elder Chapmans traveled to Osakis. They hailed from Newcomerstown, Ohio, and…*came Sunday and are spending the week at the Claude J. Palmatier home. Miss Claudette Palmatier will arrive Thursday and Miss Manuella Palmatier will also be present for a family reunion.* The Local news made much of this reunion (*Osakis Review*, October 13, 1938) and the long distance trip created a familial and geographic link between individuals in Minnesota and Ohio. Perhaps this was the first time the two families met each other.

The tie between family members living in Minnesota and in Ohio strengthened in early January 1940. Local News reported that Winston Palmatier had left the previous fall to work at Heller Brothers Company File and Rasp Works in Newcomerstown, Tuscarawas County, Ohio, which was Hilda's hometown. Wharton worked in the printing department of the same company where he printed a monthly, magazine-sized publication, *Blues Blaster*, which contained news about the plant and its employees (*Osakis Review*, January 4, 1940; *The Coshocton Tribune*, December 6, 1939).

I imagine that Wharton played a role in Winston's securing the job.

Family ties were strengthened further: *A baby daughter was born to Mr. and Mrs. Wharton Palmatier of Newcomerstown, Ohio, Tuesday, the birthday of President Roosevelt* (January 30) *Now its Grandpa and Grandma Claude Palmatier* (*Osakis Review*, December 1, 1940).

In December 1941…*Mr. and Mrs. Wharton Palmatier and daughter and son from Newcomerstown, Ohio, arrived last week to spend a vacation over the holidays with his parents, Mr. and Mrs. C. J. Palmatier* (*Osakis Review*, December 18, 1941). World War II had begun for the United States and three Palmatier children were working in Ohio; Wharton, Monnie, and Winston. 1941 was the first Christmas that Monnie spent away from her parents; it must have been lonely for this woman just in her mid-twenties.

The record of Wharton's war time employment is incomplete. He was at the printing company in Newcomerstown, Ohio, but the *Osakis Review* reported he worked at Goodyear Aircraft in late 1942 where his father also worked (*Osakis Review*, December 3, 1942). Efforts to secure his personnel files from that period were unsuccessful.

Wharton and Hilda raised four children, but divorced in 1973. She divorced him on August 15, 1973, because of…*gross neglect and extreme cruelty*. The record is confusing, but it sounds like he left Hilda in Ohio before their divorce. From his obituary I learned that in 1960 he had a work-related accident and left the printing business. He was rehabilitated and maintained bowling equipment in a Twin Cities, Minnesota, bowling lanes until full retirement. Then he went to Elmwood, Wisconsin. In 1987 he moved to Tennessee where his brother, Winston, had gone in 1979 with his second wife, Mary Boling. Wharton married his second wife, Naomi Hall Cook, in Madisonville, Monroe County, Tennessee.

Hilda Isabelle Chapman was born in Ohio on December 30, 1917, to Edwin Bernard and Nellie Jane Chapman. In 1940, she and Wharton had one child, Carol Lynn, born on January 30, 1940. They later had three boys: Bernard, David, and Paul.

Hilda was an accomplished musician as identified in this Local News article… *Mrs. C. J. Palmatier is in receipt of a concert program given by the Coshocton Symphony Orchestra of Ohio, in which her daughter-in-law, Mrs. Wharton Palmatier is one of 16 1st violinists of the personnel of one hundred musicians. The conductor is Giovanni Baletti* (*Osakis Review*, March 24, 1938). That the name of the orchestra and its conductor was given indicates the importance of this announcement in the newspaper.

Hilda, a "Rosie the Riveter" at Bell Aircraft, Marietta, Cobb County, Georgia, assembled aircraft as verified by her children, by the information within her obituary, and by articles in local Ohio newspapers during that time. This confirms that their family was living in Marietta, Georgia, during the war or at least during part of the war. I was unable to find the dates of her employment. I*n addition* …*Wharton Palmatier of Marietta, Georgia, is visiting his family at the home of Mrs. Palmatier's parents, Mr. and Mrs. E. B. Chapman at Wolf* (*The Coshocton Tribune*, June 9, 1944).

Hilda was a talented musician and from a well-to-do family. She graduated from Newcomerstown High School in 1935, attended Kent State University and later taught elementary school. Her social activities, and those of her parents and her children, were chronicled principally in *The Coshocton Tribune*, but also in the *Dover Times Reporter* and the *Dover New Philadelphia Times Reporter* throughout her life.

Hilda was touted for her violin solos at social and church events, was a member of the Order of the Eastern Star, and the Garden Club, and was involved in the local Boy Scouts. The parallels between Hilda and her mother-in-law, Emma Belle, are reflected in their education, music performances, teaching, and the fact that their comings and goings were considered newsworthy.

She died in Torrance, Los Angeles County, California on December 12, 2006, but is buried near her parents in Newcomerstown, Tuscawaras County, Ohio (*The Times Reporter*, April 15, 2007).

~Winston "Wynn" Erret Palmatier

Winston "Wynn" Erret Palmatier, born May 5, 1918, in Osakis, was the youngest child. The information about Winston's childhood was gleaned from the *Osakis Review* and from the *Sikaso Hylite* from October 1932 to November 1940, and his adult life/military career from the *Osakis Review* 1941 to 1945. His passion from childhood was in the field of agriculture, which fit his growing up in a rural farming community. He was an active Boy Scout: Tenderfoot in 1932, Second Class Scout in 1933, patrol leader in 1935, Life Scout in 1936, and who continued to be a Scout well into 1937 after he had graduated from high school. He chose to work on Scout Merit Badges that prepared him for his later education and work in agriculture: poultry keeping, cooking, safety, and civics. He passed his swimming tests, and he was a champion checker player (*Sikaso Hylite* In: *Osakis Review*, February 7, 1935).

Winston's membership in 4-H helped prepare him for his post-secondary education. The summer after high school, he entered 4-H club events at the County Fair. Expenses for the 4-H club were paid by Great Northern and the Soo Line Railroads. He was later employed by Great Northern Railway for a short time. He continued to be active in 4-H in 1937 and wrote the *Osakis 4-H Club News* for the high school newspaper (*Sikaso Hylite* In: *Osakis Review*, June 24, 1937). *Winston Palmatier Describes 4-H Trip to University Farm* was a detailed article he wrote about a three-day conference for 4-H members to agriculturally-related industries, classes, crops and poultry judging contests, and a music contest (*Osakis Review*, June 24, 1937). To top everything else, in 1937, he won 1st Place for green peppers (*Fall Festival Prize Winners Are Announced* in *Osakis Review*, September 23, 1937). His mother, who normally competed in that festival, did not enter in 1937.

He was from a musical family and played drums in the Beginners Orchestra (*Sikaso Hylite* In: *Osakis Review*, October 13, 1932), and was a member of the High

School Mixed Chorus which won first prize in the Division C District Music Contest (*Osakis Review*, May 4, 1933). He also lettered in music in high school: *In presenting the music letters Miss Pittingsrud pointed out that so many letters were earned in the field of music because the pupils had done exceptionally well at the district music contest by winning four firsts and one second place* (*Osakis Review*, June 8, 1933). Winston acted in small plays and became a member of the Senior Mixed Chorus.

To round out his school years, Winston played basketball as a guard on the "second team." I wondered at this, since Winston's full adult height was 5 feet 6 inches. Academically, he did well and was on the Honor Roll several times. As a senior, he lettered in music, earning a total of three letters that year for music and other activities. He graduated in June 1936 in a class of thirty-four students. The Class Motto was: *Life Is What We Make It*. Prophetic for those growing up during the Great Depression. In a small school, all students could participate in a large number of activities. Winston took advantage of that and appears to have developed a well-rounded extra-curricular life.

Winston Palmatier's graduating class, Osakis High School. He is seated, second from right, on the brick stoop. 1936. Source: Sharon Frederickson, Osakis Area Historical Society.

He was introduced to military life just after he graduated from high school when he attended the Citizens Military Training Camp at Fort Snelling, Minnesota, with five other young men from Osakis. *The boys…report that they enjoyed the camp. That they had good food, and that there was something to do all the time. There are some of them who did not like the drilling very well, though, strange to say. Most of them look straighter and browner and that's something* (*Osakis Review*, August 6, 1936).

He enrolled in the West Central School of Agriculture, Morris, Minnesota, in September 1937 (*Osakis Review*, September 30, 1937). Doubtless his scout and 4-H club experiences were beneficial. WCSA is now the University of Minnesota-Morris.

I believe Winston's first post-high school job was described in this Local News piece: *Winston Palmatier left Sunday for Wyoming, Minn., near Minneapolis, where he is employed at the state game farm in bird conservation work…Mr. and Mrs. C. J. Palmatier motored there also Sunday* (*Osakis Review*, April 14, 1938 and May 5, 1938). The job was at the Carlos Avery Game Farm (*Osakis Review*, August 18, 1938). The game farm helped to build populations of dwindling game bird species, such as the bob white quail, the chukar partridge, and the ring-necked pheasant. This is now the Carlos Avery State Wildlife Management Area, Anoka County, Minnesota, and is a reserve for deer, waterfowl, and other woodland animals and birds.

In 1940, Winston worked for Great Northern Railway, Barnesville, Minnesota, ninety-four miles from Osakis. Great Northern Oriental Limited stopped in Osakis as early as 1920 from Chicago during the tourist season (*Memory Refresheners from 1920, Osakis Review,* June 6, 1940; July 11, 1940, and September 19, 1940).

Winston's Draft Registration Card, signed October 10, 1940, stated he was employed by Great Northern Railroad. He was 5'6", 140 pounds, and on the top of the card, in red, is written *Disc.* Nov. 1945. The actual date was November 7, 1945. He was a T4US Army.

Winston applied to the War Department prior to September 1941. He took a week's vacation to visit his parents but…*He is now chief clerk in the office of the Erie Proving Ground outside of Toledo, Ohio* (*Osakis Review,* September 4, 1941). He accompanied Manuella to Ohio in mid-September where she expected to be employed by Erie Proving Ground. He worked at EPG for eleven months, September 1941 to August 1942.

In August 1942, Winston was inducted into the United States Army and was scheduled to report for duty on September 1. He was…*chief clerk in the star-gauge department of Erie Proving Ground…*(*Osakis Review,* August 20, 1942). He was assigned to the finance department, Army Air Corps, Colorado (*Osakis Review,* September 10, 1942).

He was in the army from August 31, 1942 to November 7, 1945, serving three years, two months, and nineteen days. At the time, his permanent mailing address was the R. Lupkes residence in Alexandria where his girlfriend/fiancé, Joyce Dorothy Lupkes, lived. In February 1943…*Sgt. Winston Palmatier returned to Osakis last Saturday to spend a 10-day furlough with his mother, Mrs. Claude Palmatier. Winston is stationed at Buckley Field, near Denver, Colo* (*Osakis Review,* February 11, 1943, News of Men in the Service).

Also… *Miss Claudette Palmatier of Princeton, Minn., and Miss Joyce Lupkes of Nelson spent the weekend at the home of Mrs. Claude Palmatier* (*Osakis Review,* February 11, 1943). Everyone in town must have realized there was a budding romance between Winston and Joyce, who had come with his sister to visit his mother. That his mother is mentioned in the article. but not his father indicates that Claude Palmatier was already in Akron, Ohio, at Goodyear Aircraft.

As local men enlisted or were drafted, and young women joined the WAC or WAVE, the Local News section grew and later was accompanied on page one with a column entitled News of Men in Service. One-hundred fifty-two names in Our List of Servicemen listed Winston Palmatier's name with the others (*Osakis Review,* November 12, 1942).

Winston's Certificate of Honorable Discharge provided more information. He was married, and had been a civilian clerk typist, and his military occupation was as a finance clerk. He took his Oath of Enlistment on August 18, 1942, and assumed active duty on August 31, 1942 (Inactive Service Enlisted Reserve Corps {ERC}). He earned a World War II Victory Medal (issued to all members of the US military who served from December 7, 1941 through December 31, 1946 – no particular length of service was required), a Good Conduct Medal (AR 600-68 1943) (awarded for exemplary behavior, efficiency, and fidelity for a three-year period of continuous active duty), and an American Theater Ribbon (refers to the continuance of American defense after the attack on Pearl Harbor), the latter earned for continual service. He did not serve in combat. He was honorably discharged giving *Dependency* as the reason.

He was married twice. He married Joyce Dorothy Lupkes of Nelson, Minnesota, but they divorced on September 9, 1977. He and Joyce had two children. They lived for many years in Eagan, Dakota County, Minnesota, where he retired from the Civil Service. Joyce Lupkes Palmatier died on December 11, 2011, at the age of eighty-seven, outliving Winston by two decades.

Winston married a second time to Mary Boling from Washburn, Bayfield County, Wisconsin, on June 9, 1979. He was sixty-one and she was thirty-six. They moved to Tennessee. Winston died April 29, 1990, at seventy-one, of heart failure in Cleveland, Bradley County, Tennessee. He is buried in Tennessee's Chattanooga National Cemetery, a military cemetery. He passed six weeks prior to Wharton's death.

The Family in the 1930s

~ Emma Belle Wharton Palmatier

Emma was the center of Palmatier family life. Family visits, social activities, luncheons attended by Emma Palmatier, "motoring" to the Twin Cities, musical performances, and news about the children's activities, were part of the social fabric for Osakis in the late 1920s. The social and business life of the elder Palmatiers was a regular feature in Local News from 1928 to 1945, particularly the activities of Emma Palmatier. The Great Depression did not seem to curtail Palmatier social and family activities. Mention of Emma's activities appeared at least sixty times between 1928 and 1945 in the local newspaper including the number of times she was mentioned with her husband. She was identified the majority of the time as "Mrs. C. J. Palmatier." She and Claude had married October 30, 1907

By the 1930 *U. S. Census*, Claude and Emma lived with their two youngest children, Manuella, fourteen, and Winston, eleven. The elder children Claudette, twenty-two, and Wharton, twenty-one, were living outside the Osakis home.

Emma often had guests for lunch, hosted the Presbyterian Choir (of which she was a member), traveled to visit her children, was in charge of the music program for a Girl Scout troop, went to her elder daughter's graduation from St. Cloud Teachers College, hosted the Galilina Campfire group in her home, participated in a group that put on an annual musical, was often the accompanist on piano or organ for funerals, church programs, choirs and choruses, and she sang soprano solos. According to a contemporary, Emma had an operatic voice.

Emma's ties with her birth family were evident in the effort her brother made to keep in touch. *Rev. and Mrs. W. W. Wharton and little granddaughter, Doris, of San Antonio,*

Texas, motored up from the cities last evening to spend a few days at the lake. Rev. Wharton is a brother of Mrs. C. J. Palmatier and this is his first visit to his sister in several years. The party had been called to Des Moines, Iowa, on a business trip and their visit here was unannounced and came as a delightful surprise to relatives (Osakis Review, June 4, 1931).

Even Emma's gardening and food preparation skills were noteworthy. *Mrs. C. J. Palmatier holds the record for growing early tomatoes by July 15* (Osakis Review, July 22, 1936). Her sweet doughnuts won first prize at the Osakis Fall Festival (Osakis Review, September 21, 1933). Among the *Fall Festival Premium Winners* listed Mrs. C. J. Palmatier, mixed relish-first…(Osakis Review, September 20, 1934) The Fall Festival Premium Winners were announced in September 1935 and noted *Mrs. C. J. Palmatier, 2nd sweet doughnuts; 2nd, crab apple pickles; 2nd, raspberry jam; 1st, mixed relish.* Apart from the sweet doughnuts, my own mother, Dolly Cargill, "put up" these same items; holiday dinner tables held a sea of home-canned goods.

In the article entitled *Premium Winners At Osakis Fall Festival, Pamatier, Mrs. C. J., 1st, canned tomatoes; 1st, sweet doughnuts; 1st, plum jelly; 2nd, currant jelly; 2nd chocolate fudge* (Osakis Review, October 1, 1936). She did not enter anything in 1937, leaving the prizes to go to her son, Winston. It looks like Emma stepped up her game in 1938, because her chocolate angel food cake took 1st prize in *Fall Festival Program Brings Crowd Here: Premium Winners* (Osakis Review, September 15, 1938). The importance of home canned, preserved, or dried food stuffs cannot be over-emphasized. Given food rationing and the scarcity of tin, a metal used in commercial canning, homemakers were encouraged to use these practices to stretch the food budget.

In her 1952 obituary Emma Palmatier is described as a…*graduate of Drake University School of Business and who attended the Chicago Conservatory of Music.* Further, Emma…*was well known for her varied activities in music circles and for her work in local churches. As a music teacher she especially endeared herself to the many young people whom she helped and were her pupils* (Osakis Review, Obituary, June 26, 1952).

The Family in the 1940s

The 1940 *U.S. Census* gave sparse information about the elder Palmatiers. Claude remained at his job as barber; he was fifty-eight, and would move to Akron, Ohio, to serve on the home front in 1943 when he was sixty-one. Emma continued to be a church organist and taught music. Their youngest son, Winston, twenty-one, was a laborer in conservation and had finished one year of college.

In a November 1940 note…*Mrs. C. J. Palmatier received one dollar for her musical question sent in to Kitchen Quizz WCCO. In thanking for it she did so with some of her original poetry. This poem was read over the air last Saturday on this program* (Osakis Review, November 14, 1940).

Small articles or announcements in the town newspaper continued to provide glimpses into their lives. *Miss Claudette Palmatier has returned from a 2-week visit with relatives and friends at Davenport, Iowa and Greene, Iowa and Springfield and Chicago, Ill.* (*Osakis Review*, Local News and Social Events, August 21, 1941). Among those she visited would have been her paternal grandfather, Hod Palmatier.

Mr. and Mrs. H. Palmatier and C. J. Palmatier and family made up an automobile party that drove to Eagle Bend Browerville, Sunday (*Memory Refreshers 20 Years Ago, Osakis Review* August 28, 1941). The article was a remembrance about a family trip that took place in 1921. The family's activities were newsworthy to Osakis readers.

Clues to Claude's desire to work in a defense plant appeared cryptically in Local News. He took…*a business trip to the Cities Monday*…seemed a note without substance when the pattern of sharing news in Local News was to include the reason for a trip. He had nieces in the Cities whom he visited before on Emma's side of the family. No names or relationships were given (*Osakis Review*, March 5, 1942).

Then in October 1942, Claude visited his son, Wharton, and daughter, Manuella, in Ohio (*Osakis Review*, October 15, 1942). Again, there was no explanation about why he traveled alone to visit the children. He stayed in Ohio and was employed by Goodyear Aircraft for three years, but in what capacity remains unknown (*Osakis Review*, December 3, 1942).

By the 1940s, all four Palmatier children had professional or technical training and jobs that could support them. This reflects the strong work ethic within the family; everyone worked outside the home.

Thanksgiving and Christmas in 1942 was probably a lonely one for all the Palmatiers. In Osakis, Emma and Claudette share the holidays with C. H. Bronson and his wife. He was the editor and owner of the *Osakis Review* and often a guest at the Palmatier home (*Osakis Review*, December 3, 1942; and December 31, 1942).

By 1943, life had utterly changed for the elder Palmatiers: *Mrs. Claude Palmatier left on Wednesday of last week for Akron, Ohio, to join her husband who is employed there* (*Osakis Review*, Local News, March 4, 1943). She left on the trip during the last week of February to be with Claude, who had been in Ohio since October 1942. The phrasing in the statement did not say Emma "visited" her husband, but "joined him." I wondered if she had moved to Ohio to be with Claude for the duration of the war. My hunch was confirmed by the severe reduction of the number of stories about the Palmatiers in Local News from March 1943 to August 1945. I realized that Emma had been the source of all the news about her family prior to 1943. In addition, she, her children, and her husband, were barred from discussing their war work, especially being admonished as home front workers not to gossip in public (*e.g.*, "loose lips sink ships").

Just before she left for Ohio, Emma entertained Claudette and Joyce Lupkes, Winston's future wife (*Osakis Review*, February 11, 1943). I imagine this was a sad farewell to Emma, a central figure in the lives of her children.

The closeness of the family and its ties to Osakis was reflected in a poignant article in the newspaper. *Send Word of Thanks. Mrs. Claude Palmatier wishes to thank her friends for the nice cards and letters received while she was confined 3 weeks in St. Thomas Hospital following a major operation. Manuella was with her at the time and Claudette is spending her vacation with her mother and father in Akron* (*Osakis Review,* July 12, 1945).

The notice confirms that Claude and Emma lived together in Akron, and their daughters were devoted to their mother. Manuella had been married just four weeks prior and her new husband was in Minnesota. Claudette used her summer vacation to attend to her parents. Emma's illness and hospitalization came just eight weeks prior to Claude's passing at the same hospital on September 5, 1945.

Claude's initial obituary was printed in the *Akron Beacon Journal* (September 5, 1945). With a follow up call to Eckard Baldwin Funeral Home in Akron, I learned about his final arrangements in Ohio - a "calling hour." Goodyear paid for the funeral: $356 for the casket, and $52.22 for clothing and for shipping his remains by rail to Minnesota. He was a member of *Pa-4169 Hillwood Lodge,* and he was 63 years 8 months and 2 days at death. Eckard Funeral Home was considered to be a "blue collar" funeral home, making arrangements for Goodyear workers who were not executives. Families of company executives used a second funeral home down the street. This information confirmed that Claude was not an executive with Goodyear, but did not state what he did at the plant.

A more personal version of his obituary was published on the front page of the *Osakis Review,* September 13, 1945, and summarized his life. Below are excerpts.

C. J. Palmatier Funeral Service Held Wednesday

Funeral services for Claude Palmatier, who passed away at Akron, O., on Wednesday of last week, were held at Presbyterian Church here Wednesday (yesterday) afternoon at two o'clock…Interment took place at Lakeside cemetery…

Claude J. Palmatier was born in Downs, Kan., Jan. 3, 1892 {this should be 1882}, the only son of Horace and Mary Palmatier. He died at St. Thomas Hospital, Akron, Oho, Wednesday, September 5, 1945…

He lived in Wadena and Staples, Minn., for 25 years, during which time he was married to Emma B. Wharton, October 31, 1907, at Jackson, Iowa, before coming to Osakis, which has been their home for 31 years, during which time he owned and operated a barber shop…

During the past three years he was employed by the Goodyear Aircraft Company at Akron, Ohio…

He leaves to mourn his sudden departure his wife, Emma B. Palmatier, and four children, Claud{ette} L. of Osakis, Wharton H. of Derea {Berea}, Ohio, Sgt. Winston E. of Camp Bowie, Texas, and Mrs. Al Payton (nee Manuella) of Alameda, Calif…

He was a devoted husband and father and will be missed by many friends…

The Government Clerk, Monnie Palmatier at Erie Proving Ground

Starting the Job

There is a history of Palmatier family members, including those who married into the family, serving in the military during World War II or serving on the home front. The information on each member was gleaned from the National Archives, from aircraft company archives, library resources, local historical societies, newspaper archives, military societies, or general online information about each war defense plant.

The greatest source of information for what life was like for these home front workers came from the employee newsletters each defense plant or military installation published: *EPG Echo* (Erie Proving Ground where Monnie worked), *Bell Aircraft News* (Bell Aircraft where Hilda Isabelle Palmatier worked), and *The Wingfoot Clan* (Goodyear Aircraft where Claude J. Palmatier and Wharton Palmatier worked.)

From the 1940 *US Census*, I knew that Aunt Monnie was a beautician who trained and worked in Minnesota, and from her 1945 marriage certificate, I knew she worked as a "government clerk" in Port Clinton, Ottawa County, Ohio. What I did not know from the Census was how a young beautician from Minnesota got to Ohio to work nor what she did during the war.

In October 2018, I requested her personnel records from the National Archives and Records Administration, St. Louis, Missouri. A scant six weeks later, I received a two-inch stack of documents about Aunt Monnie's war work, which included the following materials: four individual Narrative Personal History Reports for War Industries (background checks); Application for Employment and Personal History Statement (September 9, 1941); her signed Oath of Office; pay schedule with War Bond Authorization; Certificate of Medical Examination (referencing her congenital heart condition); Notice of Civilian Employment (September 9, 1941); Supplemental Information (September 9, 1941); Employees Clearance Sheet (to work at Erie Proving Ground); Confirmation of Temporary Appointment (September 20, 1941); Job Sheet for Field Civil Service Appointment (September 20, 1941); Ratification of Appointment (letter); Job Sheet for Field Civil Service Appointments (job duties/ gross salary); War Department Recommendation for Field Personnel Action (July 16, 1942 change in position title); Ordnance Department, Credit Application (May 12, 1943); letters citing "Special Report – For" Work Efficiency; Notification of Personnel Action; Reports of Field Personnel Action (1942-1944) (showing changes in status from Under Clerk Typist to Junior Clerk to Assistant Clerk to Clerk); Conduct Reports (1942-1944); Resignation and Exit Interview (June 11, 1945) requesting Leave of Absence to marry; Report of Efficiency Rating (March 31, 1945); and official letters surrounding her resignation (August 11, 1945).

Of singular note among the documents, are the four Narrative Personal History Reports for War Industries. The questions, with their typed responses, were used by investigators in four locations: Port Clinton, Ohio; Osakis, Minnesota; Minneapolis, Minnesota; and Long Prairie, Minnesota. The top quarter of each form provided clear guidance and instructions to the investigators for the nature of the personal data to be collected. The answers to the questions reveal a woman of "good character." However, the responses speak volumes to the manner in which the questions were asked and reflect the tension within a war time atmosphere.

I cannot completely discern Aunt Monnie's reasons for moving from Minnesota to Ohio to work during World War II. Her reasons may have been patriotic in nature, or that she knew she could make more money working in a war industry than if she continued as a beautician. She was certainly part of the "defense migration" alluded to by Alistair Cooke.

Her application and acceptance for employment must have been completed in Osakis and mailed to the War Department in early 1941. Monnie was still in Osakis in early September, but traveled to Ohio the second week. At this time, Winston worked as a civilian at Erie Proving Ground. *Miss Manuella Palmatier left the first of the week for Newcomerstown, Ohio, where she will visit her brother (Wharton and Hilda Palmatier) She expects to go from there to Texas. Winston accompanied her, but went to Toledo, Ohio* (*Osakis Review*, September 11, 1941). It read as though Monnie were given the impression that her war service, or the training for it, would be in Texas. She may have been trained in Texas for a month but the record is unclear. Later, the Local News reported that…*Miss Manuella Palmatier has a stenographic position at Port Clinton, Ohio, working with the War Department* (*Osakis Review*, October 16, 1941).

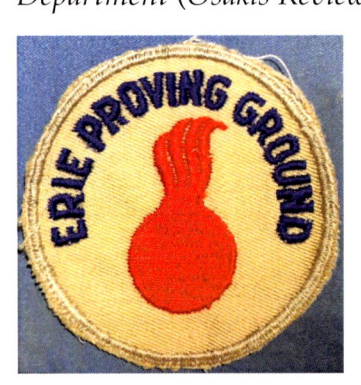

Manuella J. Palmatier was accepted for employment in early September 1941. The paperwork involved in becoming an employee during the war understandably included basic application forms, medical and health checks, a voluntary Employee's Declaration, an Oath of Office, and detailed background checks from four sources. I received over sixty pages of information about her work at Erie Proving Ground.

Erie Proving Ground patch worn on employee uniforms. World War II.

The completed <u>Application and Personal History Statement</u> was returned to *The Commanding Officer, Attn: Chief, Civilian Personnel Section, Erie Proving Ground, La Carne, Ohio*. The form came with this warning: *All answers must be stated correctly; any false statement is sufficient cause for rejection of the application or dismissal after appointment*. A background check was administered on applicants so that the veracity of their statements could be corroborated, the warning was serious.

In her handwriting, Manuella Joyce Palmatier signed and dated the form September 9, 1941. She gave her address as "General Delivery" in Port Clinton, Ohio. She was a citizen of the United States, age 25 years, and born January 12, 1916.

A tiny woman at 98 lbs. and 5' 2.5" tall, Monnie had completed high school and one year of professional training (later identified as attending a beauty college). She indicated she preferred the positon of "typist," would not accept a temporary assignment of one month, and stated her salary requirements as "$1260 per year." She had not taken the Federal Civil Service Examination, and had never been employed as a civilian by the United States Government. She was not employed at the time of her application, and she indicated she had no "physical defects or infirmities." This latter assertion would prove to be inaccurate.

Monnie graduated from high school in June 1933 and chronicled her employment history from September 1934 through March 1, 1941. She had extensive clerical skills and identified her former job duties as "stenographic," "typist," and "reception, clerk, typist." Her places of employment were all in Minnesota: Red Wing, Parkers Prairie, Osakis, St. Paul, Long Prairie, with the last job in Minneapolis. From personal conversation with one of her brother's sons, he opined that the work ethic in the family was strong and was necessary as Monnie's father, Claude J. Palmatier...*did not make that much money as a barber.*

The Supplemental Information form which accompanied her application, was typed. It is not known if Monnie typed it or if she gave answers to a typist; I think the latter is the case as it seems this process would be handled by an employee and not the applicant. The questions on the form probed her possible employment in "civilian service ...with the U.S. Government," asked if she had worked in any "legislative or judicial branches of the Government," and asked if she had been a "...member of the National Guard, Naval, Marine Corps, or Enlisted Army Reserve, or Officer's Reserve Corps." Answers to each of these preliminary questions was "no."

Manuella "Monnie" Palmatier's official employee identification photograph. The scale behind her makes her look much taller than she really was – 5'2.5". At the bottom is her Employee Badge Number. She is twenty-six.
Source: National Personnel Records Center, National Archives Records Administration, St. Louis, Missouri.

Question nine probed deeper into her life with this: *Are any members of your family or relatives (either blood or by marriage) in any part of the service of the United States (executive, judicial, legislative, military or naval); or the District of Columbia? If so, give name, address, position, relationship, and whether married or single in the case of each person.* Monnie's response provided the first clue about her decision to leave Minnesota and go to Ohio for work: *Winston Palmatier, brother, Erie Proving Ground, single.* It seems likely that Winston, her younger brother who worked for the United States Army at EPG, may have influenced Monnie's decision to seek employment there.

Monnie provided her father's name, Claude J. Palmatier, and his address in Osakis, Minnesota, as the person to be notified…*in case of accident or serious illness… and the person…to whom unpaid salary should be paid in case of death.*

The remaining four questions concerned whether or not Monnie belonged to…*any political party or organization which advocates the overthrow of our constitutional form of government in the United States,* and questioned whether or not she had…*resigned any position under compulsion,* asked if she had…*ever been arrested or fined, or convicted of any offenses*, and wanted to know if she had…*ever been barred from a U.S. Civil Service examination.* Her answer was "no" in each case. Had she answered "yes" in any instance, she would have been required to provide a lengthy explanation. The form was signed on 9/9/41; her name was typed under her signature.

I initially assumed a third, detailed form, the Employee's Declaration, was completed at the time of her application for employment. Instead this was dated July 27, 1942, almost a year after her employment at Erie Proving Ground. This form was typed and verified much of the information she had given a year earlier. Additional information, however, linked the names of her former employers to the Narrative Personal History Report for War Industries (background check files): C. H. Bronson (Osakis, Minn.), L. S. Harbo, (Osakis, Minn.), St. Paul Beauty Academy (St. Paul, Minn.), Mrs. L. C. Johnson (Long Prairie, Minn.), Miss Laura Paulsen (Minneapolis, Minn.), and Mrs. Mary Ann Martin (Minneapolis, Minn.). With regard to these six places of employment, Monnie worked from at least seven months in one location to four and a half years in another. In each case, she changed employers in her search for a better job. Her jobs paid her between $15 and $20 per week or about $1,040 annually. She verified that the Position and Character of Work had been…*typist, typist and filing, student and stenographer, general work, beautician, and beautician and reception clerk.*

Under the Statement of Membership in Organizations (since 1930) included organizations such as…*military, athletic, vocational musical, trade, professional, social, fraternal, political),* was typed *Camp Fire Girls. Social. St. Paul, Minn. (principal office). 10 years.*

She had no violations of the law, and under the Statement of Fingerprinting it said Monnie had been fingerprinted on September 9, 1941, at Erie Proving Ground. She agreed that to the stipulation that…*such fingerprints will be forwarded to the Federal Bureau of Investigation.*

She had never been bonded or insured nor spent any time outside the United States since 1930. The final request was for…*three references, not relatives or former employers or fellow employees, who are more than thirty years of age and United States citizens, business or professional men or women, including your family physician or your family lawyer, and who have known you well during the past ten years.* She first listed *Mrs. Clifford Olson (Osakis, Minn.), Housewife, Osakis, Minn., 10 yrs.* The second reference was *Terry Tano (Port Clinton, Ohio), Contractor, Port Clinton, O., 1 yr.* The final reference was *Dr. Clifford (Alexander {sic}, Minn.), Doctor, Alexander {sic}, Minn.), 20 yrs.* The town cited in the third reference is likely Alexandria, Minnesota, in Douglas County, just ten miles from Osakis.

The form was signed by *Manuella J. Palmatier*, witnessed by *L. M. Pincura, 1st Lt., Ord. Dept., and signed on July 27, 1942*. It contains the signature of *C. A. Loder, Notary Public, Ottawa County, Ohio, whose right to be a Notary expires July 14, 1945*.

One final form, signed by Lt. L. M. Pincura, on July 27, 1942, was the <u>Personnel Security Questionnaire</u> addressed to the Secretary of War, which contained Monnie's full name, her Social Security number, and stated she had been employed for ten months at Erie Proving Ground. Her job was...*Charge of proof unit, proof reading.*

Although the form was not verification of loyalty, the wording just above her full name was certainly strident: *To enable the undersigned to discharge its obligations under the Espionage and National Defense statutes and regulations thereunder, the following facts are submitted for the information of the Government of the United States. This questionnaire is not intended to cast doubt upon the loyalty of any citizen of the United States, but, on the contrary, is intended to establish mutual confidence among loyal defense workers by obviating any suspicion which might be cast upon them, and by making as difficult as possible the employment of agents to foreign governments who by subversive and sabotage tactics might endanger such loyal workers and the work under performance.*

The <u>Personnel Affadavit for the War Department</u>, Ordnance Department, for EPG is a daunting iteration of the Hatch Act, approved by the 76th Congress, on August 2, 1939. With its formal language, it is clear that the employee understands that s/he cannot have...*membership in any political party or organization which advocates the overthrow of our constitutional form of government in the United States.* To do so, and found out, the employee would be...*removed from the position or office held by him.* Violation of the Hatch Act would result in the employee's being...*guilty of a felony and, upon conviction, shall be fined not more than $1,000 or imprisoned for not more than one year, or both, and that the above penalty shall be in addition to, and not in substitution for, any other provisions of existing law.*

Just above her signature, Monnie agreed that...*I will not advocate nor become a member of any political party or organization that advocates the overthrow of the Government of the United States by force or violence.*

In addition, Monnie's signature appears on the <u>Oath of Office</u> relative to employment at Erie Proving Ground. The oath, dated September 9, 1941, is a familiar one:

> *I, Manuella J. Palmatier, do solemnly swear (or affirm) that I will support and defend the Constitution of the United States against all enemies, foreign and domestic; that I will bear true faith and allegiance to the same; that I take this obligation freely, without mental reservation or purpose of evasion; and that I will well and faithfully discharge the duties of the office on which I am about to enter.* **So Help Me God.**

With this form signed, Monnie was appointed as an *Under Clk.-Typist, CAF-1*.

Interestingly, the four background checks on Aunt Monnie were completed after her 26th birthday in 1942, and well after the start of her employment at EPG the previous September. The heading on each, with a cautionary notation, was as follows.

Narrative
Personal History Report for War Industries

Acct. No. 39317
Date of Filing:
Palmatier, Manuella Joyce
Pt. Clinton, O. 609 Jackson Dr.
Erie Proving Ground, LaCarne, O.

File No. Month-Day-Year

Caution to Customer: *In accordance with our agreement, this report is released with understanding that information in this report is STRICTLY CONFIDENTIAL; not to be communicated to person reported on or to anyone else.*

The branch office location was typed on each form: Toledo and Minneapolis. This was followed by the city in which the Report of Investigation occurred: respectively, Port Clinton, Ohio, and Minneapolis, Osakis, and Long Prairie, Minnesota.

Each <u>Narrative Personal History Report for War Industries</u> asked for the same basic information: name and address of the person being investigated, age, whether loyal to...*our government, a statement of personal reputation, and whether the person is satisfactory to employ in war industry.* The statement about Racial Descent was variously answered three times as *French-American*, and once as *French-Anglo Saxon*.

Each Narrative provides background data for the person being checked, but, more importantly, the questions and answers speak to the paranoia of the time. The interviewers summarized or truncated the answers given by informants and the phraseology speaks to the subjective nature of the answers and the apparent conclusions each interviewer derived from the answers to his questions. Not all of the information given by "witnesses" was accurate because peoples' memories about their neighbors' lives can become fuzzy as time and events move on.

<u>File No. 9-14-42, dated 9-17-42</u>, taken in Long Prairie, Minnesota, through the Minneapolis Office. This report is the briefest of the four - just 176 words. *This investigation has been conducted at the applicant's former address, Long Prairie, Minnesota. Manuella Joyce Palmatier is 26 years of age and of French-Amer. racial descent. She graduated from Osakis High School with a good record. {Mrs. L. C. Johnson employer}. The applicant worked for this lady as a hairdresser for four and one-half years. She had a good record there and was considered competent. She left because she wanted to find a job in the city. The applicant is native born and her parents are also native born. We do not learn of any acts of disloyalty to our government or acts of friendliness to foreign government. The applicant was not active in civic or*

fraternal organizations while here nor was she an active church member. Criminal records have been checked with negative results. The applicant is single and has no dependents. She boarded while here and her home surroundings were congenial. She is dependable and honest and we do not learn of any ill health or handicaps. Her associates were loyal and respectable citizens.

The *Osakis Review* fills in Monnie's history as a hairdresser. *Miss Manuella Palmatier left Monday morning for St. Paul where she will attend the Paul's School of Hairdressing and Cosmetology* (*Osakis Review,* September 5, 1935 and September 19, 1935). There also appears to be an error in the length of time given for Monnie's work at the Beauty Nook. In 1936, Monnie transferred to Lois Johnson's second beauty salon located in Long Prairie; she was the manager there. Therefore, Monnie worked for L. C. Johnson for 4.5 years.

Her employment in the winter of 1936/1937 was interrupted. Monnie contracted scarlet fever just before Christmas and her mother traveled to Monnie's home in Alexandria to care for her (*Osakis Review*, December 24, 1936). Emma did not return home until January 5, 1937, and Monnie followed to recuperate (*Osakis Review*, January 7, 1937). Scarlett fever was epidemic in Minnesota during the winters of 1935/1936 and 1936/1937. Monnie may not have returned to work full time until mid-February 1937.

As will become apparent later, not all statements about Monnie's health are accurate.

<u>File No. 9-14-42, dated 9-18-42</u>, taken in Osakis through the Minneapolis Office provided more information. *Inquiry made of above through three merchant-neighbor sources who knew applicant while she was employed as below and while she was living with her parents in this village all her life prior to 1936. Miss Manuella Joyce Palmatier is 26 years old, and is of French descent. She graduated from the local high school. We are unable to contact either of applicant's former employers in this city, since both have moved out of town, but the following is a synopsis of her past employment history as recalled by informants: 'After graduating from high school, applicant secured a position as typist under Mr. C. H. Bronson at the Osakis Review, local newspaper. She was there from 1934 until 1935, but was laid off when her employer sold out the business. She then was employed on C.W.A. under Dr. L. S. Harbo on a library project in this village until the spring of 1936. At that time she went to St. Paul, Minnesota, where she took a beauty course for about six months. After completion of this course, she secured a position as operator in a beauty parlor operated by Mrs. L. C. Johnson at Alexandria, Minnesota. She was in that city from the late fall of 1936 until the winter of 1937, when she went to Long Prairie, Minnesota to manage a beauty parlor for Mrs. L. C. Johnson. In about January of 1940, she went to Minneapolis, Minnesota, where she was employed by a Miss Laura Paulsen in a beauty shop until November, 1940. She then secured a better position under Mrs. M. A. Martin as an operator at the beauty shop in the Curtis Hotel in Minneapolis, and was so employed until about January, 1942, when she secured a position at a Government proving grounds in Ohio.' Applicant is regarded locally as a capable, industrious, and ambitious young lady with favorable future prospects.*

Further, informants attested that: *American born of native parents. 100% American in every respect, loyalty to U.S. Government unquestioned. Has one brother in the U.S. Army. In checking for any criminal record, the investigator found: Police files checked with negative results.* Final information on her personal character: *Single, lived with parents, a good laboring class section of village among Scandanavian and Anglo-Saxon people of good repute. Worth about $500, honest and dependable, financially responsible. Personal reputation as to habits, morals, and associates is of the best. Health good. Social activities were confined to the usual dates of young people, but applicant belonged to no lodges, clubs, or associations. Father is Claude Palmatier, barber in this town since 1914. Business, financial, and personal reputation good. American born of French descent, loyalty to the U.S. Government unquestioned. Has one son in the U.S. Army.* On her Personal Statement, Monnie indicated she had belonged to Camp Fire Girls for ten years. Apparently this document was not available to the investigator or, perhaps, her activities as a child were disregarded.

The information in this background check is not entirely accurate. Monnie may have worked at the *Osakis Review* from 1934-1935, but her time with the Civil Works Administration (CWA) could not have been in 1935-1936, as reported. The CWA only existed from November 1933 to April 1, 1934. It was the initial program in President Franklin Roosevelt's New Deal. It employed four million men and women – the men worked on physically strenuous construction/improvement projects, while the women were employed as seamstresses or in other inside work. Monnie's "library project" would have fit with her skill set (writer, typist, high school and town newspaper work), and with her petite physical stature.

Monnie was employed at Lois Beauty Nook in Alexandria in April 1936, just before she took her license examination (*Osakis Review*, April 2, 1936). She...*received her permanent license last week and is now assistant operator at the Lois Beauty Nook in Alexandria* (*Osakis Review*, May 21, 1936). By July 1937, Monnie was a beauty shop manager in Long Prairie. She was in Ohio in January 1942, no longer a beautician in Minneapolis.

Even though the time cited above about her employment in Ohio (January 1942) does not jibe with the official government records, it is apparent that small towns are a world unto themselves. Osakis was populated by individuals whose knowledge of their neighbors in the 1940s rivals any data that can be found on the internet! It was (and is) a small town of probably fewer than one-thousand seven-hundred people in 1940, her father was a barber, and her mother a musician who performed throughout the County, she graduated from a small high school, and her first job was with the local newspaper, and her parents socialized with the editor/ owner of the newspaper. I am sure that Aunt Monnie's every childhood move was well-known in the community, compiled, and evaluated!

File No. 9-12-42, dated 9-18-42, taken in Minneapolis, Minnesota, was quite long. *This investigation has been conducted through two former Minneapolis employers, and a personal acquaintance in this city. An informant was also interviewed at 1005 6th Ave. S., a former Minneapolis residence address. Coverage was obtained in Minneapolis from 1939 until*

August of 1941, when the subject left the city. Manuella Joyce Palmatier is 26 years of age and of French-Anglo Saxon descent. She was graduated from high school and also took beauty operator's training in a school in St. Paul. Full details of present employment are not known here, but is known that she is employed in Ohio, on some government job. She has been away from Minneapolis since August of 1941. {Mrs. Mary Ann Martin-Curtis Hotel-Owner of Beauty Parlor} Mrs. Martin was interviewed, was unable to supply any exact dates, but reports that Miss Palmatier was in her employ from early in 1940 until about the middle of August, 1941. At that time she resigned her job giving ill health as her reason. She left in good standing and is eligible for re-hire. Monnie had already planned to move to Ohio, so her excuse of ill health was not true.

{*Miss Laura Paulsen-owner of beauty parlor} Miss Paulsen was interviewed and reports that the subject was in her employ for approximately 8 or 9 months starting in the summer of 1939. She was a beauty operator and finally resigned of her own accord presumably to take another position. However, Miss Paulsen states that the subject was not dependable and although not discharged, she would not re-hire her. Nothing more definite could be obtained from this employer in the way of criticism of the subject, and the inspector received the impression that Miss Paulsen was prejudiced, for some reason not disclosed.*

Prior to 1939, Miss Palmatier was employed by Mrs. L. C. Johnson, now of Long Prairie, Minn., who previously operated the beauty parlor at Alexandria, Minn., where the subject was employed. An informant who knew here there reports that she was well regarded at the latter point.

Her birthplace is in this country and her parents were also native born. She is not known to have made any trips abroad and has no known foreign relatives. She is not active in civic or church affairs here. Her attitude toward the international situation was favorable. Her name does not appear in criminal apprehension records, district court records or subversive activity lists.

She was single, had no dependents, and worth was estimated at $500. She rented an apartment with another young woman at 1005 6th Ave. S., which is in an Anglo Saxon and Scandinavian working class district. Home surroundings were desirable. There was no criticism of habits, or associates. Informants other than Miss Paulsen considered her dependable and honest and of good character. The subject is a very small girl and of frail build. It is unlikely that she would be able to stand any type of work requiring a great deal of strength.

The above investigator is the only one who commented on possible limitations to Monnie's employment based on her physicality. He is the only one who referred to her as a "subject" rather than an "applicant" as did the other three investigators.

The exact dates given for Monnie's employment do not exactly match the information taken from Local News in the *Osakis Review*. Since informants' memories can be incorrect, I used the data from the newspaper because it was printed in real time.

<u>File No. 9-14-42, dated 9-24-42</u>, taken at Port Clinton, Ohio, provided overall information about Monnie's employment at Erie Proving Ground. *This investigation has been conducted through landlady, and through close neighborhood sources. Manuella Joyce*

Palmattier {sic} age 26, and of French-American Descent. Informants here have only known here {sic} in recent months and would regard her as having at least a high school education. Applicant for the past 10 months, has been employed by the Erie Proving Ground, at LaCarne, O. No other employment, locally. Is native born, has no relative in foreign countries, has never traveled abroad, shown no acts of disloyalty. Is not active in local or civic affairs. Not attended church since coming here. Is a loyal American. All informants here agree that your applicant has no police or criminal record. Single, has no dependents, and has worth estimated at $400, she and three other girls rent a small bungalow adjoining the Alano Home, a better class residential part of this city. Home surroundings are pleasant, Anglo-Saxon residents. Associates with other girls also employed by the Proving Grounds, and is well regarded. Activities consists of an occasional visit to the movies, and the girls attending dances at the local service center, this being the Armory building. She conducts herself in a normal manner, and is honest, dependable, and temperate in habits, never known to drink to excess. Good health, and has no handicaps, parents are not known by local informants.

An Undiagnosed Medical Condition

Manuella Joyce Palmatier had a basic physical examination prior to beginning her work at Erie Proving Ground, but apparently, not a thorough one. She had an undiagnosed congenital heart disease that was not discovered, or at least not acknowledged by her, until her hospitalization at the EPG Post Hospital in 1944. Captain Paul Chrenka, Medical Officer, oversaw several tests performed on Aunt Monnie: *Two electrocardiograms, x-rays and a fluoroscopy report.*

Another document provided by NARA is a request to Lt. C. R. Quellmalz, on September 20, 1941, to the Proof Division, Planning Section, where Aunt Monnie worked. The statement is brief and reads like a memo: *Please advise Miss Manuella J. Palmatier that her Certificate of Medical Examination has not yet been received by the Civilian Personnel Office. It is requested that she take care of this matter as soon as possible.* The typed request was initiated by J. W. Tettau/jer on 20 September 1941. This request to complete the medical examination was not followed up for thirty months, either by bureaucratic oversight, or because Aunt Monnie did not want her condition known.

Along with the medical data sent by the National Archives and Records Administration, was the Electrocardiograph Report, dated March 16, 1944, well after she was assigned her war-related duties. She was designated a Federal Employee whom Captain Wertheimer described as having the following diagnosis: *Heart disease since birth. EKG shows left axis deviation with to-and-fro murmur heard throughout the chest with thrill (systolic over aortic and pulmonic areas). Bruit heard over the large arteries and thrill felt in supraclavicular notch. Slight cyanosis of finger nails and toe nails. Parrot nails. Congenital heart disease without evidence of failure. Can do light work only.*

The assignment to light work was suggested two years earlier by the Minneapolis investigator who completed a background check on Monnie. Her brothers, Wharton and Winston died of heart failure in their eighth decade, as did her father, Claude J.

Palmatier in his early sixties. Heart failure eventually took Monnie's life at the age of fifty-three. Clearly, heart problems were endemic in this family. Sadly, Monnie's heart condition caused her and Alfred Payton to decide not to have children, reportedly something they both wanted.

The <u>Certificate of Medical Examination</u>, which was completed before the above tests were done, was a document of the United States Civil Service Commission, and was dated March 7, 1944. It was signed by both the attending physician and Manuella Palmatier. This exam was defined as a Physical Re-Check. Her eyes, ears, nose and throat, veins, feet and so forth were normal. However, under question seven, the doctor wrote…*loud and blowing double murmur heard best over tricuspid area and also heard over other areas.*

The physician completed the question asking for his opinion regarding her duties: *capable of performing duties involving <u>light only</u> physical exertion. Further, under remarks, he wrote…Gives history of vascular leakage since birth – EKG to be taken – slight blueness of nail but no clubbing of fingers or toes – no evidence of decompensation.*

On January 26, 1943, one record states Manuella Palmatier, *Badge No. 20-516, Proof Division, Record Bldg. #88 Section, has been vaccinated for small-pox. December 1941. Post Hospital.* The form was signed by Dorothy E. Huss, RN, Nurse, First Aid Station No. 2. Smallpox vaccinations were essential in the early part of the 20th Century because of the horror of this disease. There were one-hundred-thousand cases in the United States in 1921, and an epidemic in Minnesota from 1924-1925 with five-hundred-four deaths. There was no global campaign to eradicate the disease until 1959.

Later, between March 9, 1950 and April 25, 1950, letters were exchanged between Dr. David W. Feigal, MD, Wayzata, Minnesota, and Colonel John J. Donovan, AGD Commanding, regarding access to the medical records on Manuella J. Palmatier (now, Payton), during the time she was at Erie Proving Ground. The initial request for medical records made by Dr. Feigal was deflected by Colonel Donovan whose March 24, 1950 letter states in the second paragraph: *It is not the policy of the Department of the Army to furnish medical information contained in official records unless the release is authorized by the former patient concerned. It is therefore, suggested that your request be supplemented by a statement signed by Mrs. Payton indicating her desire that the records be furnished. Upon receipt of such authorization, your request will received {sic} prompt attention.*

On April 14, 1950, (Mrs.) Manuella Palmatier Payton typed a request to the Chief, Civilian Personnel, NARA, St. Louis, Missouri to request that her medical records be sent to Dr. Feigal. Her language is clear, professional, and very polite:

> *Dear Sir:*
>
> *I was just notified by Dr. Fiegal of Col. Donovan's letter to him Mar. 24. As Dr. Fiegal told you, we are trying to get the medical records or copies of the examinations that were made of my heart condition at Erie Proving Ground during the war. I originally wrote Erie Proving Ground and was referred by them to you and it was suggested at that time that I have my doctor write you.*
>
> *My heart condition is very unusual and my doctor is planning on taking me through the new heart clinic soon to be in operation at the University of Minnesota. We would like very much to have the records and tests made by Capt. Chrenka at the post hospital at EPG in order to determine whether or not there has been any change since that time.*
>
> Monnie went on to list the tests for which she needed copies, and indicated the records would be under her maiden name. She ended her request with…
>
> *I feel sure that we can count on your cooperation in this matter. Thank you.*
>
> *Sincerely yours, (Mrs.) Manuella Palmatier Payton.*

On April 25, 1950, Colonel John J. Donovan mailed Dr. Fiegal the…*photostatic copies of Certificate of Medical Examination dated 7 March 1944 and Electrocardiograph Report dated 16 March 1944*. A copy of the letter went to Monnie.

I do not know what medical treatment Aunt Monnie received for the rest of her life. However, their move to Arizona in the 1950s may be a clue to extending her life by living in a less harsh climate than that afforded to her in Minnesota.

Work at the US Army Ordnance Department

Taken from an on-line history entitled *The History of Ordnance in America*, I learned that the Ordnance Department (OD) is one of the United States Army's oldest branches, going back to the Colonial era. OD expanded in number and scope (including seven proving grounds and other installations) when President Franklin Roosevelt developed his Arsenal of Democracy to combat the Axis forces during World War II. Seventy-six installations focused on ammunition and explosives.

To operate these facilities the number of officers increased from three-hundred thirty-four to twenty-four thousand, and from four-thousand to three-hundred twenty-five thousand enlisted, and from twenty-seven thousand eighty-eight to two-hundred sixty-two thousand civilians, the latter of whom included eighty-five thousand Women Ordnance Workers (WOW).

EPG was originally known as Camp Perry Proving Ground. At EPG nearly all World War II artillery and tank armament received final acceptance tests. The installation employed five-thousand people who tested armor plate and weapons systems, and developed and tested new types of ordnance. This area was a heavily militarized zone, secured and operated by the United States Army. Camp Perry is now a National Guard training facility.

The war was very personal to Port Clinton residents, and to the civilian and military employees at EPG. Many Port Clinton soldiers were part of Company C, 37th Tank Company, of the 192nd Tank Battalion, who were the first to engage the enemy in a tank-to-tank battle during World War II. They fought in the Bataan Peninsula, Philippine Islands, and surrendered on April 9, 1942, after months of combat. Those surviving were interned by the Japanese until December 1944. The war was <u>very</u> personal.

As I worked through the material on EPG, I learned that two groups of prisoners of war were housed at Camp Perry. *World War II Prisoner of War Camps in Ohio* informed my thinking with a detailed and accurate portrayal of life for POWs in northern Ohio. There were both Italian and German POWs; I focused on the Italians only. The first group of Italians arrived on October 10, 1943, after Italy's capitulation that fall. They formed the Italian Service Unit (ISU) and, by all accounts, worked hard and were model prisoners who helped with the labor shortage in the United States by filling in for local residents whose family members were serving in the military. One-thousand Italian POWs worked at Erie Proving Ground as grounds sweepers, PX workers, and cafeteria waiters. Significantly, several ISU members were assigned to recondition and service artillery guns (40-mm and 90-mm anti-aircraft guns), and to load and unload trucks. Italian POWs worked alongside civilian workers.

> Erie Proving Ground's Strategic Importance
> Proof-fired/shipped 70% of mobile artillery for the U.S. and its Allies
> 90,000 artillery units (all calibers) shipped = greatest volume in U.S. history
> 50 rail carloads shipped daily
> 70 truckloads shipped daily
> Adapted from Van Kueren, p. 50

While the POWs cooked, ate, and lived a seeming world apart from their civilian co-workers, the ISU members' integration into daily life, and their social intercourse with people from Toledo, Ohio's large Italian population largely made them welcome. I do not know if my Aunt Monnie interacted with these workers, but surely their apparent pleasant presence must have allowed her and other civilians to learn more about Italy and its people. I wonder at what conversations could have occurred.

Aunt Monnie began her job at Erie Proving Ground on September 9, 1941, as an *Under Clerk Typist, Ordnance Department at Large*. The War Department kept careful records of its employees and the National Archives Records Administration provided those, including: <u>Ordnance Department-Notices of Civilian Employment; Individual Record of Class A Pay Reservation Payroll Deduction and War Bond Issues; Individual Earning Record (by the Half-Calendar Year); Reports of Efficiency Ratings</u>; and letters of recommendation for her many promotions within the fifty-seven months she worked in the war effort. Some documents were duplicated and sent to, and signed by, more than one person. I placed these documents on a timeline which allowed me to get a clearer picture of what she was asked to accomplish (see Appendix 2, p. 177).

The <u>Notice of Civilian Employment</u> was a fill-in-the-blank typed document formatted like a memo. From the Erie Proving Ground Commanding Officer to the District Manager of the Sixth U. S. Civil Service District in Cincinnati, Manuella J. Palmatier (badge #20-315) was officially appointed an *Under Clerk Typist, CAF-1*, citing her oath of office as September 9, 1941, the same day she began working. Her badge number had changed.

She was paid $1260 annually. Her appointment was granted by telephone, citing Section 2, Rule VIII. The official stamp of approval stated she was *Approved for temporary appointment under Sec. 2, Rule VIII, pending register of eligibles*.

On September 20, 1941, an Erie Proving Ground Captain, Administrative Officer, completed the <u>Job Sheet for Field Service Appointments</u>, which delineated Monnie's job tasks. Her immediate supervisor was 1st Lieutenant C. R. Quellmalz, Ordnance Dept., U.S.A. *The Description of duties, with approximate percentage of time spent on each major operation: Typing 70%, Clerical work 20%, Sorting, arranging, and filing records 10%.* A notation just to the left of this time allocation, was stamped EMERGENCY ALLOCATION; and was initialed by *h.s.*

A written request to ratify her temporary appointment was sent to the *Secretary of War, Washington, DC, Thru Manager, Sixth U.S. Civil Service District, and Chief of Ordnance*. The letter was dated September 20, 1941, and asked for approval of Monnie's *position as Under Clerk-Typist, CAF 1, at $1260 per annum, effective 9 September 1941… Other papers pertaining to the employment of the appointee have been previously forwarded to the office of the District Manager*. Captain J. A. McNerney, Administrative Officer, signed the letter.

A memo was sent from the *Secretary of War, War Dept., Ordnance Office, Washington, D.C. November 3, 1941*. The War Department returned a form to the Commanding Officer, Erie Proving Ground, on November 5, 1941, which stated *Nature of Action: Confirmation of Temporary Assignment*. The <u>Confirmation of Temporary Appointment</u> was issued after she had been working for eight weeks. The Erie Proving Ground Commanding Office received a copy of the confirmation on November 10, 1941. She was official, retroactive to September 9, 1941.

NARA Documents included many <u>Report of Efficiency Rating</u> forms from March 1942 to July 1945. Each was tied to a promotion earned by Manuella J. Palmatier. The first was dated March 31, 1942, after she had been employed for eight and a half months. The report evaluated her job performance retroactive to September 9, 1941, as she functioned as an *Under-Clk Typist, in the War Ordnance Department, Industrial Division, Proof Section*. She was rated by Captain Carl R. Quellmalz Ordnance Department on May 12, and countersigned by Major Eddy, Ordnance Department on May 13, 1942.

In answer to the summary question...*On the whole, do you consider the conduct of this employee to be satisfactory?* They answered *Yes*. Interestingly, they did not rate any of the thirty-one skill sets separately listed on the form. Twenty were pertinent to the job, with an additional eleven used to rate supervisors. That section of the form was blank. On a four-point scale, Monnie was rated...*VG* (Very Good), just below excellent.

General skill sets for this job included maintaining equipment, skill in the application of techniques and procedures, accuracy and attention to detail, interpersonal skills, ability to complete assignments in a timely fashion, physical fitness for the work, cooperativeness, initiative, resourcefulness, and dependability. I thought the skill called *Industry* was interesting, and really have no idea what was meant by that.

On June 12, 1942, the Chief, Civilian Personnel Section, approved the EPG <u>Recommendation for a Change in Status</u> for Aunt Monnie's promotion from *Under Clerk Typist, CAF-1 to Jr. Clerk, CAF-2*. She received an increase in annual salary from $1,260 to $1,440. She increased her war bond contributions as she earned her promotions. The reason given for her promotion was: *This employee is now performing the duties of a Junior Clerk in a very satisfactory manner*. She was promoted after nine months on the job.

With this promotion came a change in job duties as indicated on the <u>Job Sheet for Field Civil Service Appointments</u>, signed June 22, 1942. The breakdown in percentage of time for each job duty clearly underscores the change of status: *Supervision of preparation of artillery material firing records 50%, Sorting and arranging firing records for typists 20%, and Checking artillery material firing records for accuracy in transcription, completeness, and legibility 30%*. She was supervised by Captain Carl R. Quellmalz who indicated she needed *moderately close guidance during progress of tasks by Captain, Ordnance Dept*. She supervised five Under Clerk Typists. By July 9, 1942, all departments had received the <u>Notification of Personnel Action</u> regarding her promotion which was initiated by the War Department. She worked in the Ordnance Department at Large.

About eight months later, something changed. On March 31, 1943, Aunt Monnie received only a *Good* overall rating on the <u>Report of Efficiency Rating Retroactive to March 31, 1942</u>. She was rated by Captain Carl R. Quellmalz on April 17, 1943. She was Supervisor of the Proof Reading Room, but the <u>Conduct Report</u> noted Monnie had taken 30 days off: *14 days S.L. {sick leave}, 13 5/8 days A.L. {annual leave}, and 2 3/8 days N.S. (1 s.l. and 1 3/8 a.l.)*. I do not know why she was away from her job, but, apparently, her supervisor did not approve even though her time off is tagged as sick leave, and annual leave. This may have been a time she traveled to Akron, Ohio, to visit her mother and her father.

To add to the confusion, on June 10, 1943, Monnie received a form signed by Lt. Colonel N. H. Strickland, Chairman, Efficiency Rating Committee. Although she was informed that her March 31, 1943...*adjective efficiency rated for the period ending 31 March 1943 is Good...In regard to the element of conduct, you are advised that, on the whole, same was considered **not** {emphasis as given on report} satisfactory*. There was no explanation or description of the unsatisfactory conduct.

Whatever happened in March 1943 did not prevent Aunt Monnie from receiving a second Change in Status about six weeks later. On June 30, 1943, her promotion, which had been granted on June 1, 1943, was approved and recorded on the Report of Field Personnel Action. She was moved from Junior Clerk to Assistant Clerk, with an increase in annual salary from $1,440 to $1,620. This was considerably more money than she was making in 1940 in the civilian world as a beautician. On the form it stated: *Acton taken as results of recent survey of graded positions at this establishment by Office of the Chief of Ordnance*. Perhaps an evaluation of job duties and persons assigned to them along with office protocol or procedures, came as a result of the unsatisfactory conduct rating. No clear picture can be discerned at this point.

The poor conduct rating in March 1943 did not deter her rise in civilian rating and her pay schedule confirms that as indicated by the Recommendation for Change In Status, dated January 18, 1944. The Report of Efficiency Rating, covering her performance from April 1, 1943 to March 31, 1944, netted Aunt Monnie eight *Outstanding* scores for the basic job duties she performed, and five *Adequate* check marks for those duties earmarked as *Supervisory*. She still fell short in her interpersonal skills in the view of the Principal Clerk, CAF-5.

On November 13, 1943, the Chief, Records Section, completed a Special Report Commending a Group of Employees (there were eight women), of whom *Miss Manuella Palmatier CAF-3*, was listed. Following that, on November 26, 1943, Major C. B. Potter, Ordnance Department, sent a separate letter to *Miss Manuella Palmatier, Proof Division*, which stated:

Dear Madam,

In accordance with the orders of Major C. L. Sidinger, Chief, Proof Division, a "Special Report – For", dated 13 November 1943, has been permanently filed in your service record.

This report states that you are to be commended for your fine spirit of cooperation and conscientious efforts in planning and carrying out a program resulting in the simplification of work in your section, thus making possible the release of seven (7) Clerk Typists to other divisions where they were badly needed.

You are reminded that this report and letter may be referred to for personal reference purposes at any time.

For this Commanding Officer:
    C. B. Potter, Major, Ordnance Department, Chief,
    Civilian Personnel Branch

The <u>Special Report For Group of Employees</u> referenced in the letter, went on to state: *In the spirit of making some contribution which might aid in easing the present man-power shortage, these supervisors carefully analyzed their work and effected changes which ultimately permitted seven (7) Clerk Typists to be released for other work. In addition, their experience and knowledge of their jobs were vital factors in accomplishing work simplification, the benefits of which have not yet been fully realized. Their attitude is highly commendable and it is felt that the high echelons of command at this station should know about the good work that these people are doing.*

The eight women were listed by name; one was a CAF-5, one a CAF-4, and the remaining six were CAF-3s, including Monnie. The form with the letter were received November 23, 1943, by Civilian Personnel.

Apparently, Aunt Monnie rose above the criticism leveled against her the previous spring, in order to be cited in this singular fashion. The letter and report became part of her permanent record. It is unknown if Monnie had formally appealed her poor conduct report or if her continued good work was sufficient to change the minds of her supervisors.

By January 18, 1944, the <u>Recommendation For Change In Status</u> moved Monnie from Assistant Clerk (CAF-3 at $1,620 annually) to Clerk (CAF-4 at $1,800 annually). Her new job made her a supervisor who served…*as working leader of the checking group in the checking of all completed Proof Firing Certificates and Firing Records for accuracy and form prior to mailing. As working leader, performs the following duties:*

60% - receives all incoming Firing Records and checks them for correct nomenclature, legibility, and grammatical correctness.
30% - Assigns Firing Records to various groups for typing according to type of material.
10% - Prepares a daily report of work completed by this unit.

In addition to the above, Monnie performed these duties…*Under general supervision responsible for checking of remarks in the completed Firing Records and Certificates for clearness.* Finally, she supervised…*three CAF-2 Clerk Typists, $1,440 P.A.*

On January 22, 1944, the <u>War Department Report of Field Personnel Action</u> was signed by the Commander of the Ordnance Department, and officially announced Monnie's promotion to Clerk, effective February 1, 1944. The form was sent to the U.S. Civil Service Commission, Washington, D.C.

A month later, another <u>Report of Efficiency Rating</u> was completed for Monnie covering April 1, 1943 to March 31, 1944. This time, ten of the twenty skills in the general skills column and three of the eleven skills in the supervisory column were marked. She received a plus sign indicating *Outstanding* for techniques, accuracy, effectiveness, completing her work, cooperation and being resourceful. Her supervisor stated the work she produced was based on production records. However, they gave her only an *Adequate* check mark for…*effectiveness in meeting and dealing with others* and in *dependability.*

In the column asking for the assessment of supervisory skills, Monnie received only *adequate* check marks in three areas: *effectiveness in directing, reviewing, and checking the work of subordinates; effectiveness in instructing, training, and developing subordinates in the work; and effectiveness in promoting high working morale.* Her overall official adjective rating, however, was *Very good.* It was March 1944 when the full report of her medical contition as made known.

As Clerk CAF-4, Monnie received another Report of Efficiency Rating. This would be her last one, as she left to marry Chief Alfred James Payton, U.S. Navy, in June 1945. The report covered her employment from March 31, 1944 to March 31, 1945. On it the evaluator, Gerald T. Flynn, Administrative Assistant, submitted his findings on April 5, 1945. It was reviewed on April 5, and approved by the Efficiency Rating Committee on April 28, 1945. She received a rating of *VG* (Very Good). However, in the column listing individual skill sets, she received *Outstanding* plus marks showing improvement in *Dependability*, a skill set that was underlined by the evaluator. She received a plus mark for...*Attention to broad phases of assignments;* this was underlined. But she received only an *Adequate* check mark for *attention to pertinent detail.* She was not evaluated on her supervisory skills on this final form.

Her final Conduct Report was dated July 12, 1945, by 1st Lt. L. C. Humble, Jr. Monnie was: *Eligible for a periodic pay increase on 1 July 1945 provided employee's conduct has been satisfactory.* On July 13, 1945, A. B. Johnson, Major, Ordnance Department, Chief, Proof Division, wrote: *I certify that the conduct of the above employee (has) (has not)* been satisfactory. {*cross out one}* She left her employment in everyone's good graces, after all.

Resignation as a Government Clerk

Resigning from her job was not an easy process for Aunt Monnie. After working at Erie Proving Ground for forty-five months, her Resignation and Exit Interview (REI) was begun on June 11, 1945, and signed by Manuella J. Palmatier, Badge No. 22-274. The REI was a three-part form forwarded in triplicate and each copy was signed. Her badge number had changed again.

Part 1 was addressed to the Commanding Officer, EPG, LaCarne, Ohio. Aunt Monnie stated her resignation was to become effective June 13, 1945, and gave "leave of absence" as the reason for submitting the form. Gerald Flynn, Board Section, Administration Branch, acknowledged and signed the REI on June 13, 1945.

Part 2, Divisional Interview and Remarks stated: *Employee has been granted a month's leave of absence – to return 19 July 1945.* James S. Stewart recommended acceptance of the request when he signed for A. B. Johnson, Major, Ordnance Department, Chief, Proof Division.

Further typewritten remarks were: *Employee's fiancé just returned from overseas and she has been granted a leave of absence for one month during which time she plans to be married. Will return at end of that time if he is sent back overseas, but will remain with him otherwise. Employment satisfactory. Clearance forms checked.*

The final part of the REI was signed by L. C. Humble, Jr., and stamped 1st Lt. Ord. Dept. Typewritten on the lower left corner was the name of her supervisor, Gerald Flynn, and this was date stamped Jun 20 1945. The form was forwarded in triplicate.

The <u>Check Sheet for Resignations</u> summarized her basic employment data: name, badge number, address, designation and grade (clerk), rate of pay (CAF-4 $1800 $2166 p.a.), birth date, social security number, and an indication she was a white female, and a Non-V (non-veteran). Left blank was the Effective Date and the *Last Day Paid Through.*

Aunt Monnie marred Alfred J. Payton on June 16, 1945, just before Al's birthday, then he left Ohio for Minnesota and California, where he was eventually mustered out of the United States Navy. She remained for a few weeks in Ohio to care for her mother who had been hospitalized. Their marriage was announced in her hometown newspaper:

Palmatier-Payton

Mr. and Mrs. C. Palmatier announce the marriage of their daughter, Manuella, to Chief Petty Officer Alfred J. Payton, son of Mr. and Mrs. H. E. Payton of Wayzata, Minn.

Chief Payton recently returned to the states after serving 26 months in the Pacific as a newsreel and aerial photographer. They were married June 16 in the T.T. Lano home in Port Clinton, Ohio, where the bride had made her home for nearly four years while employed by the Army Ordnance Dept. at Erie Proving Ground.

Osakis Review, Local News and Social Events, June 28, 1945

Sadly, Al's nephew, Johnny Payton Cargill, died on June 15, 1945, in a ranching accident in Montana, Monnie's mother had a serious operation in Akron in late July, and her father, Claude J. Palmatier, died on September 5, 1945, in Akron. Those summer months were filled with joy, happiness, and incredible sorrow.

Apparently, the process to affect her resignation was misunderstood as she received a letter dated August 11, 1946, from the Office of the Commanding Officer, Army Service Forces, Ordnance Department, questioning her reasons for her continued absence. Someone did not read the Resignation and Exit Interview form which clearly stated her intentions.

The letter to her was a formal one and seemed strident in its tone:

> Dear Madam,
>
> Records in this office disclose that you were granted a leave of absence by your division chief, from 13 June 1945 to 17 July 1945. Upon the expiration of this leave, you were expected to return to duty at this establishment; however, word was received from your division that you had been granted a brief extension as you were uncertain about returning.
>
> You will understand, however, that it is impossible to continue carrying you on the rolls indefinitely; therefore, it will be necessary for you to forward an immediate reply in writing stating the reason for your continued absence and the probable date of your return to duty at this establishment.
>
> You are hereby notified that failure to report for work or furnish a satisfactory explanation of your absence by 20 August 1945 will constitute grounds for removal for abandonment of your position, and such action will be effected as of that date.
>
> If separation is effected, it will be necessary for you to return all government property in your possession, such as identification badge and pass, supplemental gas books, tools, etc., before final pay for services rendered and any accrued annual leave to your credit can be released.
>
> Very truly yours,
>
> L. C. HUMBLE, JR., 1st Lt. Ord Dept Assistant

On August 17, 1945, a woman living at Monnie's Port Clinton address signed for the registered letter sent by 1st Lt. L. C. Humble, Jr. Aunt Monnie responded within three days and on August 20, 1945, she addressed a letter to the Personnel Division, Erie Proving Ground, Attn: Lt. Humble. Her handwritten, one-page letter was clear and apologetic. It was postmarked August 22, 1945, sent Air Mail (8c postage stamp!), with a return address in Alameda, California.

> Attn. Lt. Humble,
>
> In answer to your letter of 11 August, I hereby tender my resignation. I was unable to do this sooner as we were moving according to my husband's Navy orders and our status was too indefinite. Now that he is being discharged, I am resigning.
>
> All my identification papers, cigarette card, pass, etc. were turned in before I left the Proving Ground.
>
> I am sorry if my inability to write this sooner in any way inconvenienced you.
>
> Sincerely yours,
> Mrs. A. J. Payton
> (nee Manuella Palmatier)

Although Aunt Monnie's letter is certainly polite, I suspect she was not sincere in her final apology.

In order for her to receive her final pay, the EPG Civilian Employee Clearance Sheet needed to be completed. There was very little data, but the effective date of separation was listed as...*close of business on 24 August 1945*. The form was prepared, signed by *A. F. Signore, 1st Lt., Ord. Dept. cak*. I believe the signature was written by an assistant, given the small letter "cak" – a clerical practice used to expedite paperwork, and the paper was date stamped *Aug 27 1945*.

The Clearance Sheet was redone and these words were hand written at the top in pen: *corrected copy*. In pencil across the main body of the form, was hand written *Resignation corrections*. The interesting thing about the "corrected copy" was its incorrectness. The employee named was *Palmatier, Manuella J.*, but the badge number noted was *38-924* from the Maintenance Department. The separation date was given as *20 August 1945* and signed again by the assistant to A. F. Signore, 1st Lt. Ord. Dept. The date stamp was *Oct 15 1945*.

The paperwork got back on track on October 10, 1945, when the War Department Notification of Personnel Action (FIELD) summarized Aunt Monnie's employment and stated clearly she was leaving as: *Clerk, CAF-4, $2100 p.a., ASF Ordnance Department, EPG, LaCarne, Ohio, Proof Division*. Under remarks was typed: *Requested by mail to be resigned. Did not give pay period notice. Tontine* (a type of investment plan) *is not refundable. Accrued annual leave: none.* The Nature of Action was resignation...*Effective Date August 24, 1945*.

In the right column were ten forced choice questions requiring short answers or check marks. Not all the questions were answered. This Permanent Civil Service Report Series indicated Monnie was a white female, non-veteran, and hers was a Civil Service Retirement, meeting Public Law 106 (War Overtime Pay Act).

Following this are two more War Department Notification of Personnel Action forms. The first one indicates the Nature of Action was *Resignation – Correction*, and dated November 29, 1945. While the second such form indicated the Nature of Action was *Resignation – Correction – Correction* and was dated December 14, 1945. In both cases, the effective resignation date was August 20, 1945. The form dated in November changed the effective date of resignation from August 24 to August 20 and moved the Organizational Unit from Proof Division to Maintenance Division. The form dated in December indicated a raise in her salary from *$2100 p.a. to $2166 p.a.*

While Monnie's name, date of birth, and social security number are correct on these forms, I found no other indication that she worked anywhere at Erie Proving Ground but in the Proof Division. In addition, she left Ohio in June 1945, returning only in July 1945 to attend to her mother, and again in September 1945 when her father died.

It appears that it was as complicated to retire from her job as it was for Monnie to obtain it. The documents may have confused Aunt Monnie with someone else. The mountain of paperwork needed on the home front was handled through personal interview, by telephone or by hand, in triplicate, using typewriters, ditto machines, then forwarded by courier or through the mail to multiple levels of oversight within a military structure. EPG was a large facility with many buildings, and with a complex set of jobs for its five-thousand employees to perform, all overseen by a military administrative system. Confusion in paperwork processing is understandable.

Chief Petty Officer Alfred James Payton

The story of my uncle's life was reconstructed by my using his military records, documents from the Civilian Conservation Corps, navy history websites, naval cruise books, photographs from northern Minnesota history centers, consultation with navy archivists, photographs from his personal collection, newspaper articles, vital records and family remembrances. Titles of documents pertaining to his service are underlined.

Al was the eighth child of thirteen, and the second of five sons, born to Herbert Edwin Payton and Eugenie Ann Hollis Hinson on June 18, 1915, in Wayzata, Minnesota. He grew up in poverty even though his father was employed as a plasterer. Within ten years after his birth, his mother gave birth to five more children. The family's food and material resources were stretched almost beyond comprehension.

He had completed the eighth grade and, in 1930, dropped out of the William Hood Dunwoody Industrial Institute, Minneapolis, at age fifteen. His family background included many male ancestors employed in the trades, so his decision to attend a trade school fit with the family pattern. Al had enrolled in shop classes, applied science, and general social studies, but he was absent a good deal and his enrollment was terminated in December. From 1933 to 1934, Al was in the Civilian Conservation Corps. Just short of his twentieth birthday, in 1935, Alfred James Payton enlisted in the U.S. Navy. After two stints in the U.S. Navy, he continued on a career path in the trades, and maintained his naval status by serving in the United States Navy Reserve.

Civilian Tour of Duty: Civilian Conservation Corps

Accounts of Al's participation in the Civilian Conservation Corps (CCC) and his two stints in the United States Navy are based on records secured from the National Park Service (CCC records), the Civilian Conservation Corps Legacy, the National Archives and Records Administration (U.S. Navy service records), augmented by naval vessel records (Fold3), as well as documents and photographs from the Minnesota Digital Library. I also reviewed several YouTube videos about life in the United States during the 1930s and the Great Depression for background information.

According to family stories, and in his obituary, Al joined the Civilian Conservation Corps (CCC). The program was a public work relief program formed through the

Emergency Conservation Work Act of March 31, 1933, and correlated with the Reforestation Relief Act 1933. The CCC was operational from April 7, 1933, when the first enrollee was inducted, to its end on July 1, 1942, six months after the United States entered World War II. The CCC was designed to employ unemployed, unmarried men from relief families, ages eighteen to twenty-three initially, later including ages seventeen to twenty-eight. In Minnesota 87,000 workers were in one-hundred four camps and worked on projects to build forests and their infrastructure, for soil conservation and cleanup of the Red River, and to establish forest fire training schools.

On June 5, 1933, Alfred Payton, just before celebrating his eighteenth birthday, signed his Oath of Enrollment to join the CCC at Fort Snelling, Minnesota, and was assigned to CCC Company 1721 at Camp F-17, Ely, Minnesota.

The U.S. Army transported the men from the site of induction to their work site, Camp Isabella, forty miles southeast of Ely. Service terms were six months in duration, and Al re-enrolled periodically to at least the end of November 1934. It appears he was part of the CCC for seventeen months continuously. He was given room and board, outfitted with a uniform, and paid $30.00/ month, of which he was allowed to keep $5.00. The remaining $25.00 was sent to his father in Wayzata. The CCC men were well fed, as suggested by the recruitment poster on the right.

On the day he initially enrolled, he was given the first of three doses of typhoid fever vaccine which was completed over the next ten days. He also was vaccinated for smallpox at induction.

Al was about 6'3" and weighed only 169 pounds - a pretty scrawny guy. He had all his teeth and was considered, in later documents, to be of… *good character*. The application stated Al had…*no regular employment*…and had finished the eighth grade.

Academic and vocational classes were offered to the CCC "boys." Fifteen vocational tracks were offered, including photography. A state-wide committee of educators, including the Assistant Director of the Minneapolis-based William Hood Dunwoody Industrial Institute, prepared a detailed instructional manual. The photography class was taught with the notion that the enlistees could use these skills after they left the CCC camp to find gainful employment. The photography class taught all aspects of the field, including basic skills of photography, an appreciation of it as a vocation, kinds of cameras, darkroom procedures, and developing film.

Since Al trained as a photographer in the navy, I wondered if he had enrolled in the CCC photography classes. He could have used the class content to leverage better duty in the navy. The names of the classroom participants were not given in the camp newsletters. However, it seems logical that Al may have taken the class because in 1942, shortly after the United States entered World War II, he was rated as a photographer's mate and experienced regular changes in rating.

Company 1721 published a small two-page typed newsletter, *Isabella Trail Blazer*. An anniversary edition dated June 21, 1935, appeared after Al left the CCC. It contained a summary of the CCC projects assigned in Minnesota: *Forestry work projects have included: liberation, fish and game improvement road construction, surveys, rodent control, hazard removal, acquisition and construction work.*

See a photograph of Al's CCC Company 1721, F-17, Camp Isabella, or Dunnigan, Ely, St. Louis County, Minnesota in Appendix 3 on page 179.

U. S. Navy Tour of Duty: Interwar Years

Al's eldest brother, George Herbert Payton, served in the U.S. Navy during the interwar years 1924 to 1928; he was seventeen at induction. There is a long history of Payton family members serving their country. Their father, Herbert Edwin Payton, enlisted in the British Army at eighteen and served in The Royal Garrison Artillery from 1897 to 1904 during the Second Boer War. As a sergeant, he was a guard of Afrikaner prisoners of war transported from the battlefronts in South Africa to a prison camp in Bermuda. There he met his future wife, Eugenie Hollis Hinson, a young widow.

In December 1934, Al lived with one of his elder married sisters, Edith St. John (nee Henrietta Edith Payton), her husband, and their three daughters in Fargo, North Dakota. He worked as a printer during this time. Then on May 14, 1935, Al pledged to serve his country for four years after completing his enlistment papers for the United States Navy from Minneapolis, Minnesota. He was nineteen years old and would celebrate his twentieth birthday four weeks later.

As he was close to his sister, Al named her as beneficiary on his Application For United States Government Life Insurance: $2,000 coverage for which he paid $3.52 monthly. He signed the application at the U.S.N. Training Station in San Diego, California, on July 17, 1935.

He remained in San Diego until August 1935 when he was assigned to the USS *Arizona,* a *Philadelphia*-class "super-dreadnaught" battleship berthed in Long Beach, California. Al often stated that this was his favorite ship; he kept a small model of it on his desk. The *Arizona* published a newsletter on board ship: *At 'Em Arizona* is archived on-line by the National Park Service. I reviewed the collection from April 1921 to August 1941 although the issues are intermittent. It is not clear if the NPS collection contains all that were published. The newsletter was… *Published by and for the crew of the United States Ship Arizona*. Later this wording was changed to read… *A ship's paper published on board the U.S.S. Arizona in the interest of the ship and the Navy.* That subtle change in wording occurred in 1937.

Notices in the *Arizona's* newsletter were of interest to diverse populations. For example, there were announcements about weekly religious services including those for the Jewish High Holy Days. At that time, African American men served in the navy, but in a truncated role: *Colored mess attendants are now being enlisted as Mess Attendants third class at all main recruiting stations. To be eligible they must, of course, be United States citizens and the age limit has been set between 18 and 25* (*At 'Em Arizona,* August 17, 1935, p. 2).

In an article entitled *Hello Stranger!*, newcomers on board were welcomed by name and rate. Included were transfers from the Naval Training Station in San Diego, California:…*Payton, A. J., AS*, (Aviation Support Equipment Technician) (*At 'Em Arizona,* September 7, 1935, p. 2).

On this initial tour of duty Al became part of the "Black Shoe" navy – a traditional ship's company. He served three years, eleven months, and twenty-nine days, and was honorably discharged as a Sea1c – Seaman, First Class, aboard the USS *Arizona*. He mustered out on May 12, 1939, just one-hundred thirteen days before World War II started when England declared war on Germany on September 3, 1939, for its invasion of Poland on September 1, 1939. He returned to live with his elder sister, Edith St. John, and to work as a painter, earning $700 in 1940.

U. S. Navy Tour of Duty: World War II

For his second tour of duty, Al re-enlisted with the U.S. Navy in Minneapolis, Minnesota, on September 9, 1940, just a week before the Selective Service Act was signed on September 16 {the draft began on October 10, 1940, the first peace-time draft in American history}. He maintained his rank of Sea1c. Al was twenty-five when he again pledged to serve his country for four additional years. He was immediately transferred to Norfolk, Virginia, for general duty. He was assigned to the USS *Wyoming*, which was berthed near the Norfolk Receiving Station on October 31, 1940. The information I received did not specify the type of training he received, but it seems he was in Norfolk for six months. During this tour of duty, Al was involved with naval aviation, so became part of what is euphemistically called the "Brown Shoe" navy named for the brown flight boots worn by pilots and air crew and the brown shoes worn with their service khaki uniform. They are referred to as "Airdales." The war in Europe had been ongoing for a little over one year.

Briefly, Al's service record showed that he had several Changes in Rating (CR) which moved his rate on a regular basis throughout his career in the navy. He entered his second tour as a Sea1c Seaman First Class, a carryover from his first tour of duty. He was moved to SC3c – Ship's Cook Third Class within seven months, and to P3c - Photographer Third Class seven months after that. His rating was P2c - Photographer Second Class in 1942, a rate which he held until late that year. By early 1943, Al was a PhoM2c - Photographer's Mate, Second Class, a rate he held until June 1943, when he became PhoM1c – Photographer's Mate, First Class. By February 1944, Al was CPhoM – Chief Photographer's Mate. He mustered out with the rate of Chief Petty Officer in mid-1945. In sixty months, his rate was changed six times; three of those changes occurred when he served in the Pacific Theater.

Three more of Al's brothers, all younger, served during World War II: Richard Hollis Payton was twenty when he was drafted in 1942, and served in the U.S. Army in the New Guinea Campaign; William Arthur Payton, seventeen, enlisted with his father's consent, in the U.S. Navy and was part of *Operation Torch* in the Allied invasion of North Africa; and Douglas John Payton was drafted at twenty in the U.S. Army, but did not serve. He was incarcerated in Leavenworth, Kansas, for one year and a day, according to the 1940 *US Census*.

On April 28, 1941, Al was FFT (For Further Transfer) to the USS *Pocomoke* (AV-9), a *Pokomoke*-class seaplane tender in service from 1941 to 1946. The ship was attached to Task Group 4.3 of the Support Force, Atlantic Fleet, stationed at Argentia Bay, Newfoundland. The ship tended two patrol planes which scouted waters approaching the harbor in search of German U-boats which threatened supply convoys to England. On January 9, 1942, she departed Argentia Bay for Norfolk, Virginia for alterations. She served in the Atlantic Theater and in the Pacific Theater transporting supplies from the continental west coast to Pearl Harbor and other islands in the Pacific, including the Philippine Islands.

Al remained aboard the USS *Pokomoke* (AV-9) from April 28, 1941, to November 19, 1941, when, as P3c, he was transferred to Naval Air Station, Pensacola, Florida for a *…course of instruction in photographer school…* The Naval Photography School was renowned for its instructors, especially U.S. Navy Lieutenant Joseph Janney Steinmetz, a nationally-known commercial photographer. He contributed significantly to the development of aerial reconnaissance photography. In addition, Edward Steichen was a commercial photographer and chief photographer for the magazines *Vogue* and *Vanity Fair*, had been curator for the Museum of Modern Art, New York, and had exhibited his paintings in Paris salons. He joined the navy in January 1942, when he was in his sixties, and commanded the Combat Photography Units.

By March 31, 1942, Al was a Naval Air P3c. By April 1942, he was assigned to Naval Air Station, New York, New York…*For instruction at Fox Movie Tone News (6 wks) completed 5-30-42*. Later Al referred to one of his skills as *photojournalist*. This training became important to his personal life about a year later. Essentially Al was in photographic school, then Movietone News, followed by a transfer to the Photographic Science Laboratory from November 1, 1941 to April 1943. The training and practice he underwent was extensive.

The Office of War Information within the Office for Emergency Management was put into place by President Franklin D. Roosevelt on June 13, 1942. OWI's task was six-fold: provide accurate information to the American people; depict the issues of the war; describe the goals and characteristics of the enemy; present the notion of an Allied coalition; emphasize the importance of domestic production; describe the role of civilians on the home front; and describe the realities faced by servicemen and women. OWI became the official arm of government propaganda. Movietone News films would have been reviewed for publication by OWI.

World War II was moving fast and military personnel were transferred to wherever they were needed, at any time. Al was assigned to temporary duty as a Photographers Mate, Second Class Petty Officer (PhoM2c) at Anacosta Naval Air Station, then transferred…*to photographic science laboratory for duty.* Campbell reported that…*the rating 'Photographer' had been re-designated 'Photographer's Mate' with the addition of warrant officer rank in its rating structure.* Photographer's Mates served on board all the navy's air stations, aircraft carriers, aircraft tenders, battleships and new cruisers (Campbell, 2014).

The Photographic Science Laboratory was established at Anacostia NAS on February 24, 1943…*to provide photoservices to the Navy and to develop equipment and techniques suitable for fleet use* (Campbell 2014). Also the Center had sound stages to produce films for training, information, and recruiting purposes.

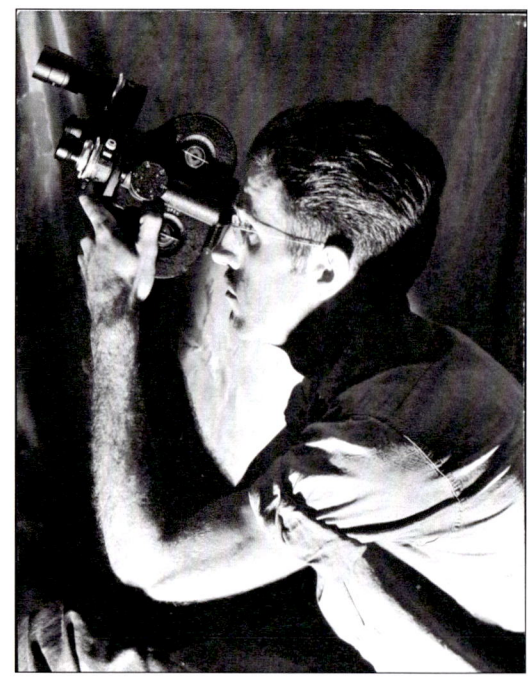

Al Payton using a movie film camera. Al's personal collection. Undated.

From April 1943 through December 31 of that year, he worked out of Newport News, Virginia, aboard the aircraft carrier USS *Yorktown* (CV-10). It was aboard this ship that Al worked as a combat reconnaissance photographer, with a rate first of Photographers Mate, Second Class Petty Officer (PhoM2c), then Photographers Mate, First Class (PhoM1c).

Al Payton boarding a North American Aviation T-6 (SNJ), the navy's term for the "Texan." This two-seater intermediate trainer (instructor and student) was used at the Naval Air Station in Pensacola, Florida. He is holding a Kodiak K-24 Aerial Surveillance Camera.

He wrote on the back of the photo: *the cameraman caught me unawares.* Al's personal collection, 1942.

The K-24, mounted in the plane, had two basic functions: night reconnaissance and orientation, and verifying a bomber's position over a target when the bomb was released.

The aircraft allowed the photographer to roll back the aircraft's rear canopy to provide an unobstructed and wide view of his subject. Generally, the aircraft was unarmed, as the addition of armament would have slowed the aircraft, making photography a hazard during battle.

The USS *Yorktown* (CV-10), The Fighting Lady, was one of twenty-four *Essex*-class aircraft carriers built during World War II for the U.S. Navy. Named after the *Battle of Yorktown* of the American Revolutionary War, it was the fourth U.S. Navy ship to bear the name. Originally the ship was to have been named *Bon Homme Richard*, but was renamed *Yorktown* while under construction to honor the eponymous ship sunk during the Battle of Midway in June 1942. It was built by Newport News Shipbuilding and Drydock, located in Newport News, Virginia.

The *Yorktown* was launched January 21, 1943, with First Lady Eleanor Roosevelt in attendance as sponsor. On April 15, 1943, it was commissioned in a traditional ceremony. The commissioning ceremony is the final act before the ship enters into service for the U.S. Navy. The *Yorktown* was given her USS designation for the first time and became a member of the battle force.

Since Al was on board, he and his crewmates each became a "plank holder" – a member of the crew to first take a ship to sea. After launch, there would have been a "shake down" cruise to ensure the ship was sea worthy and that all the ship's machinery functioned properly. The process could take several weeks to complete: the *Yorktown* cruised from May 2, 1943 to June 17, 1943 on its "shake down." There would have been little reason for Al to be on board for this initial cruise. He would have been detailed to other tasks. The carrier completed repairs on July 1, 1943, and cleared the Panama Canal on July 11/12, arriving in Pearl Harbor on July 24, 1943.

While the ship was undergoing its initial cruise and subsequent repairs, I believe Al's talents as a newsreel photographer came into play at a different location: Erie Proving Ground. The U.S. Navy sent naval personnel wherever they were needed to complete myriad tasks. Al could have completed the newsreel in upstate Ohio, and easily rejoined the *Yorktown* before final launch in Virginia. The story of how Al met Manuella has been stated by family members as "they met during the war."

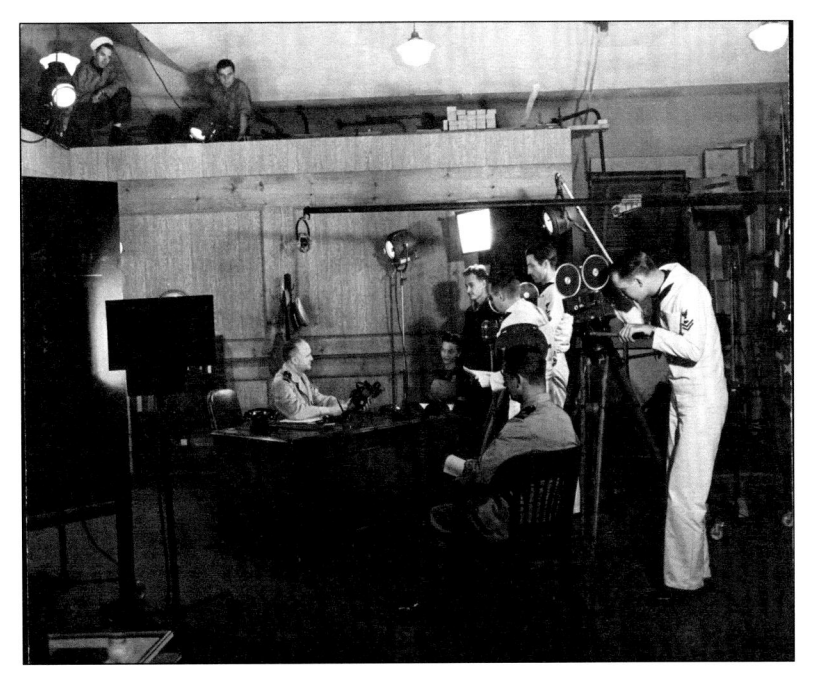

News crew interviewing U.S. Army officer, believed to be at Erie Proving Ground. May 21, 1943. Al is the tallest man in the room, standing in the center. Al's personal collection.

Since there was no other record of their having met until I read the Movietone News Cameraman's Dope Sheet, dated May 21, 1943, I pieced together a probable meeting of the two (University of South Carolina, Moving Image Research Collection).

The Dope Sheet outlined what was to appear on the newsreel: *Testing Guns, on 25th, Anniversary of Post in LaCarne, Ohio* (*i.e.*, Erie Proving Ground). The newsreel depicted…*girls firing 40 and 90 mm anti-aircraft guns, and firing the 105 mm Howitzer*… Monnie worked in the Proof Department, and, along with other women, would have been the focus of the news crew's attention for business and for socializing. That they met and corresponded throughout the rest if the war is plausible. This is the only clue to their meeting that I could find; it is speculation.

That August, the *Yorktown* left Pearl Harbor for her first combat cruise. Al was aboard the *Yorktown* from at least June 1943 through February 1944, and would have photographed fighter and bomber action.

The ship initially was assigned missions carrying supplies and aircraft between San Francisco and Pearl Harbor. She performed these duties in September 1943.

In a salute to *The Fighting Lady,* a seven part film series, dated 1943 to 1944, shows ship life (galley, hospital, post office, laundry, movie night, soda fountain/Gedunk, and so forth), officers and men in action, pilots and air crews ("Airdales"), ship ordnance, and dozens of gun-mounted synchronized camera shots of battle action. The films were produced by the U.S. Naval Communications and production was supervised by Commander Edward J. Steichen, USN, one of the photo reconnaissance instructors at Pensacola. While the films chronicle the accomplishments of the *Yorktown*, they are propaganda films designed to stir civilian viewers. I cannot confirm that any of Al's photography is part of the films, but it seems reasonable that his work would have been included. These films may be viewed on-line through Periscope Film LLC.

The films take the viewer through the Panama Canal with the crew on its way to the Pacific and the west coast and to Pearl Harbor on July 24, where she conducted a month's worth of exercises in the Hawaiian Islands. On August 31, 1943, they attacked Markus Island with both the fighters and the bombers the ship carried. This was a combat debut for the *Essex*-class carrier. The Japanese stronghold was decimated.

On October 5, 1943, the ship launched strikes on the Japanese strongholds on Wake Island. In Al's effects, there were photographs of this attack. The ship returned to Pearl Harbor on October 11, and conducted training operations for a month.

From November 10-19, 1943, the ship participated in the assault of the Gilbert Islands, and amphibious assaults on Tarawa, Abemama, and Makin. It made passing raids on other small islands before returning to Pearl Harbor on December 4, 1943, then went to Pearl Harbor where the crew conducted air training exercises for a month.

The *Yorktown* was ordered to battle in *Operation Flintlock* from January 31 to February 4, 1944, at Kwajalein Atoll in the Marshall Islands. Following that the crew saw action at the Truk Islands, a Japanese fortification that had been under construction for twenty years. Most of the Japanese fleet had moved so the *Yorktown* pilots strafed the enemy transports and cargo ships. The *Yorktown* went back to the Marshall Islands to rendezvous with other carriers, battleships, and supply ships.

The *Yorktown* then went to the Mariana Islands (*i.e.*, Guam, Rota, Tinian, and Saipan) in preparation for what would become an enormous battle. The fliers' personal health needs were addressed when they were told to "scrub up" before the battle to lessen infection in case of their being wounded. The film showed the men writing a last letter home followed by participating in "divine services" - communion and prayer before battle - all three-thousand men went to these services.

Just south of the Marianas, the Allies encountered the Japanese Imperial Navy on June 6, 1944. The Battle of the Philippine Sea became known as the *Great Marianas Turkey Shoot;* three-hundred sixty-nine Japanese planes were shot down and seventeen Japanese war ships were severely damaged. The *Yorktown* crew counted the number shot down - Zekes, Vals, and Kates are the names the Allies gave to some Japanese aircraft.

I can verify Al's presence on board the USS *Yorktown* for the following military operations in the Pacific Theater: Marcus Island – August 31, 1943; Wake Island – October 5-6, 1943; Gilbert Islands – November 19 to December 5, 1943; Marshall Islands, Truk, Marianas – January 29 to February 23, 1944; and Palau, Hollandia, Truk – March 29 to April 30, 1944.

The ship and its crew earned twelve battle stars - the air crew conducted…*11,346 sorties over enemy targets* - and earned the Presidential Unit Citation.

CITATION: For extraordinary heroism in action against enemy Japanese forces in the air, at sea and on shore in the Pacific War Area from August 31, 1943, to August 15, 1945. Spearheading our concentrated carrier-warfare in forward areas, the U.S.S. YORKTOWN and her air groups struck crushing blows toward annihilating the enemy's fighting strength; they provided air cover the our amphibious forces; they fiercely countered the enemy's savage aerial attacks and destroyed his planes; and they inflicted terrific losses on the Japanese in Fleet and merchant marine units sunk or damaged. Daring and dependable in combat, the YORKTOWN with her gallant officers and men rendered loyal service in achieving the ultimate defeat of the Japanese Empire.

For the President, *James Forrestal*, Secretary of the Navy.

When I scanned the photographs and read the text of *Into The Wind*, the Yorktown's Cruise Book 1943-1945, I noted the segregation of African Americans from the other sailors. Of the one-hundred pages in the book, the majority of group photographs, taken by unit or task or event, identified each sailor by name. There were three photographs only of African American sailors on a page entitled S-2. These men were the cooks who served over eight million five-hundred meals to a total ship's company of 3,105 officers and men. In the photos, the cooks were in uniform, and in one photograph they were posed to use the onboard anti-aircraft guns. There was no text. No man was identified by name.

The *Yorktown* went on to serve in the Korean War, Vietnam, and other duties in the Pacific. It was formally dedicated as a memorial on the 200th anniversary of the U.S. Navy on October 13, 1975. It is currently berthed at Patriots Point Naval and Maritime Museum, Mount Pleasant, South Carolina.

After the battle at Kwajalein, February 25, 1944, Al's military record contains a letter changing his rate from PhoM1c—Photographers Mate, First Class Petty Officer) to CPhoM—Chief, Photographers Mate. The Photographer's Mate organized and directed operations of naval photographic units. He operated "still" and motion picture cameras, and took photographs under all conditions. He developed negatives and made prints, and, for all this, earned under $130/ month. The letter changing his rate was signed by the Personnel Officer, Photographic Reconnaissance & Interpretation Section, Intelligence Center, Pacific Ocean Areas, San Francisco, California. Al was aboard the USS *Yorktown*, where the record states he was serving...*temporary duty*.

He was on the <u>Muster Roll of the Crew</u>, US Navy Yard, in Pearl Harbor, Territory of Hawaii, for the quarters ending January 1944, March 31, 1944, and June 1944. By December 11, 1944, Al was stationed aboard the USS *Sanborn* APA-193, an attack transport ship, with the rate of CPhoM. He was assigned to the Joint Intelligence Center.

Photo-intelligence developments were enhanced by the establishment in 1942 of the Photographic Reconnaissance and Interpretation Section, Intelligence Center at Pearl Harbor. This unit created a group of photographic interpreters that could be used by advance units in the Pacific Fleet. Their intelligence was useful in planning and executing operations, and for strategic planning.

1945 was a busy year for Al; the <u>Service Record</u> provided by the National Archives did not photocopy the month, only the day and year for January through September 1945. I used ancillary data to fill in the blanks. In early 1945 he was aboard the USS *Auburn* (AGC-10) for temporary duty. The *Auburn* was a *Mount McKinley*-class amphibious force command ship. It was a floating command post with advanced communications equipment and extensive combat information spaces to be used by amphibious forces/ landing forces commanders during large-scale operations. It was berthed in Pearl Harbor.

From the paperwork I reviewed, it seems – at war's end – there was a rush of forms, letters, and events that happened all at once. Al was posted to CINCPAC Advanced Headquarters (Commander In Chief Pacific Fleet Headquarters) for duty in Pearl Harbor in 1945. This was the headquarters of Admiral Chester W. Nimitz. From there he went to San Francisco for further transfer (FFT) in early June and on to Ohio to be married.

He was in Port Clinton, or at least on leave, for about five weeks. He traveled to Minneapolis on July 24, 1945, was after his marriage to Monnie Palmatier in mid-June. She began the process for her resignation as a Clerk CAF-4, on June 11, 1945, when she indicated in a letter to her superiors that she and her new husband would be moving to California.

From a partially completed summary dated July 5, 1945, I learned that Al was listed as not having been a *gunner*, but had been in…*Motion Picture Production in Aerial Photography, Journalist Combat Photographer NAS Pensacola – PhoM – 16 wks…New York – Motion Picture – 12 wks*. This jumble of words and abbreviations laid out what he was expected to do for the war effort.

On September 5, 1945, Al was transferred to *ComFair, Alameda, NAS, Alameda, California FFT to Personnel Separation Center, Alameda, California for separation from the Naval Service*. ComFair (Commander, Air Western Pacific). Points to Discharge (Points System or Advanced Service Rating Score) were calculated by the age of the serviceman, time served, and service overseas. The system was used to determine who would go home first. The Alameda Naval Air Station was home to seventeen naval vessels during the war, including the USS *Hornet*, which had transported Doolittle's Raiders into position to bomb Tokyo on April 18, 1942. In Minneapolis, Al was assigned to Fleet Air Wing-81 (FAW-81) although some records say FAW-8. The final entry in Al's Service Record states: *For Duty HEDRON* (Headquarters Squadrons) *FAW-8*. His father-in-law passed from a heart attack on September 5, 1945. It is not known if Al attended Claude's funeral the next week in Minnesota.

Photographic Reconnaissance

The training that naval aerial photographers underwent was extensive. They were called upon to record battles, invasions, bombings, and both military and civilian personnel. The first U.S. Navy aerial photographs were taken in 1913 in support of fleet exercises off Guantanamo, Cuba. The last aerial photo plane in the navy's inventory was retired after flying to the Smithsonian's Air and Space Museum Annex at Dulles International Airport in Fairfax County, Virginia. Appendix 5 is the table of contents from one of four training manuals, courtesy of the U. S. Naval Aviation Museum, Pensacola, Florida. (p. 185)

According to the Naval Aviation Museum, the cameras used from 1941-1945 were the following: Fairchild F-1, (rapid action, oblique photography); Fairchild K-17 (vertical aerial); Fairchild K-18 (best for high altitude aerial); Fairchild K-20 (hand-held light weight, rapid action observation photos) was famously used by the tail gunner positon in the B-29 *Enola Gay* to photograph the nuclear mushroom cloud over Hiroshima; and the Fairchild F-56 Aerial Camera (made primarily for U.S. Navy reconnaissance).

The importance of aerial photography to Allied military operations in both the Pacific and Atlantic Theaters cannot be overstated.

Marriage in a Time of War

Al's marriage to Monnie is explored in greater detail on pages 55 and 65, and the Marriage License Application below provided useful information. As indicated above, it seems reasonable that they met during the war at Erie Proving Ground..

Probate Court, Ottawa County, Ohio
No.14021 Marriage License Application

Alfred J. Payton and Manuella J. Palmatier respectfully make application for a Marriage License for themselves…{he states further} he was 29 years of age on 18th of June, 1944. Born and resides in Wayzata, MN. His occupation was 'Navy.' Parents: Herbert Edwin Payton and Eugenia {sic} Hollis. He was not previously married and had no wife living.

Manuella J. Palmatier was 29 years of age the 12th of January, 1945. Her residence was Port Clinton, Ottawa Co, OH and she was born in Osakis, MN. Her occupation was 'government clerk.' Parents: Claude Palmatier and Emma Wharton. {She further attested} She was not previously married, is not a widow or divorced woman and she has no husband living.

{They both attested}: *That neither of the parties is an {sic} habitual drunkard, epileptic, imbecile or insane, or under the influence of any intoxicating liquor or narcotic drug.* They were married by the Rev. Reynolds. They signed in front of the Probate Judge and his Clerk. Port Clinton, Ohio.

Dated 11th Day of June, 1945

Servicemen had to sign the WWII Draft Registration Card after having served during the war. Al signed on September 17, 1945, in Moorhead, Clay County, Minnesota. It seems he and his new wife were visiting his elder sister again as his real address was Box 21, Wayzata, Minnesota. The Card read that Al was 30, born June 18, 1915, that he had no employer, and was 6'3", 160 lbs. with a dark complexion, brown hair, hazel eyes.

It was signed after he had served two tours in the United States Navy, one before, and one during World War II. The date of Al's signing was just twelve days after his father-in-law passed.

U. S. Navy: Navy Reserve

Al joined the Navy Reserve, *on or before 15 Aug 45*. One record shows he was Honorably Discharged from the reserves on January 14, 1955. The Computation of Service For Retirement was prepared April 1, 1957, and calculated prior to July 1, 1949. The form indicates he started earning USNR points for days of service on February 1, 1947; the computation ends June 30, 1949. The computation included age, time served, and service overseas.

Chief Petty Officer Alfred Payton and his bride, Manuella "Monnie" Palmatier. June 15, 1945. Author's personal collection.

He requested a transfer to Phoenix, Arizona, on December 12, 1957, taking him permanently from his home in Wayzata. In Phoenix, on March 17, 1958, when the paperwork was actually submitted/received, he agreed to remain a member of the Ready Reserves until March 17, 1960, when he would be forty-four.

In December 1952, the Chief of Naval Operations sent the Commander of Air Wing-81 a letter of commendation to be placed in each staff member's permanent record, including Al. The unit received the Noel Davis Trophy for...*high efficiency standards in competition with eighteen other air wing staffs*...in the Naval Air Reserve Training Program.

NAS Minneapolis patch and insignia, designed by Walt Disney Studios.

Life after the War

From 1945 to 1957 Al and Monnie lived in Wayzata, Minnesota, his home town. He was self-employed in Excelsior, Minnesota, as a painter and decorator of old and new building, residential and commercial, interior and exterior. He had been doing the work for ten years. They moved to Flagstaff, Coconino County, Arizona, in 1957 where he was self-employed as a painter and paperhanger until 1979.

An advertisement for his business appeared in *The Sun*, Flagstaff, Arizona, on Saturday, October 14, 1961, under Business Directory: Painting and Decorating.

> **Painting and Paperhanging,
> Expert Personal Service,
> Free Estimates.
> Al Payton PR4-2012.**

Monnie's suffered a stroke in 1967, and died in 1969. Al married Martha Ballard, a military veteran, in July 1972. Then, separated from his second wife in 1979, he moved to Olympia, Thurston County, Washington. He lived close to his younger brother, William Arthur Payton, a United States Navy World War II veteran, and his family. Al was divorced on September 22, 1981. He died at his home in Lacey, Thurston County, Washington, on November 26, 1982, at the age of sixty-seven.

Among his effects were fifty large black-and-white war-related photographs that he took during World War II. Forty-four were of combat missions, aerial shots of the invasion of Wake Island, photos of U.S. Navy personnel, shots of dead Japanese soldiers, and so forth. In November 2019, I donated the combat-related photographs to the Department of the Navy's National Naval Aviation Museum, Pensacola, Florida, for use by other researchers. The signed <u>Deed of Gift</u>, dated December 5, 2019, was returned to me just before Christmas that year.

I used military and civilian archives to understand my uncle's movements. Many documents were hand-written during a time of strife and are difficult to discern. Since chronology places history into context, I found it useful to create a timeline of service so that I could make sense of what my uncle was asked to do from the early 1930s to his death in 1962. (See Appendix 4, p. 180)

Profile of Al Payton. Undated, but likely after World War II. Al's personal collection.

Al Payton in his later years. Photo courtesy of Sally Seward Pesta, Al's grand-niece. Undated.

Thank you for your decades of service, Uncle Al. Thank you for keeping the pledges and oaths you signed to serve our country – four times.

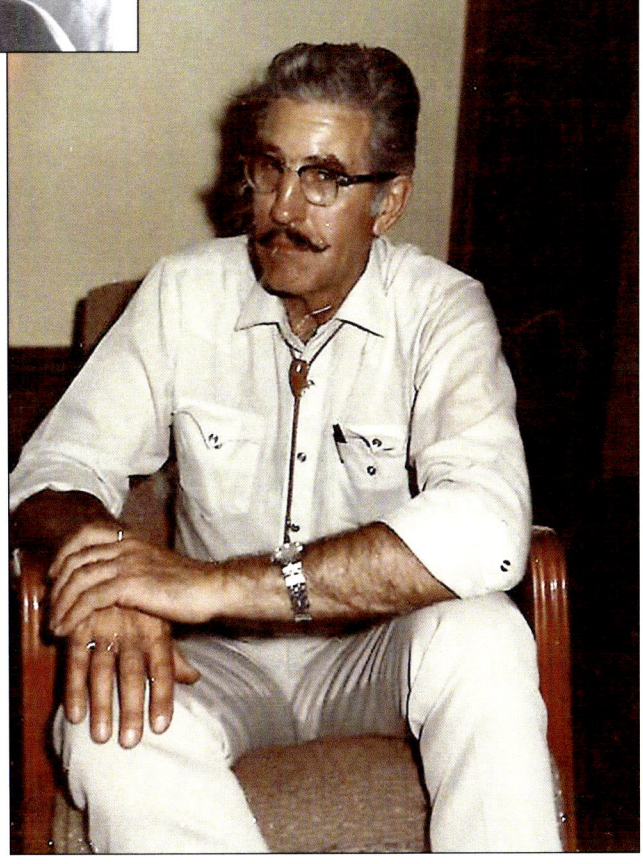

Employee Newsletters Provide a Glimpse of Life in Defense Plants

War disrupted the lives of every American citizen: sons, brothers, fathers, or uncles either enlisted or were drafted to serve their country in increasing numbers as the war progressed. Thousands of women joined the WAC, WAVE, Marines, or SPAR. Meanwhile, thousands of mothers, sisters, daughters, and sweethearts took positions in defense plants or at military facilities. Often, workers, such as my Aunt Monnie, moved hundreds of miles from their home to take temporary housing near where they worked.

Many defense plants employed a cross-section of Americans – American Indians, African Americans, midgets, women, sightless workers, and those who were "deaf-mutes." The diversity in the workforce for each plant surprised me, although I came to learn about the segregation of employees by socio-economic status and by ethnicity. What did not surprise me was the anti-Japanese and anti-Nazi rhetoric expressed by employees as reported in company newsletters.

Defense plants became a center for production and a center for social life. Clear communication was a must. Young women had to grow up fast and older women had to adjust to working outside the home. Many went to work because it was good money for families that had just come through the Depression.

Since Monnie's father and elder brother worked in Akron, Ohio, at Goodyear Aircraft, and her sister-in-law worked for Bell Aircraft in Marietta, Georgia, with family ties in Newcomerstown, Ohio, I wondered if she traveled to visit her family members while she worked at Erie Proving Ground in Ohio. I calculated the distance between Port Clinton and Akron, and between Port Clinton and Marietta. Gas, rubber, and tires were rationed, so Monnie likely would not have driven to visit family, even with the remote possibility of car-pooling. Such travel by car was frowned upon because gas and rubber were needed by the military. Further, the distance to Georgia was over five-hundred miles, and too great for any visits between family members. Wharton and Hilda Palmatier did visit Hilda's family in Newcomerstown, Ohio, a distance of one-hundred sixty-four miles from Marietta, but it is unknown if Monnie traveled there to join her brother and sister-in-law.

I thought Monnie may have traveled to see her father, or to visit with both parents, when her mother came to Akron in March 1943. In fact, Monnie took just over thirteen days annual leave between March 31, 1942 and March 31, 1943. The specific dates were not noted on her timesheet, so I can only speculate on any travel plans for her outside of Port Clinton. It is possible that she went to Akron to see her parents, a distance of one-hundred miles. It would have been feasible by bus or by train. By train, she would have taken a ferry across Put-in-Bay from Port Clinton to Sandusky then east to Cleveland, and south to Akron. I can only speculate on any long-distance travel she may have made during her time at Erie Proving Ground.

I obtained photocopies of employee newsletters to understand what everyday life was like for those working on the home front. Many employees, including Aunt Monnie, had relocated from other states, and lived near EPG in small apartments or rented rooms from local citizens. Life revolved around the work each was asked to do and socializing with co-workers was very common. When I accessed company employee newsletters, I was nearly overwhelmed by the shear amount and variety of information available for research. I came to understand that there was a mountain of paperwork generated by war and war production before the advent of the computer.

The weeks spent reading the newsletters essentially compressed the information; readers at the time would have had days to consider the information they were given, and would have had co-workers they could talk to about joyous or upsetting news. The workers did not realize during the war that war never really ends; there would be too many memories. Several times I had to pull away from the research as the emotion I assumed the workers felt – a juxtaposition of fear, anger, joy, happiness, confusion, grief – about the news they read each week became too much. Breaks in research were necessary for me to gain perspective.

Employee newsletters tied plant workers together by printing articles about such things as: war news; vignettes of employees or their loved ones serving in the military and, later, of employees whose husbands, fathers, sons, and brothers were missing in action, killed in action or who became prisoners of war; employee complaints about the cafeteria; beauty contests; War Bond purchasing contests between departments; employee wedding/engagement/birth/death announcements; special pages with news/gossip; team sports and recreation for men and women such as movies, plays, choruses, small concerts; employee social activities such as picnics, dances, get-togethers; the positive impact workers' production had on the war effort; spread of anti-Nazi and anti-Japanese sentiment; the ever-present admonitions to comply with food rationing, to save gas and tires, and to recycle other commodities such as metal; and the imperative for ride-sharing, timeclock protocol, safety protocols, and safe tool use.

The book covers a number of topics taken from the newsletters to give readers an idea of what life was like working in a defense plant or on a military installation. I did not write in detail about many other topics such as: famous entertainers who came to encourage workers, worker housing, inter-department contests, the strong push for workers to recycle scrap (rubber, metal, paper, carbon paper, and paper clips), women's fashion outside the workplace, or articles about credit unions and insurance. Nor did I cover tips to women on self-improvement, household hints, recipes, or home decorating contests.

I left undiscussed the myriad articles about sports and team standings (baseball, basketball, horse shoes, archery, bowling, softball, shooting, hunting, swimming, and so forth), nor did I discuss in detail the many picnics and outings employees organized nor the more formal recreation clubs started by companies or by employees. Celebrations of birthdays, marriages, engagements were acknowledged and employee illness or family deaths were announced. Many employees attended skills training classes, but these are not discussed in detail, and companies hired college educated counselors to address employee's personal problems affecting their work. Details about what the problems might have been were not delineated, leaving the readers of newsletters to discern for themselves what those problems might have been.

The large number of avenues for historical and anthropological research was simply too much for this brief look at home front culture. I leave unexplored topics to future researchers.

Workers were encouraged to suggest improvements in production processes, to participate in Red Cross blood drives (those giving the most blood were recognized), to volunteer in the community, or to make suggestions to enhance safety on the job. Workers were admonished to avoid absenteeism, to keep a positive attitude, to wear their employee badges, park their cars in the correct lots, to turn in scrap, to recycle, to not complain about shortages, and to keep working. Above all, keep working. The tone of the articles varied from being simply informative, to admonishing, to shaming, and to blaming. Many articles did celebrate success in production, especially as they related to successes reported from the battlefront.

The newsletters became a rich source of information - so much that it took me several weeks to go through the issues to tease out only a few themes of daily life, just so that I could begin to understand the home front culture surrounding the employees, particularly the culture that the women experienced.

All the articles - this onslaught of information - intertwined to increase employee morale, to push productivity, and to enhance feelings of patriotism. Newsletters were both personal and public in the writers' choices of newsworthy material. These elements could not be separated.

I used photocopies of the *EPG Echo* from Erie Proving Ground, Port Clinton, Ohio, from May 20 through July 29, 1943. It was not published after that. Both Aunt Monnie and her younger brother would have read these. Copies of the *EPG Echo* from 1943 were provided by the Ottawa County Museum in Port Clinton.

The *Bell Aircraft News* was published weekly and I reviewed the issues from May 21, 1943 through May 13, 1944, and from June 24, 1944 through August 24, 1945. Monnie's sister-in-law worked in the Marietta, Georgia, plant and I wanted to understand what was available to her and to other workers. I obtained the *Bell Aircraft News* in hardcopy from the University of Georgia Libraries, Athens, thoughtfully printed and shipped by a doctoral student. The Bell newsletters were printed every two weeks on either Friday or Saturday, and were between four and eight pages in length. And I received mid-1944 through August 1945 issues from Emory University.

I reviewed the *Wingfoot Clan Aircraft Edition*, published by and for employees of Goodyear Aircraft, Akron from January 7, 1942 through August 22, 1945 and *The Wingfoot Clan Akron Edition* from August 1945 through December 1945 to learn what

Monnie's father and elder brother experienced. *The Wingfoot Clan*, a weekly four to ten- page publication, generally printed on Wednesdays, had been digitized and was readily available on line through the Akron-Summit County Public Library.

I found that each production facility created a complete world unto itself and fostered a culture designed to keep employees motivated to work hard while attending to their need for some form of normality. Life in the defense plants discussed next is seen through the writings of newsletter staff. To paraphrase Alistair Cooke (2006), the articles talked about the things that were closest to employees' interests and fears – and collectively let future readers surmise employees' feelings about the war.

Home life was far from customary for anyone; lives changed utterly when World War II began. Elements of war became central to people's lives. Managers and supervisors who lead production facilities or directed departments were aware that a sense of "family" needed to be created to keep employee morale at its highest level while asking people to work harder, faster, longer hours, more safely, and remain patriotic – to be "soldiers of production" as stated in one newsletter editorial in *The Wingfoot Clan Aircraft Edition*, written by Paul W. Litchfield, an American industrialist, who served as superintendent of Goodyear Aircraft.

Establishing the Culture: Work in a Time of War

Erie Proving Ground

Erie Proving Ground (EPG) was a U.S. Army installation associated with Camp Perry, located just five miles away in Port Clinton. EPG was an artillery and air defense artillery proving ground from 1918 to 1965. *From Proof to Depot to Troops* was the installation's motto, printed on each copy of the employee newsletter. Housing was available to employees at Erie Gardens, a quickly-constructed community in which just EPG employees could buy or rent a home. There were two-hundred fifty-nine two-family homes (duplexes). Civilians also rented rooms to workers, as in the case of my aunt (*EPG Echo*, June 3, 1943, p. 1).

Trailer camps were also available as indicated in ***Applications of EPG Employees Eligible For Trailer Homes In Pt. Clinton Should Be Made to Welfare Branch, Bldg. 1***. The Welfare Branch was part of the Civilian Personnel Division and applicants for either the trailer camps (490 trailers) or Erie Gardens had to be *employees who in-migrated because of the increase in war work in this vicinity…Trailers will be arranged in groups of four with streets and sidewalks built, and electricity and water facilities planned accordingly. Oil stoves will be used. Dishes, silverware, and linens will be furnished by the renters* (*EPG Echo*, June 3, 1943, p. 1)

Of particular interest, EPG employed 1,000 Italian prisoners of war, creating the make-up of its personnel different from those at Bell Aircraft and Goodyear Aircraft. There were five thousand EPG personnel. The summary below is adapted from Van Keuren's 2018 description.

The nation underwent a severe labor shortage because thousands of men were needed for the armed forces. Camp Perry was a base-camp, and oversaw the administration of nine sub-camps in Ohio. There were 2,732 German POWs also housed at the camp. Germans and Italians were housed separately with a road between the living quarters. There was one distinct difference between the two groups: the Italians were allowed to work in ordnance at the proving ground after October 1943 when Italy capitulated. The Italians worked with civilians and proof-fired some ordnance, and they did make bombs, despite the rules of the Geneva Convention that would prohibit those activities. It is not known if Aunt Monnie interacted directly with the Italian prisoners of war. Surely she knew they were working at EPG, but I cannot confirm any professional or personal interactions.

The German POWs were not allowed to work at the proving ground because their country did not surrender until May 1945.

The POWs were treated well and had many privileges or amenities not available to local Port Clinton residents: filling meals cooked by the POWs, recreational activities (carving, painting, card playing) and a 'date-hut' to allow conversations with Italian females visiting from nearby Toledo. Food was rationed, but apparently the POWs had access to eggs, meat, milk, and sugar from which they made cookies, among other pastries. There were understandable feelings of resentment among local citizens.

Though not a culture expressly created by women, they were surely integral to its development. For example, Women Ordnance Workers (WOW) were a front and center element in the EPG's culture which overall was military in tone. They often were photographed at their jobs. They were…*featured in one of the Paramount Studios' releases of Unusual Occupations within the next four months. Women's work in ordnance will be described…Permission for the taking of these films was granted by the War Department…* (*EPG Echo*, May 20, 1943, p. 8).

Erie WOWs At Work was a photo collage of seven images showing women ordnance workers at task on large caliber guns, specifically the 155 mm field artillery guns.
EPG Echo, May 20, 1943, p. 2.

EPG WOWs Entertain Soldiers at Port Clinton USO Center, read the headline about these women being among the first to become hostesses when the USO of Port Clinton was created in September 1942. Almost 140 women gave part of their time to the USO. Entertainment was nightly and included movies and formal and informal dances (*EPG Echo,* July 15, 1943, p. 3). The article included a collage of ten photographs showing women and men talking and dancing.

At each victory by Allied forces, EPG employees were reminded that…*we have contributed directly to this victory…These coordinated efforts are the goal, which, when total victory is won, will be recorded as a glorious tradition of Erie Proving Ground* (*EPG Echo,* May 20, 1943, p. 4).

All employees were evaluated, and because EPG was Ohio's only proving ground, the Proof Department employees played a central role in EPG's mission. The Proof Department, where Monnie worked, was singled out for praise because a majority of the employees purchased safety shoes for work. This set an example for the rest of the employees. The department also planned a War Bond party and dance and offered a War *Echo* Bond to a lucky ticket holder. Social activities were overshadowed by war. In addition, the Proof Department was often the subject for tours by the War Department, and visits by the press (*EPG Echo,* May 20, 1943, p. 3). I believe this access by the press was integral to Monnie's meeting her future husband Alfred Payton.

Bell Aircraft

The federal government awarded the contract to build fighter aircraft to Bell on February 19, 1942. Construction began on Bell Aircraft's bomber plant in Marietta, Georgia, in March 1942; the company originated in Buffalo, New York. It employed 28,158 at its peak (caveat: employment totals vary by source). The complex covered 4.2 million square feet. About ninety percent of the employees were Southerners, thirty-seven percent were women, eight percent African-American, and six percent physically disabled. Advancement opportunities for women and Blacks were limited, and job sites were segregated by race and disability. Pay scale for all workers was higher than that found in other Southern industries, according to the New Georgia Encyclopedia.

Assembly lines began functioning in the spring 1943, and Bell employees built 663 Boeing-designed B-29s for the United States Army Air Force by December 1945. It was the nation's largest and longest-range bomber produced.

The following is a message from senior leadership at Bell - one of three editorials. This one is a strong admonition and is shaming in its tone (*Bell Aircraft News,* May 28, 1943, p. 2).

> ### *Speaking of "All-Out" Effort*
>
> The tinkle of time clocks punched right on the minute at quitting time would no doubt delight the ear of the house painter of Berchtesgaden, who professes a taste for things aesthetic as well as gory.
>
> It would warm his barbarian heart to see workers strolling down hallways a few minutes before the bell in order to avoid standing in line two or three minutes with their more conscientious fellows.
>
> No doubt these gun-jumpers believe themselves justified in getting a head start in the head house handicap. They probably feel they are due some adjustment because they punched in a few minutes early.
>
> Hitler would like that.
>
> He would like to multiply those minutes by the total number of gun-jumpers in American industry, then divide them into man-hours
>
> "This talk about America's all-out war effort," he would chuckle, "is a lot of bunk!"

Goodyear Aircraft

Goodyear Aircraft initially produced zeppelins to advertise its products. It manufactured two airships for the United States military in the early 1930s. During World War II, the company manufactured one-hundred-four airships (blimps) for the military at its Akron facility for patroling the country's coastline. The company also built the F4U *Corsair* for the United States Navy, which was flown in combat in the Pacific Theater by the marines and from aircraft carriers by the navy. In 1939, Goodyear employed about thirty workers and by 1942 the company consisted of thirty-five thousand employees. These employment statistics vary by source; some say Goodyear had sixty employees in 1939, and thirty-three thousand by 1942. It was one of the ten largest aircraft producers in the United States.

Admonitions to employees about the manner in which they conducted their work lives is exemplified in a short article entitled: **Change of Time**. *Every man, woman and child in the United States will sacrifice an hour of their time toward the nation's war effort beginning Monday when 'war time' goes into effect at 2 o'clock a.m. Employees are advised to move the clocks ahead an hour before going to bed* (The Wingfoot Clan, February 4, 1942, p. 4). The tone of the article is strident (*i.e.*, sacrifice), but did alert employees to a Congressional ruling that "war time" would go into effect on February 9, 1942; this national act was not repealed until September 30, 1945. It was instituted to conserve resources.

Production leadership imbued their editorials or messages to employees with patriotic rhetoric, typical in a time of war, and designed to increase morale and to spur production. Goodyear Aircraft's slogans were: **America First in the Air**, and **Keep 'Em Flying**. The latter slogan was repeatedly interspersed between articles printed in the employee newsletter. Goodyear referred to itself as Aircraft without the specific name of the company in keeping with its marketing as a pre-eminent war aircraft assembler From the tone in the Goodyear newsletters, it is apparent that wording was used to bolster morale and to increase employee pride as they were asked to work harder and faster.

Patriotic messages to employees were common. One of Paul W. Litchfield's earliest such messages appeared in the December 10, 1941, Goodyear company newsletter, scant days after Japanese aircraft attacked the American base in Pearl Harbor:

We Are At War

The hour of war has struck.
Our people have been attacked by a foreign foe.
They must be given blow for blow – and more.
I do not say we must unite – I say we have united.
Internal differences are automatically resolved.

Capital, labor and management are as one, shoulder to shoulder in the common and paramount determination – to wipe these sinister enemy forces from the face of the earth.

Every resource and facility owned by Goodyear, every bit of our talent and man power is the President's to command.
This is offered without reservation or qualification.

As individuals and as a corporation, we have worked hard during the past months to be ready for this situation.
Now we shall double and redouble our efforts.

P. W. Litchflield

The Wingfoot Clan – Aircraft Edition, V.1, No.28 December 10, 1941
The Wingfoot Clan – Akron Edition, V.30, No.37, December 10, 1941

Management took advantage of every piece of war news to inform home front workers, to emphasize the need for greater effort, and to relate that effort to winning the war. After James "Jimmy" Doolittle's Raid on Tokyo in spring 1942, P. W. Litchfield wrote this to his workers (*The Wingfoot Clan*, March 11, 1942, p.1):

> Unless and until America is the most powerful nation in the air, our safety, our freedom and our standard of living will not again be what it has been in the past.
>
> *Our Rising Sun*
>
> Japan is known as "The Land of the Rising Sun," but America is showing the Nipponese and the Nazis that "Our Rising Sun" is growing brighter and brighter every day. It is the American industrial production – and women of America are playing a very important part in the program.
>
> At Goodyear women already are "manning" machines, wielding drills, trimming metal sheets, driving rivets and performing other tasks – and they're making good jobs of their undertaking.
>
> One Goodyear shop foreman said that after a week's training women have shown a marked proficiency in metal work. Women who have come to Goodyear to take their places at the benches of freedom are turning out vital products our country needs to crush aggression. In the months to come women will continue to bolster the factory front as vast new plants now being built go into swift production, and others, like Goodyear, are converted to war work…
>
> It behooves the Axis powers to keep an eye for "Our Rising Sun."

A cartoon accompanied the above editorial; it depicted a large Sun with the words *American Industrial Production* radiating around it. The Sun's heat was rapidly melting a snowman, with the word *AXIS* written on it; it looked like a sad and worried Hitler.

Becoming "Soldiers of Production"

Lt. Colonel Abraham Robert Ginsburgh, Aide to the Secretary of War, Office of the Assistant Secretary of War, stated succinctly: *This is a war of production* (*The Wingfoot Clan*, December 10, 1941, p. 3). These words were designed to set a tone or create an attitude in the minds of civilians: war is a competition and this war would be won (and was won) by out-producing the enemy. In the European Theater, Allies principally attacked material-making industries. In the Pacific Theater, Allies focused on regaining the captured countries to re-acquire badly needed resources and raw materials.

Erie Proving Ground

Defense plant and military facility workers were constantly reminded that their efforts had a direct and positive impact on individual soldiers and on the war effort as a whole. Erie Proving Ground was Ohio's only proving ground. The military culture in which employees worked was controlled directly by the U.S. Army. All employees' records were reviewed and signed off by military personnel assigned to the installation.

Women Ordnance Workers (WOW) were depicted in recruiting posters.

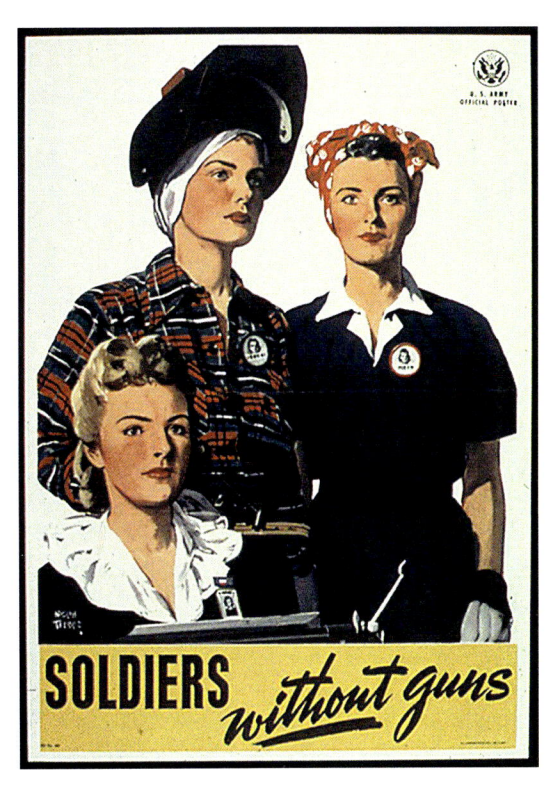

The *EPG Echo* was printed only for a brief period of time and strived to give information alongside personal news about employees, their children at war, and those who were lost. The motto at the top of page of several issues said: **From Proof To Depot To Troops.** Military vocabulary used at EPG was reflected and reinforced in the newsletter. Specific words to describe ordnance were routine. In addition, other words highlighted the military culture, such as: *civilian, Civilian Personnel Branch, Civil Service* (referring to employees who were not in the military), *V-mail* (Victory mail), *officers' mess* (referring to the area in which officers had their meals), and so forth.

Photos in the *EPG Echo* accompanied vignettes of EPG commanders in uniform. There were articles in the column *Men Serving in Uniform*, next to a gossip column entitled *Rapid Firing*. There were articles about the activities of the EPG Civilian Club differentiating them from military social activities. One issue listed hundreds of men in an *Honor Roll of Military* who were furloughed (*i.e.*, on leave of absence), including Monnie's younger brother, Winston Palmatier, who served at EPG during part of the time she was there.

Civilian Club of Post Will Be "Reactivated": Plans For Summer Outings Will Be Given Approval. Ostensibly, the Club would promote recreational and social activities for employees. But…*official military sponsorship and assistance will be given*…It seems the military structure was superimposed on all employee activities – on and off the job (*EPG Echo*, June 3, 1943, p. 1).

There were pictures of military personnel giving jeep rides to boys, and articles about the…*high school boys given* **Pre-Induction Training Classes. First Course Is Completed by 28 Youths**. The class was an 18-week course (three days/week at three hours/day) in which the young men received training on guns (material, assembly, and disassembly), shop math, shop theory, and precision instruments. The course was a thinly veiled enlistment tool; the first class had three military inductees, and seven took examinations for the Army Air Corp when group photos were taken (*EPG Echo*, May 20, 1943, p. 5). At least two civilian women employees were course instructors.

Below is one of the most direct reminders of the task assigned to EPG. It is included here because Aunt Monnie worked in the Ordnance Department in the Proof Testing Division (*EPG Echo*, July 15, 1943, p. 7).

Big Guns are Ready to Crack Hitler's Fortress

The Ordnance Department has immediately available various types of hard-hitting guns to crack Hitler's bristling European fortress. These include rugged, mobile guns and howitzers, ranging from the 75 mm howitzer to the 8-inch gun. The majority have split trail carriages and are stable in all firing positions.

EPG employees engaged in the proof testing program of this Post are familiar with many of these guns.

Howitzers, which have shorter barrels than guns of the same caliber, fire projectiles in a high arching curve. Howitzers may therefore be hidden from the enemy behind a hill.

The baby 1-ton 75 mm Howitzer can be transported by plane and accompany paratroops. The field howitzer may be towed on its pneumatic-tired carriage. The pack howitzer can be carried in several loads on pack animals.

The 105 mm howitzer was developed to replace the 75 mm gun of World War fame and to provide greater firepower for divisional field artillery. The unit weighs slightly more than 2 tons, and is capable of hurling a 33 pound projectile nearly 7 miles. This weapon is the "workhorse of the Army," being used as a bombardment and anti-tank weapon. It is best for "Hit and run" tactics.

Now that the Nazis have been driven within this strongly fortified "fortress of Europe" the fighting may revert, for a time, to siege warfare. In that event, Army Ordnance has ready such heavy long-range guns as the 8-inch gun, and the 240 mm howitzer.

The 8-inch howitzer is capable of firing a 200 pound shell through a plunging trajectory nearly 11 miles.

The 8-inch gun and its companion piece, the 240 mm howitzer, are the largest mobile field pieces used by the Army. Each of these guns in firing position weigh over 30 tons. They will be used in bombardments.   *EPG Echo*, July 15, 1943, p. 7

In the column *Services in Uniform*, a two-star mother (*i.e.*, she had two children serving in the military) worked in the Proof Department, where 20-mm ammunition belts for proof firing 20-mm feed mechanisms were installed in U.S. Army aircraft. One of her sons wrote: *P.S. Gee, Mom, it sure does make me think of you when I see that EPG stamp*. A stamp was placed on armament that had been proofed. The articles created a culture that personalized employee jobs; they learned about the immediate result of their hard work and its impact on their own children (*EPG Echo*, July 15, 1943, p. 4).

Bell Aircraft

I thought one article accompanied by an editorial, was unusual until I realized how important cotton was to the war effort. ***Cotton Pickers Needed to Save Crop for Army and Cotton Pickin' Time*** gave Bell Aircraft workers an opportunity to assist local cotton farmers, whose children were in the military or working in industry, with the fall harvest. The autumn season was especially dry in 1943 and the cotton bolls were opening at the same time, hence the need for an immediate harvest. Cotton was needed for military clothing, and cottonseed oil and other plant by-products were used in making munitions. The editorial urged office workers to pick cotton, while the lead article asked for night workers to do a short five-hour day shift as well. The pay was $1.50/ hundred pounds (*Bell Aircraft News*, October 15, 1943, p. 1/ p.2).

In its March 1944 report of company successes, Bell Aircraft cited dramatic increases in sales and production: 1943 saw a great increase in the production of the P-39 *Airacobra*; scheduled production of large bombers in Marietta; began production of a new fighter (likely, this was the P-63 *Kingcobra* that was produced from 1943 to 1945); became the first U.S. company to…*design, build, fly, and put into production jet propulsion planes…*; perfection of the Bell helicopter (first flight June 26, 1943); and expanded its ordnance division by moving it to Burlington, Vermont. The company and its employees were…*commended by the army and the War Production Board* (*Bell Aircraft News*, March 18, 1944, p. 1).

Goodyear Aircraft

The U.S. War Department and other highly placed politicians kept the pressure on employees of all installations to increase production. A telegram printed on the front page of one Goodyear newsletter is illustrative.

> 1942 Jan 24 PM 10 43
>
> TELEGRAM FROM WASHINGTON DC
>
> The Employees of Goodyear Tire & Rubber Co., Akron Ohio
>
> The Army is calling on you soldiers of production to back up our soldiers on the front lines with every ounce of your energy. The Army looks to you to provide the weapons of victory. The fighting weapons we lacked yesterday at Wake and Manilla we must have today. Your contribution must be production and more production. American is confident of your answer.
>
> Patterson Under Secretary of War

Robert P. Patterson was Under Secretary of War and served under President Franklin D. Roosevelt and his successor, President Harry S. Truman. The Battle for Wake Island lasted from December 7 to December 23, 1941, with a victory for the Imperial Japanese forces. The Battle of Luzon, part of the Philippine Islands, occurred between December 8, 1941 and January 8, 1942, and resulted in a victory for Japan.

Clearly, the telegram from Under Secretary of War Patterson was timely, designed to energize the home front workers, and written to point out that if the U.S. had proper weaponry, it would not lose other battles.

While all three facilities – Erie Proving Ground, Bell Aircraft, and Goodyear – took their jobs seriously, The Aircraft 8 Campaign imposed on its employees by Goodyear was over-the-top, albeit responding to a national requirement. *Our Job A Plane Every 8 Minutes* appeared on a special edition of the newsletter and several articles addressed this campaign. The company leadership stated that…*the task of America's aircraft industry for 1942 as set by our Commander-In-Chief, President Roosevelt: there must be one fighting plane every eight minutes in 1942 if America is to emerge victorious in our struggle for life.*

The Aircraft 8 Campaign, then, was part of the…*overall war production program that called for…60,000 fighting planes…45,000 combat tanks…20,000 anti-aircraft guns…8,000,000 dead weight tons of merchant ships in 1942* (*The Wingfoot Clan*, April 14, 1942, p. 1). Goodyear produced aircraft parts as a subcontractor.

As I read the newsletter's articles, and subsequent newsletters, I could barely comprehend the effort mandated by the President, and the combined management-labor organizational time and effort that went in to meeting those goals. I truly realized at this point, that World War II was a war of production and that the shear effort by home front workers was almost unimaginable.

Thousands of Aircrafters Hear Plans For More Planes: Problem American Is Facing Is Dramatically Presented. This was followed by a sub-headline: ***Workers Gather At Sunrise For First Rally To Hear Representatives of Labor, Management, Army, Navy Ask For "All Out" Effort***. The staging of this presentation was calculated to engender maximum effort by employees. In a later article, employees were asked to repeat the Aircrafters Pledge (and to sign it) to support the objectives of the joint labor-management production committee so that an American war plane would be produced every eight minutes (*The Wingfoot Clan*, April 22, 1942, p. 1, with Pledge on p. 5).

Pledge of the Aircrafter

To the end that American war plane production may reach the rate of one every eight minutes or a total of 60,000 for 1942 –
To the end that there not be "too little, too late" on the battle fronts where our fighting men are offering their lives for the preservation of my country –
I solemnly pledge my full support to the great objectives of the
Joint Labor-Management Production Committee of Goodyear Aircraft Corporation.

By the end of April, ***Aircrafters' Pledges Rolling In For Support of 8-Ball Program*** the article stated thousands of employees pledged their full support of the 8-Ball Program. When all the cards were collected, they were sent to Donald Nelson, Chairman, War Production Board. The article talked about a...*seriousness prevailing in everyone's actions...in fulfilling the nation's task of producing a war-plane every eight minutes in 1942... to make sure that Hitler, Hirohito and Mussolini wind up 'behind the eight-ball* (*The Wingfoot Clan*, April 29, 1942, p. 1).

Contests within the plant were continuous, and employees were urged to suggest ideas to...*speed up production, eliminate waste, and improve conditions*... In the article ***Special Prizes Offered Besides Regular Awards for Suggestions In Aircraft's 8-Ball Campaign***, an extra $1,500 would be awarded during the three-month special campaign (*The Wingfoot Clan*, April 29, 1942, p. 1).

The pressure to produce and subsequent competition between departments, each of which had specific production goals, was encouraged. ***8-Ball Flag For Production Goes To PBM-3: Each Week Winner To Be Adjudged On Department's Effort***. Production figures were charted, displayed, and compared to the previous month's production, and to the cumulative effort since the start of the campaign (*The Wingfoot Clan*, May 6, 1942, p. 1).

For example, by mid-May the jig crew in Consolidated PB2Y3 assembly beat the schedule by five days; they earned a photo on the front page. ***Strong In 8-Ball Campaign – Beat Schedule Five Days*** (*The Wingfoot Clan*, May 13, 1942, p. 1).

All In 8-Ball Production Race: Banner Now On Display In Every Department of Aircraft Division. Parts Manufacturing was declared the overall winner of the six-week contest, with second place held by the Wheels and Brakes Division, third place by K-Ships (blimps), fourth by Grumman (parts for Grumman Aircraft), and fifth by Martin PBM-3 (flying boat used by Naval Air Transport Service, Pacific Theater). Each employee got a lapel pin (*The Wingfoot Clan*, June 17, 1942, p. 1). Goodyear's part of the national campaign was touted as a success. Later statistics indicate forty-six thousand nine-hundred seven combat and support aircraft were built in 1942, while in 1943, eighty-four thousand eight-hundred fifty-three combat and support aircraft were built.

Here Tokio, {sic}***Chew On This! 'Fine Job, Aircraft!' Says Donald Nelson***. Nelson, chairman of the War Production Board in Washington, D. C., praised Aircraft workers for increasing production more than ten percent. He had been following the Eight-Ball War Production Drive. He thanked each worker for her/his effort and sent his letter at the conclusion of the 8-Ball Campaign (*The Wingfoot Clan*, July 29, 1942, p. 1). By July 1943, the United States was building seven-thousand aircraft per month, but ten-thousand were needed (*The Wingfoot Clan*, July 21, 1942, p. 1).

Efficiently building aircraft meant saving and recycling scrap. The entire Akron community asked Goodyear to participate in a community-wide effort: ***Aircraft Asked To Take Prominent Part In "Give-A-Gun."*** This was a city-wide program to retrieve scrap metal by city employees and taken to Akron's community scrap site. *Based on the fact that a 30-caliber machine gun requires 25 pounds of steel, and that half this steel is manufactured from scrap, the drive is expected to produce thousands of "machine guns" from the Akron district* (The Wingfoot Clan, August 26, 1942, p. 1).

Goodyear rubber plantations in the South Pacific were overrun by Japanese forces in early 1942 and rubber was needed in aircraft assembly. The nation felt the pinch. ***Let's Get Into Scrap By Turning In Scrap: Entire Goodyear Organization Urged by Mr. Litchfield to Assist Nationwide Drive For Rubber, Metals, Etc.*** Rubber items such as these needed to be turned in: soles of shoes, raincoats, bath mats, bathing caps, boots and overshoes. Metal included household items such as iron beds, appliances, kitchen utensils, lamps, garden/porch furniture, auto parts, tools, chairs, wire fences, and so forth (The Wingfoot Clan, July 22, 1942, p. 1).

The Quota Ship was a designation given to an aircraft that met the quota for the month or the year. The construction of the F4U *Corsair* at Goodyear was one of its most successful planes…***Mostly Women From Plant D To Build FG-1 Ships***. The article stated that by June 1, 1943, the company would have three-thousand five-hundred more workers, mostly women (The Wingfoot Clan, April 28, 1943, p. 1).

By September 1943, Aircraft had a well-developed program for employing young men in their late teens. ***16, 17 Year Olds Will Alternate Job and School: About 50% Continue on Four Hour Basis When Classes Resume Within Next Few Weeks***. Some boys would divide their time between school and work each day. Vocational school boys would work two weeks and attend school two weeks, other would work a full shift and attend night high school (The Wingfoot Clan, September 1, 1943, p. 3). The Allies were making headway in Europe and the Pacific and more men were called to duty, necessitating creative ways for Aircraft to maintain a work force and make sure boys - children, really - finished high school.

The Quota Campaign was launched in December 1943, with an increase in the number of F4U *Corsairs* built, and a corresponding winding down of blimp construction. America needed more fighter/bombers. A contest was proposed to employees. If the quota were met, all could autograph the aircraft. Men and women worked on its assembly; ***"Quota Ship" Ahead of Schedule*** (The Wingfoot Clan, December 15, 1943, p. 1).

Employees signed a scroll that was turned over to navy personnel:

> We, the members of Goodyear Aircraft Labor-Management, sent to you, the men of our U.S. Navy, the 'Quota Ship' for the month of December 1943, and solemnly pledge to extend our greater efforts in each succeeding month until victory is ours.
>
> The Wingfoot Clan, December 29, 1943, p. 1

Aircrafters Hold Celebration As "Quota Ship" Is Finished On Time (*The Wingfoot Clan*, January 5, 1944, p. 1). The headline says it all and the celebration was a thank-you to the aircraft's assemblers. The Quota Ship scroll had over ten-thousand names when it was presented to navy personnel headed to Washington, D.C. After that, the scroll went to battlefronts where the *Corsairs* were in action (*The Wingfoot Clan*, January 19, 1944, p. 3).

American Red Cross Blood Services and Homefront Workers

The health of individual employees was important in maintaining optimum production schedules. For example, I noted on Aunt Monnie's medical records that she had been vaccinated against smallpox. This disease, now eradicated worldwide, was of great concern during World War II. Goodyear placed this announcement in their newsletter: **Warning Issued By Head of Goodyear Hospital Regarding Threat of Smallpox**. He urged employees to be vaccinated: *Even a mild epidemic could close the plants for a protracted period of time, and in a severe epidemic the death rate might be appaling* {sic}. There had been reports of smallpox in surrounding counties (*The Wingfoot Clan*, January 20, 1943, p. 1).

Red Cross Blood Services began during World War II and their blood drives reached across the United States, and into the work places of American citizens. They collected 13.3 million pints of blood for the armed forces. Blood was in short supply during the war, and citizens were encouraged to give blood to be used by soldiers wounded in battle. Local Red Cross volunteers appeared regularly with mobile units at defense plants and employees were given time during the work day to contribute. Companies often published stories illustrating the personal impact that plasma made to servicemen. Erie Proving Ground, Bell Aircraft, and Goodyear Aircraft employees were urged to give blood regularly, and blood donating contests were part pf the push; individual employees who gave regularly or gave a great quantity were singled out for praise. Competition was part of the push. Red Cross campaign posters often were reprinted in newsletters or were displayed in defense plants.

Long forgotten is the Red Cross practice of historically segregating "Negro blood" from that of other donors, a policy justified by the army surgeon general. The Red Cross Donor Program began in 1941 and went on to save many lives. "Negro blood" initially was not taken after the bombing of Pearl Harbor, so that white recipients could be assured they were getting "white" plasma. Interestingly, the director of the first Red Cross blood bank was an African American doctor who pioneered the techniques that made large-scale blood plasma storage possible. The segregation of blood began in January 1942 and was only discontinued in 1950. It is not known how blood was administered on the battlefield.

These posters are illustrative and poignant.

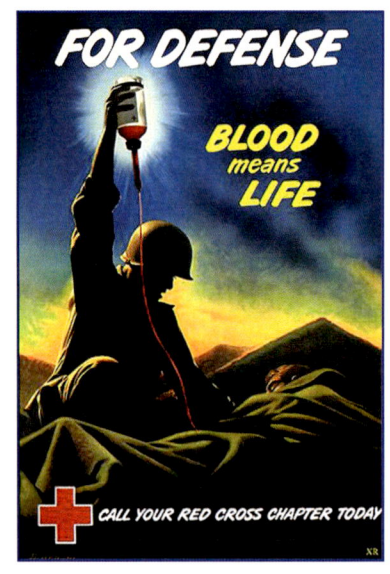

Erie Proving Ground

There was no information about blood drives in the *EPG Echo*. They may have occurred after the newsletter was discontinued or been reported in the local newspaper.

Bell Aircraft

One photo in *Bell Aircraft News* shows eight women, dressed in Red Cross dresses/hats, standing behind a long table filled with food. *They laid a fine table, right down to floral decorations, and served many gallons of fruit juices.* In another article one employee was lauded for donating eight pints, and another man for contributing four times. Both were from Tool Design (*Bell Aircraft News*, June 11, 1943, p. 4). There were regular blood donating contests between departments to increase the overall company donations.

The push to give blood was part of one Bell Aircraft slogan: *Bombers, blood, and bonds.* An article entitled **Blood Unit Due Back Jan. 6-7** set the tone for 1944. A Red Cross blood unit appeared at the plant weekly, and information was given about what to eat or not eat prior to donating blood. The final statement reiterated the competition atmosphere for giving blood: *Donations Dec. 28 and 29 moved the plant total to within striking distance of the 1,500 mark* (*Bell Aircraft News*, January 1, 1944, p. 1).

An emotional article on the front page of *Bell Aircraft News* said it all when it came to donating blood for service personnel. **Bell Worker's Son Owes Life To Plasma In Pacific Fighting**. The son of an employee received a Purple Heart earned during the sinking of the aircraft carrier USS *Yorktown* (CV-5) at the Battle of Midway. The young sailor was one of only fourteen men at two gun stations to survive the blast from a Japanese bomb which struck the carrier's stern. He reckoned he would not have made it through the battle and its aftermath if he had not had plasma. This story was impactful because it was about the child of a Bell employee. The article was placed next to one letting employees know when the American Red Cross mobile blood unit would next be at the Bell Bomber Plant. Needed were eight-hundred more successful donations to reach a three-thousand five-hundred pint goal for 1944 (*Bell Aircraft News*, April 29, 1944, p. 1).

The *Atlanta Journal* was quoted: *It's a lot easier to shed a little blood with trained attendants than to shed a lot of blood on a battlefield where your main hope of survival is the presence of blood plasma from home. It doesn't exactly make you a hero but it helps a hero keep on being one* (*Bell Aircraft News*, January 22, 1944, p. 2).

An October 1944, newsletter reprinted a **Certificate of Appreciation** *awarded to… Bell Bomber Plant…for outstanding cooperation with the…American Red Cross Blood Drive Service.* It was sent from the Atlanta Chapter of the American Red Cross to thank the company employees for…*outstanding and continuous support in this most vital supply mission* (*Bell Aircraft News*, October 21, 1944, p. 2).

In an early December issue, employees were alerted to an offer to autograph their blood donations: **1st Autograph Blood Donation**. This emotional and pointed offer said…*donors may sign the label that goes on package to the battlefront and dedicate their blood in honor of a friend or loved one in the armed services…Today the need is greater than ever before…it would be impossible to think of a finer Christmas present than a pint of blood for a wounded man overseas* (*Bell Aircraft News*, December 9, 1944, p. 4). The program allowed workers to participate in the war in a very personal manner.

Goodyear Aircraft

By early 1942, Goodyear pushed the need for employees to give blood. **Early To Register As Blood Donors** stated…*students of the Aircraft sheet metal training school were among the many Goodyearites who last week appeared among the first at The Wingfoot Clan office to volunteer their blood for the Red Cross "blood bank."* Women from the sheet metal class were included in the photograph that accompanied the article (*The Wingfoot Clan*, March 25, 1942, p. 4).

Blood drives had specific goals for states, cities, and businesses for both donations of cash and pints of blood; both were encouraged. In 1943, employees at Goodyear gave $30,000. By mid-march 1944, employees gave $27,234, which was short of the goal: **Redoubling Of Efforts Is On To Reach Mark** (*The Wingfoot Clan*, March 15, 1944, p. 4). By the next week, Goodyear employees had exceeded the goal for donations to the Red Cross (*The Wingfoot Clan*, March 22, 1944, p. 1). This article appeared just above one about the Fourth War Bond Drive. Employees were encouraged/expected to give to both types of drives.

One More Pint Will Make A Gallon Of Girl's Blood Donated To Red Cross highlighted the effort of one young woman whose brother had been killed in action (*The Wingfoot Clan*, November 1, 1944, p. 6). Her donation was personal. These types of articles were common in their linking a home-based action to an action on the battlefront.

War Bond Campaigns and the Pressure to Give

From her payroll and war bond record, I learned that Aunt Monnie was paid bi-weekly, and had $3.75 deducted each pay period to purchase a war bond at $18.75 (with a value of $25.00). Records indicate she purchased war bonds in this way for the entire time she was employed at Erie Proving Ground. In June 1944, when she received a promotion and a salary increase, the amount deducted for the purchase of War Bonds increased to $9.38/pay period. Employees were encouraged to give 10% of their salary each pay period; Monnie gave roughly 7% of her bi-weekly salary.

Liberty Bonds were issued during World War I to help finance the war effort and were sold in the United States. The last time the U.S. issued war bonds was during World War II, when full employment collided with rationing, and War Bonds were seen as a way to remove money from circulation as well as to reduce inflation. Issued in May 1941 by the U.S. Government, they were initially called Defense Bonds. The name changed to War Bonds after the United States entered World War II.

Defense plant workers were urged to invest in War Bonds, and urged to give to the Red Cross, March of Dimes, local charities, to donate blood, help put together Russian Relief Kits or assemble Food Packages for prisoners of war, give to the Army-Navy Emergency Relief Fund, and myriad other funds or special projects. The push by management to give, participate, and donate was unrelenting.

There are hundreds of examples of War Bond posters from both World War I and World War II on the internet. They depict patriotic themes or suggest horrifying results if Bonds are not purchased. They include all racial groups, countries, men in action, and children and women on the home front. Images of Hollywood actors and high-ranking military officers, such as General Dwight D. Eisenhower, were used to encourage bond purchases. While fascinating as historical recruitment tools, they are often demeaning to American women and African Americans, while simultaneously depicting the pure hatred the Allies felt for their German and Japanese enemies.

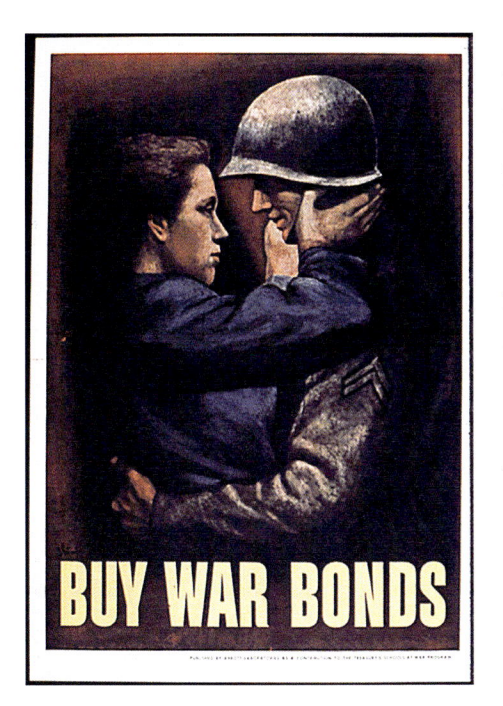

The sale of War Bonds to the American public was very successful. There were eight drives: the First Drive was November 30 through December 23, 1942; the Second Drive was April 12 through May 1, 1943; the Third Drive was September 9 through October 1, 1943; the Fourth Drive was January 18 through February 15, 1944; the Fifth Drive was June 12 through July 8 1944; the Sixth Drive was November 10 through December 16, 1944; the Seventh Drive was May 14 through June 30, 1945; with the Victory Loan Drive from October 29 through December 8, 1945. By the end of World War II, eighty-five million Americans (population 131 million people – 65%) had purchased a total of $185.7 billion in War Bonds. The pressure on individual workers to invest in War Bonds was unrelenting.

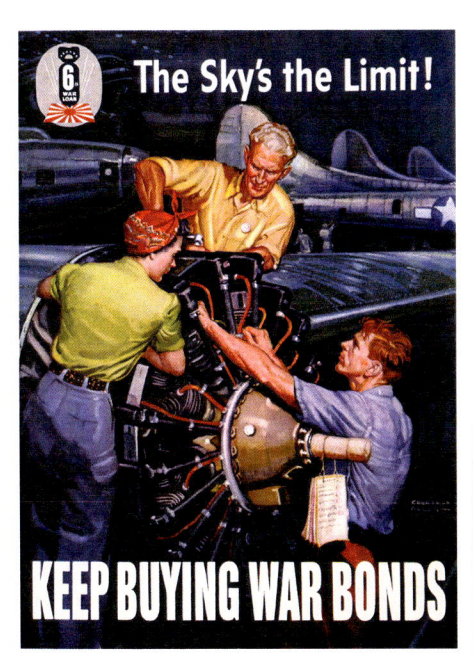

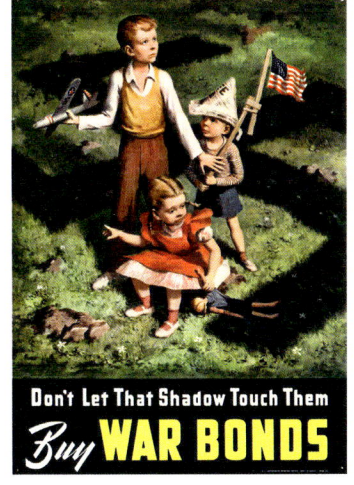

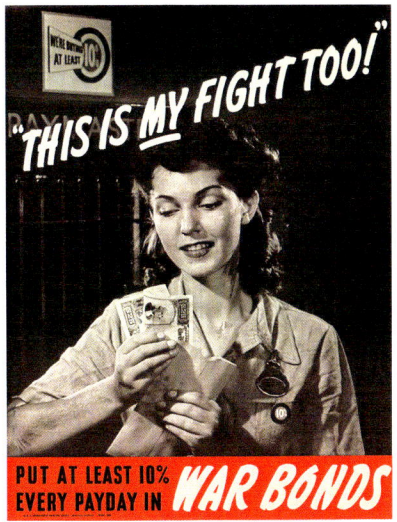

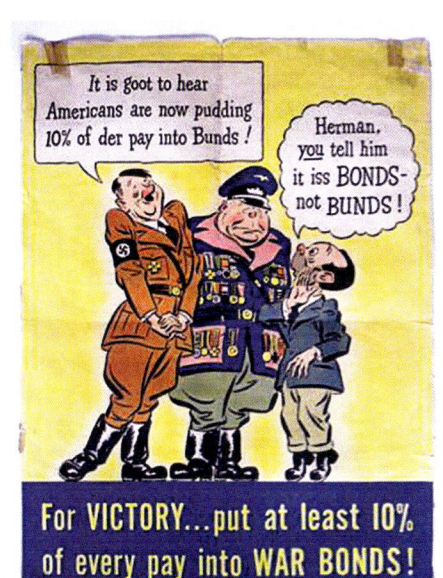

Erie Proving Ground

The Last Cartridge was likely an editorial in the *EPG Echo* (July 15, 1943, p.2). In the analogy of the last cartridge to the need to purchase War Bonds, the author stated: *Life's battle is an economic one waged with our abilities to perform a valuable service and establish monetary security. And it behooves all of us to guard our 'last cartridge' which is represented in savings and investments.* The article went on to state: *At the present time the soundest investment in the world is United States War Bonds. The interest rate paid is good and the value of bonds is not changed by market conditions.* EPG employees were told they were well paid but an analysis by management showed those same employees were way below the minimum of a ten percent investment. A concluding statement read: *Patriotism alone should offer enough incentive to the investment of ten percent of our pay in War Bonds.*

Erie Proving Ground initiated a **War Bond Honor Roll For EPG Is Planned**. *A War Bond honor roll for sections and units of EPG divisions and branches whose employees rank high in War Bond participation will be printed in the next issue of the EPG Echo. At present, Coast Time Unit of the Adm. {Administrative} Branch with a 99 per cent participation ranks highest on the Post. Special mention should be given Capt. R. V. Mackey and his section of Proof Div., and Capt. M. Phelan, EOD, and his able assistant, Ed Sprenger, who have pushed EOD away on top. The best way to save. Buy War Bonds each pay* (*EPG Echo*, July 15, 1943, p. 6). Aunt Monnie was in the Proof Division and routinely gave seven percent of her salary to the purchase of War Bonds, increasing the dollar amount with each promotion in rank and increase in salary.

The United Service Organizations (USO) centers around the United States played a key role in boosting morale for both soldiers and home front workers. The Port Clinton USO became a home to enlisted men locally. Of great importance to the local people was the statement that *the former home of the men of the 192nd Tank Co., (now captive in Bataan) is now the home of hundreds of men like them* (*EPG Echo*, July 15, 1943, p. 3). The 192nd Tank Battalion was composed of tank companies from Ohio, Wisconsin, Kentucky, and Illinois. The Port Clinton Ohio Company C was formerly the 37th Tank Company. They were deployed to the Pacific Theatre and fought alongside Philippine forces against the Imperial Japanese Army.

On December 22, 1941, the 192nd Tank Battalion became the first American tank unit to engage Japanese armor in tank-to-tank combat during World War II. The unit withdrew to the Bataan Peninsula as part of the general retreat, and ceased to exist on April 9, 1942, when the last surviving American and Philippine forces on the Bataan Peninsula surrendered. The Battle of Bataan lasted three months. Some men went to Corregidor, while others escaped into the jungle. Those who remained were part of the Bataan Death March, the forcible transfer of between sixty-thousand and eighty-thousand American and Filipino prisoners of war. They remained prisoners *of* war until the close of the invasion of the Philippines. Some prisoners at Cabanatuan were rescued by US Army Rangers on December 30, 1944. Others were sent to Japan or other parts of the Japanese empire as laborers. Of the five-hundred ninety-three officers and men of the 192nd Tank Battalion who went to the Philippines in October 1941, three-hundred twenty-eight did not survive the war.

The employees at Erie Proving Ground knew their local citizens, their "boys," were prisoners of war, a particularly horrifying thought for those on the home front. Port Clinton was a very small town. This knowledge must have spurred many to greater efforts at EPG and to purchase War Bonds. However, the horror of the Bataan Death March was not made public by the United States government until January 27, 1944.

Bell Aircraft

A page one headline in *Bell Aircraft News* read: **DEPT. 27-0 LEADS PAYROLL WAR SAVING PARADE**. The article indicated Bell Aircraft's intention to win the Treasury "T" Award which would be given to companies with at least ninety percent of their employees having purchased War Bonds. All employees were invited to participate with a goal of at least a ten percent investment of the company's payroll. Department 27.0 (Employment) was in the lead, followed by the employees in Finishing, then Employee Publications, Fire Department, Tool Crib, and Contracts. These departments were set up as examples for all forty departments; clearly competition was encouraged. A chart within the article rated departments' participation with scores of "excellent," "good," "improving," or "coming up." The system was easy for employees to participate in as any amount could be deducted from an employee's paycheck (*Bell Aircraft News*, July 2, 1943, p. 1). Virtually every issue of the newsletter carried an article about the need for employees to purchase War Bonds. The standing of each department was routinely printed.

By July 9, 1943, the newsletter stated that…*practically all departments report steady advances in the number of employees who are participating in the purchase of War Bonds in an effort to win the Treasury "T" Award for the Georgia Division* (p. 1).

Plant Life was a cartoon that appeared regularly to deliver messages about War Bonds. In the Saturday, January 8, 1944, issue, a male child is writing a math formula on a school room blackboard while his teacher looks on. Her facial expression changes when it appears that the child has not done his math correctly. He wrote: *1+1+1 = 4*. The teacher frowned until he adjusted his formula to read: *$1+$1+$1 in war saving bonds in 1944 = $4 in war saving bonds in 1954*. The teacher smiled, and the smiling child was pleased with himself.

In January 1944 the United States launched its Fourth War Loan Campaign. For Bell Aircraft the headline said: **Plant's Quota Is $500,000 In Extra Bonds**. The article acknowledged this goal was a "stiff one" but assured workers that…*Bonds of the United States are the best investments in the world today…They represent both national and personal security…The buying of war bonds under the stimulus and fervor of a campaign* *to support our men in the armed services is only part of the privilege of American…Bonds bought should be retained against any impulse to turn them back into cash, except to meet the most serious personal needs.* The push to purchase war bonds was constant *(Bell Aircraft News, January 22, 1944, p. 1).*

A moving poster about the purchase of extra bonds appeared in a 1944 issue: A soldier with his right hand in a throwing positon is ready to launch a grenade; he appears to be yelling. The poster title says: **Let 'Em Have It**. A small logo on a shield with stars appears over his right hand: *4th War Loan*. In large letters at the bottom of the poster: BUY EXTRA BONDS (*Bell Aircraft News*, January 22, 1944, p. 2).

A similar poster appeared the next month depicting a solder crouched in a jungle. He says: **No Kidding…Are You Really Doing the Best You Can, Too?** The poster logo in a shield with stars accompanies the depiction: **Buy Extra Bonds 4th War Loan** (*Bell Aircraft News*, February 5, 1944, p. 2).

The sale of War Bonds was discussed in virtually every issue of the 1944 newsletter until the goal was finally reached. Articles appear on the front pages giving the total dollars garnered to date. A film star visited Bell Aircraft to do lunchtime bond selling: one such visit garnered $38,350 in sales bringing the total to $65,000, but was still behind the goal (*Bell Aircraft News*, January 29, 1944, p. 1). A warning of a possible failure to meet the goal was given on page one of the February 12, 1944 issue. Finally, on February 16, 1944, the front page headline read: **Fourth War Bond Drive Spurred By Company's Half Million Offer.** The president of Bell Aircraft, Larry Bell, promised to match dollar-for-dollar the Marietta employees' goal of $500,000 with an additional $500,000. **Deadline Extended to Allow Workers Benefit of Pay Day For Last-Minute Purchases**; the plant was $50,000 to $70,000 short of its goal and the time to reach the goal was extended to Friday, February 18, 1944. By February 19, 1944, the headline was: **Sales Reach $1,040,000 Doubling Bond Total: Employes** {sic} **Meet Bell's Offer To Tie Plant Quota.**

In a letter to his employees, Larry Bell wrote: *It was most gratifying for me to learn that the people in the Georgia division topped their quota of $500,000 in the Fourth War Loan campaign. But the result was even more gratifying, I am sure, to our boys on the battlefronts. It indicated to them that the people at home were at least sacrificing on a temporary basis by investing in the future of America. To you who willingly gave up some of the luxuries of life in order that victory might be brought closer, my heartiest congratulations* (*Bell Aircraft News*, February 19, 1944, p. 2).

In June 1944 the United States launched its Fifth War Loan Campaign. In April prior to that, two Bell Aircraft employees' purchase of war bonds was praised in ***Investors Jump Gun On Coming War Loan Drive***. Bell employees were well motivated; they had oversubscribed during the Fourth War Loan Campaign. A senior accounting clerk gave $5,000 and an in-training worker gave $2,000 for the 1944 campaign. Bell renewed its effort to encourage bond purchases by selecting division representatives to lead the effort (*Bell Aircraft News*, April 29, 1944, p. 3).

By Christmas 1944, Bell workers were offered an opportunity to purchase ***Unique V-Mail Bond Gift Form Available Here***. This *Yule-embellished reproduction of a war bond* could be used as a gift from a relative or friend for someone overseas. There was room on the photocopy for personal messages, and the gift included the denomination and the bond's serial number. *It had been stressed by bond leaders that the giving of a bond is not merely the gift of money but it also hastens the return of the recipient* (*Bell Aircraft News*, December 9, 1944, p. 1). The bond was a gift, but came with a veiled message that not to purchase would lengthen the war.

The pressure on employees to invest in War Bonds did not abate even as many believed the Allies were winning the war. ***A Seabee Writes*** was a long letter originally printed in *Minute Man*, a field publication of the War Finance Commission of the Treasury Department and reprinted in the editorial section of *Bell Aircraft News*. The letter was anonymous. Its tone was accusative, scolding, derisive, and written as a six-stanza poem. The last stanza serves the point: *"Well, we've been tired and hungry, seared with frost and broiled in sun; mired in mud and stench and oozy slime, peppered by Jap and Hun. And we've often felt like quitting, throwing down the tools of war, for we don't see sense in fighting for the things you won't work for! Of course, that's just plain grouching, for we won't quite, you know, until we have Berlin in our hand and march in Tokyo…"*(*Bell Aircraft News*, March 3, 1945, p. 2).

Telling in their tribute to a fallen leader is ***FDR Bonds Go On Sale; Total Passes $500,000: New Securities Issued in Honor Of Fallen Chief.*** The bonds sold during the Seventh War Bond Campaign were issued in honor of President Franklin D. Roosevelt who had died April 12, 1945, at his retreat in Warm Springs, Georgia. Each bond was inscribed *"In Memory of Franklin Delano Roosevelt"* (*Bell Aircraft News*, April 21, 1945, p. 1). The sale of the bonds to honor the President was Bell Aircraft's idea. They were opened to the public at a later date by the State War Finance Committee, the only state in the union doing such (*Bell Aircraft News*, April 27, 1945, p. 1).

War Bond Goal Smashed In 7th praised Bell workers for beating the quota set for the company by 102% - $2,290,899 worth of bonds were sold in an eight-week campaign. Departmental standings were published at a later date (*Bell Aircraft News*, July 13, 1945, p. 1). The willingness of employees to invest in War Bonds when the war was nearly over is remarkable.

Goodyear Aircraft

On page seven of the February 24, 1943, *The Wingfoot Clan*, C. J. Palmatier, Aunt Monnie's father, was listed with several other employees as needing to contact the Company Cashier to retrieve their War Bonds. This was one of the first written confirmations I had of his employment at Aircraft.

Put a Bond In The Bank for a Yank: That's Slogan for Aircrafters in Sixth War Loan Campaign. The headline marked the beginning of the Sixth War Loan Campaign which began November 10, 1944. The front page article encouraged workers to buy one as a Christmas gift for…*that husband, sweetheart, brother or son now in the service of Uncle Sam*…They would be placed in attractive holiday envelopes to be shipped overseas. Each employee was asked to purchase…*at least one $100 bond*. The push was on to Japan: **Let's Help Him Finish The Job** (*The Wingfoot Clan*, November 15, 1944, p. 1).

Next to this appeal was a note of thanks from the United States Treasury for what plant employees achieved in the previous campaign: **Pat on Back For Fifth Bond Drive**: *A Citation to Aircraft from the US Treasury Dept. signed by Secretary Morgenthau, was received this week. It cited Aircraft 'for distinguished service rendered the war financing program,' through meeting its quota in the Fifth War Bond Drive* (*The Wingfoot Clan*, November 15, 1944, p. 1).

By the time the Seventh War Loan Campaign started employees learned: **Aircrafters' Quota Set At $3,382,000 Opens Next Monday** (*The Wingfoot Clan*, March 28, 1945, p. 1). They reached a 93.5% of the quota, second highest among Akron industries (*The Wingfoot Clan*, July 18, 1945, p. 1).

Conception Data Sheets (CDS)/ Suggestion Awards to Workers

Employees at EPG, Bell and Goodyear were repeatedly encouraged to suggest ideas, and were rewarded for ideas that would save time and money in ordnance work or in the production of aircraft. For example, generally companies sought ideas to simplify processes to reduce production costs and to increase production overall. The employers wanted ideas to eliminate hazards, and…*eliminate waste of time, material, tools, or energy*…(*Bell Aircraft News*, June 18, 1943, p. 3). Goodyear Aircraft and Erie Proving Ground mirrored those contest parameters.

Erie Proving Ground

Aunt Monnie received recognition for her suggestions, as cited in an official letter of commendation for her effort to simplify the work in her department, thereby allowing seven clerk typists to be reassigned to other divisions. Overall, her suggestions improved paperwork processes and procedures. There was no announcement in the newsletter and no certificate of award, and no mention of money awarded to her.

An article appeared in the newsletter to entice employees with offers of cash prizes for their suggestions. **WD Authorizes Cash Awards For Suggestions.** *War Department Civilian Personnel regulations just received authorize the awarding of from $5 to $250 in cash for employee suggestions which result in improvement or economy in operations within the War Department. Under these regulations any Civil Service employee of EPG will be eligible to receive an award for a suggestion adopted on or after 2 June 1943* (*EPG Echo*, July 15, 1943, p. 1). Suggestion boxes were placed near time clocks. Suggestions that were awarded would be forward for review by the War Department Board on Civilian Awards for a possible additional reward.

The military laid out a process for employees to follow if they wanted to submit a suggestion: *Three Named On Suggestion Committee: Civ. Pers. Branch To Maintain Routine*. There were two military officers and one civilian worker on the committee tasked with approving or disapproving suggestions. The committee also had to establish and maintain an effective routine for collecting, analyzing, and filing the suggestions. *Cash awards would be given when a suggestion results in one or more of the following: conservation of manpower, material, time or space; elimination of unnecessary procedures or records, or improvement of existing methods; improvement of conditions affecting safety and health; increased productivity; elimination of excess waste, improvement of quality; invention of a mechanical device, conservation of critical materiel previously scrapped* (*EPG Echo*, July 29, 1943, p. 3).

Bell Aircraft

Suggestions for Victory were labeled boxes placed around the plants so that employees…*may drop your thoughts about the best method of adding power to that Sunday punch the boys abroad are handing to totalitarian powers these days*. Both patented and unpatented suggestions were accepted. Employees were given recognition and a monetary award (*Bell Aircraft News*, May 28, 1943, p. 1).

Similarly, Bell Aircraft employees won awards for their suggestions for tool designs to streamline production, printed instructions for using fire extinguishers, using blunt white paper as a filler on pages that have erasures, print a warning tag for electric switches while employees are working on a particular circuit, and using a zinc-oxide paint mixture applied to welding booths to eliminate or reduce glare and radiation of ultra-violet rays. Each of these ideas was accepted by the Awards Committee for the Georgia Division and put into operation. An article about employee suggestions appeared in every issue of the newsletter. Clearly, the War Department and company management understood the need to encourage employees to identify personally with the war effort. Later, employees were named as prize recipients but sometimes their ideas were not listed or described; I assumed this was for security reasons.

Goodyear Aircraft

Put On Thinking Caps; Get Cash for Good Ideas. Employees and their awards were listed individually for their suggestions pertaining to safety, waste reduction, and production (*The Wingfoot Clan*, April 8, 1942, p. 1).

The suggestion program was popular as evidenced by *Over 20,000 Suggestions Submitted* a headline over a photo of a woman who…*Turns In 20,000th Suggestion*. She worked in Dept. 216, Riveting, Plant A (*The Wingfoot Clan*, July 5, 1944, p. 1).

At Christmas, the newsletter printed a front page article about employees who won awards for their suggestions: *Aircraft Is Santa Claus With Gifts To Workers*

Who Submit "Ideas." The long article identified two women and their ideas. *Two Plant B girl workers…Dept. 345, collaborated on a suggestion for a new rod device used in covering fabric surfaces and will split $165. The award was the highest ever offered for girl workers since the suggestion program was inaugurated at Aircraft* (*The Wingfoot Clan*, December 23, 1942, p. 1). The vast majority of awards for suggestions went to male employees.

Suggestions from employees remained a popular activity: ***63 Employees Split $1630, Woman Wins: Mrs. Dalton's Check Marks 150th Paid Out Since January 1***. She was a parts assembler, and received a check for $7.50, marking her second time as a winner. Her suggestion was not described, nor were those of the other winners (*The Wingfoot Clan*, August 25, 1943, p. 1).

Mary White suggested…*a new type jig used in the location of drilling for bolting on an idler shaft bracket of the K-ship* {blimp}. ***Seven Individual Production Merit Awards For Ideas*** were awarded to employees by the War Production Labor Management Committee, and made by a navy lieutenant (*The Wingfoot Clan*, September 22, 1943, p. 2).

Specifics about the suggestions were not always given as I suspect the company wanted to keep production ideas confidential and out of the hands of enemy spies. However, I thought one suggestion submitted by two women demonstrated some out-of-the-box thinking. They suggested a tool to be used to stretch fabric over a wing during wing assembly. Based on the curlers one woman used to set her hair, they asked the tool maker to create a three-foot version. It was very successful and this headline, with a photo of them using their suggestion, appeared: ***Newspaper Read At Sea Results In Two Aircraft Girls Learning They Got Publicity*** (*The Wingfoot Clan*, September 20, 1944, p. 6).

Cafeteria Troubles

American food production was pre-eminent so the American food supply line created a strategic advantage for the war effort. The greater portion of food went to the military, so, on the home front, some food items were rationed.

The logistics of acquiring food while meeting national rationing standards, then storing, preparing, and serving at least three meals daily to thousands of employees was a daunting, complex, and controversial problem. Rationed food items included coffee, sugar, lard, tea, meat, jam, cheese, eggs, milk, and canned or dried fruit. Fresh vegetables and fruit were not rationed, but often supplies were limited. Companies encouraged employees to create Victory Gardens to augment their diets. Articles about food storage, and meal menus were a regular part of employee newsletters. People needed to be fed nutritious meals and EPG employed about five-thousand people, Bell employed just over thirty-thousand at its peak in February 1945, and Goodyear employed thirty-three thousand people by 1945. Lessons in skilled food handling, preparation, and delivery were constantly relearned.

Erie Proving Ground

PX Expansion Underway announced to employees that a new wing of the Post Exchange would have a dining room with thirty-five booths and about forty tables … *all with formica tops with black trim. Woodwork will be yellow knotty pine.* In addition, employees were told that the cafeteria line would be modernized…*kitchen space will be enlarged, remodeled, and modernized.* The official opening was planned for July, and employees would see new electrical fixtures, overhead heating, and new decorations in the PX (*EPG Echo*, June 17, 1943, p. 4). It seems attempts were made to make the eating facilities more attractive for EPG workers.

The Erie Proving Ground cafeteria had its problems. One newsletter column, *Return Silverware, Please*, implored workers to return silverware to the PX. Apparently, 1,200 pieces had been missing since the first of the year. The writer of the article stated there was a…*veiled threat* and that the PX might have to…*resort to using wooden knives, forks, and spoon?* (*EPG Echo*, July 15, 1943, p. 3).

Another column, *PX Staff Has Dinner In New Dining Wing*, announced the opening of the dining wing with a small dinner for two valued female employees; the official opening was thought to be scheduled for August 1943. The facility was expected to be the finest in the state once all the reconstruction was completed (*EPG Echo*, July 15, 1943, p. 5).

Bell Aircraft

Bell Aircraft and Goodyear Aircraft also had trouble with their cafeteria organizational structure, food delivery, food quality and variety, all in keeping with national rationing of many food stuffs. Both plants had to deal with a rapid increase in the number of workers – from fewer than one-hundred workers to thousands of workers – in a very short time. Feeding workers who were placed in different buildings was an exercise in organization, and in serving nutritious food (hot or cold) in the time allotted for meals.

Several articles addressed employee concerns about the food quality, meal schedules, and portion size. In May 1943 a contract was awarded for all seven cafeterias with hot meals promised at Bell Aircraft by a Detroit, Michigan, catering company: *Contract Is awarded for All Cafeterias; Hot Meals Soon*. Bell management stated they recognized the need for hot meals to war workers, who would pay only a small amount for the food. An enormous kitchen equipped with large appliances was installed (*Bell Aircraft News*, May 21, 1943, p. 1).

Bell cafeterias formally opened Monday May 21, 1943; two were opened for breakfast, and four would be readied…*to serve hot, nourishing meals.* The contract with the caterer was signed (*Bell Aircraft News*, Friday, June 18, 1943, p. 1). By news time that Friday, headlines read: *New Deal in Cafeteria's Announced; Bell Moves to Take Over*

Service. Bell took steps to...*oust the contracting caterer and take over the operation of all cafeterias in order to serve better food on a cost basis*. **Cafeterias Opened—Better Service Promised Patrons: Warm Meals Served to Big Crowd**: the headline was over four photos showing employees in line and sitting at tables. *There were compliments and complaints, but it was generally understood that the new service had been hastily organized to enable the new cafeteria system to start a full week ahead of schedule*. Under Bell's management, the new cafeteria system would operate on a non-profit basis and serve tobacco, soft drinks, and candy as well as food. Bell management promised employees better food at a lower cost (*Bell Aircraft News*, July 30, 1943 p. 1).

In August 1943, the front-page headline read: **Bell Hires Engineer Staff to Operate Plant Cafeterias**. They hired a...*college trained home economist*...educated at the University of Alabama as the dietician to supervise all the kitchen work at all the cafeterias of the Bell Bomber plant. Apparently, the Army Engineer cafeteria had operated successfully for over a year, so those people took on greater responsibilities. The article repeated that food was not prepared often enough so snack bars were set up for employees who did not want or require a hot meal. This was a speedier way to serve food as those employees did not have to wait in the regular cafeteria lines (*Bell Aircraft News*, August 6, 1943, p. 1).

To alleviate a rush in the cafeteria lines, Bell **Staggered Lunch Hours Prevent Delay**. *The system of staggering noon lunch hours, recently adopted by the management, has proved effective in avoiding delays which are always irritating to those who have to stand in long lines waiting to fill their trays in the plant cafeterias. Both office and factory employees are now going to lunch in three different groups at 15-minute intervals in order to relieve congestion* (*Bell Aircraft News*, August 6, 1943, p. 2).

The reorganized cafeteria system seemed to be successful: **Workers Greet Cafeteria Opening With Enthusiasm**. The article went on to say there were very few complaints by employees, and the snack bars were popular as they offered bottled coca cola, milk, and cracker sandwiches. All six dining facilities were to be provided with snack bars also. *In addition to this were candy and tobacco counters with 16-cent cigarettes, four cents cheaper than those dispensed mechanically, cigars and pipe tobacco*. Sample menus were presented...*roast pork with brown gravy or breaded veal cutlet for 15 cents, with wieners and kraut or ham and macaroni for 12 cents. Vegetables, salads and desserts were priced in ration*. Bakery products were in the planning stages. The article mentioned employees' efforts to make the cafeteria successful, including this comment: *One woman department head, who incidentally is a veteran aircraft pilot, was seen at the luncheon rush hour pushing a broom and mop behind the new snack bars* (*Bell Aircraft News*, August 20, 1943, p. 1).

Yet another article about the cafeterias appeared on the front page of *Bell Aircraft News* (September 10, 1943, p. 1): **Cafeteria Equipment Will Be Identical**. The company planned to...*install identical counter equipment for the service of food at all cafeterias now being operated by Bell*...*the improvements*...*are in line with the management's aggressive campaign to provide the best possible food in the shortest time at the lowest possible level.*

Readers were assured that…*all food was prepared in the same kitchen and hot servings are dispatched in the basement cafeterias in insulated trucks*. The executive assistant to the manager of industrial relations appealed to readers to provide him with…*constructive criticisms… in writing…send a copy to the cafeteria manager*. The assistant to the manager was transferred to other facilities in Buffalo, New York, and Cleveland, Ohio; it is unclear if the transfer was related to the cafeteria woes. He returned to the Marietta plant in March as reported in the March 11, 1944 issue. What a saga! And not over.

Just when I thought I had read the last of Bell's cafeteria problems, this appeared: ***Equipment Shortage Is Blamed for Use Of Paper Plates***. Sufficient dish washing equipment was not available for all the cafeterias, but was on order. To avoid complaints of discrimination, all cafeterias used paper plates for a time, even though some of the cafeterias had adequate dish washing equipment. They hoped to…*return to the china standard shortly* (*Bell Aircraft News*, September 17, 1943, p. 1).

3 Top Caterers Added to Staff Of Cafeterias was a lengthy article about more changes instituted by the industrial relations office. The three men would manage the cost of food, *pay attention to a proper variety of summer dishes and sandwiches, including home-baked pastries, and would speed up the service of foods in the seven cafeterias*. The overall manager had been director of the Georgia Milk Control Board in Atlanta (*Bell Aircraft News*, April 1, 1944, p. 1). It appears that it was not only the army that traveled on its stomach.

The cafeteria continued to face complaints about food quality at Bell*:* ***Quality Is Aim Of Cafeterias*** was the headline over assurances by the company that quality rather than quantify was the goal. *Nothing but A-1 meats and produce will be purchased, and there will be no let-down in securing the best foods obtainable*. With food rationing, the term "obtainable" was the caveat. The company continued to work toward serving food faster and keeping it hot at all times (*Bell Aircraft News*, April 15, 1944, p. 1). Reorganization continued for example, to gain the improvement they sought, management put the menu at the front of the line so workers could review it before they got to the food, and in another week they saw improvements in the quality and handling of the food – a wider variety of vegetables and breakfast foods (*Bell Aircraft News*, April 22, 1944, p. 1).

By October 1944, the company tried yet another way to distribute food to its workers. ***Rolling Cafeteria Saves time, Trouble for Hangar Workers*** allowed workers…*to save the time which they would ordinarily have spent going to the lunchrooms…in other buildings. And the mobile cafeteria offered them all the benefits of the stationary cafeterias – hot meats, vegetables and soup, cold milk, dessert and a miniature cigar and candy stand*. One man, the first to be served this way, stated categorically: *Gosh, this is swell. I've been eating in cafeterias all over the project. This'll keep me from doing a lot of running around*. Management decided if the experiment were successful, mobile units would be placed in other buildings as well (*Bell Aircraft News*, October 7, 1944, p. 1).

Some uncomplicated news about the cafeterias came to light in a November issue: ***Café Employes'*** {sic} ***Fund to Cheer Transient GIs***. Kitchen employees set up a free chicken dinner fund for wounded servicemen who arrived in the C-47 transports on their way to hospitals. Employees set up a Christmas tree in the transient hangar and distributed gifts to the wounded as well (*Bell Aircraft News*, November 1, 1944, p. 3).

Missing silverware was a recurring problem in the plant. ***Cafeterias Face Silver Shortage*** let workers know there was…*a serious shortage in silverware has developed through failure of employes* {sic} *to return*…these items to the cafeterias. The cafeteria manager's threatening tone was quoted: *In the first place, these utensils are owned by the government and it is in direct violation of federal laws to remove them from cafeterias, regardless of whether or not they are stamped 'U. S.'* (*Bell Aircraft News*, November 18, 1944, p. 1). Silverware was made of critical materials and hard to replace.

Bell workers contributed to a Red Cross program that provided food packages to prisoners of war: ***Food Packages For Prisoners Main Objective***. Hundreds of Bell workers had relatives who were prisoners in German POW camps, so the appeal to them to assist was very personal. *Prisoner of war food packages contain tins of Brunch, a pork mixture, salmon, cheddar cheese, pineapple, liver, oleo, pork and beans, powdered milk, and coffee, and packages of raisins, sugar, biscuits, chocolate, cigarettes, soap and Vitamin C tablets*. The quota for purchasing the packages was set at…*six dollars a head*. To further encourage purchases, this was the final sentence: *If we could all see the look of gratefulness on the faces of our boys who receive these packages, I'm sure that any feeling of sacrifice on our part would shrink to the size of the molecule…*(*Bell Aircraft News*, March 10, 1945, p. 1).

It was a daily challenge to serve nutritious meals to large numbers of employees, but Bell praised the efforts of those who purchased and prepared the food: ***Cafeterias Serve 24,000 Daily Despite Shortages, Rationing.*** The purchaser had avoided meatless days to date by anticipating meat shortages and purchasing ahead of time. His job was a heavy one as he had to purchase milk, bakery bread, and produce – fresh to the plant each day. In addition, he was responsible for… *the purchase of cigars, candy, china, cutlery, and heavy kitchen equipment*. The article went on to discuss, in detail, how menu items were prepared, how sanitation was maintained (…*cafeteria workers are relentless dirt chasers…*), and that a meal was served to an employee every twelve seconds! (*Bell Aircraft News*, March 10, 1945, p. 1/ p. 5). The next week, employees heard about upcoming meatless days.

Food rationing was part of everyday life for civilians whether working on the home front or not, even as the war neared its conclusion. ***Meatless Days Predicted For All Cafeterias*** announced on the front page that…*meat selections in all plant cafeterias would be limited to one, effective April 1…The situation will become more acute as European lands are conquered and lend-lease demands increase, market authorities have said, and the shortage also will apply to hams, bacon, cheese and butter* (*Bell Aircraft News*, March 24, 1945, p. 1). Discouraging news for hard workers, to be sure.

Cafeteria managers reduced prices to workers on some food items in May: ***Milk, Vegetable Prices Are Cut In Cafeteria***. Prices were cut by one cent for milk and by two cents for rice, potatoes, and dried beans. The price reduction was credited to efficient management of the cafeteria by Bell itself, rather than by outside vendors (*Bell Aircraft News*, May 19, 1945, p. 3).

Finally, the employees got a real break: ***Candy –The Army Sent Us Candy –Because We're Sweet on Candy.*** Sugar rationing was nationwide because the military was given preference on this commodity. Advertised as on sale was forty-thousand pounds of candy bars at a reduced price; a box of twenty-four bars sold for $1.00, down from $1.20! The carload of candy was released by the army and the navy following V-E Day (Victory in Europe Day, May 8, 1945) and…*included milk chocolate, caramel, nougat, pecan, peanut and other assorted candy bars* (*Bell Aircraft News*, May 25, 1945, p. 7).

Cafeteria management seemed to be at its wits-end: *The plant must be full of magicians. Enough silverware has vanished to stock a silver mine – some 6,000 pieces a month at a total evaluation of about $2,000.* Management threatened to serve food with wooden forks and spoons. ***Fingers Came Before Forks – Stayed Longer*** headlined a plea to employees to return silverware to the cafeterias (*Bell Aircraft News*, June 2, 1945, p. 3). Erie Proving Ground threatened the same solution - wooden cutlery.

Later in June, the newsletter published a ***Ration Calendar*** which informed employees about the dates coupons could be used to purchase meats, processed foods, sugar, shoes, and gasoline. Next to this column was a longer article referencing the need for meatless meals: ***Accent On Sandwiches, Salads, Cold Plates In Meat Shortage***. A couple of meatless items were offered: egg salad and sausage club sandwich, or apple sauce and cottage cheese salad (*Bell Aircraft News*, June 22, 1945, p. 3).

By July 1945, Bell Aircraft began to cut back on its cafeteria service: ***B-1 Cafeterias To Close For Week-ends***. All cafeterias in the B-1 building were closed, but employees could take available transportation to the airport cafeteria for meals (*Bell Aircraft News*, July 13, 1945, p. 1).

Goodyear Aircraft

By the end of January 1942 there were new cafeterias in Plant A and B and the lunch schedule was listed by shift: ***New Cafeteria Is Equipped To Serve 8,000 In 24 Hours*** (*The Wingfoot Clan*, January 20, 1942, p. 4). I was not able to discern how many cafeterias there were on the Goodyear campus.

Aircraft tried to alleviate food delivery problems by providing helpful hints to the wives of plant workers. ***Helpful Hint About Lunch Bucket*** said: *Here's a helpful hint to wives of Goodyear men regarding the lunch bucket…* It is implied that male workers carried a lunch pail which their wives packed for them. Instructions included the need to wash the bucket and thermos daily in hot soapy water, to vary the contents of the lunch, and to use clean napkins or towels daily to wrap sandwiches and other food.

I found the article preachy and demeaning, but maybe there was a need to address overall cleanliness and food quality coming from employees' homes (*The Wingfoot Clan*, March 18, 1942, p. 3).

Goodyear provided a separate dining room for office workers, management, and production workers. One article explicitly stated: **Plant C Cafeteria Only For Plant C People** (*The Wingfoot Clan*, October 21, 1942, p. 3). By November: **New Cafeteria Building Being Constructed** (*The Wingfoot Clan*, November 11, 1942, p. 3).

Goodyear spent a great deal of time and energy in planning menus and in the efficient serving of meals. **Feeding 8,500 Daily In Plant C Cafeteria NOT EASY PROBLEM, With Rationing, Soar in Prices** was the headline over an article that discussed the logistics of creating a menu from the food the buyers were able to obtain. Plant C did have…*two huge dining rooms, large kitchen, and a 68-place private dining room*. Breakfast was often coffee and doughnuts, while the article did say the kitchen staff obtained roast beef, potatoes, butter, and milk; dinner cost thirty cents (*The Wingfoot Clan*, January 1, 1943, p. 9).

Goodyear continued to strive to properly feed its increasing number of employees: **Plant D Cafeteria, Largest At Aircraft, To Be Opened This Week: Main Dining Room Has Seating Capacity Of 1,500; Equipment Strictly Modern; Supervisor Chosen for Each Shift**. This was a twenty-thousand square-foot dining room which served six lines of employees simultaneously (*The Wingfoot Clan*, March 10, 1943, p. 3). By March 3, Plants A and B served six-thousand people daily at eight persons per minute. The new manager was noted as having a great deal of experience in the navy and the private sector (*The Wingfoot Clan*, March 3, 1943, p. 2).

In July, Goodyear's company nutritionist warned employees to take only the food they could eat, eat it all, or share food (*The Wingfoot Clan*, July 14, 1943, p. 7). Some employees must have heard the words of their mothers echoing in their heads!

Aircraft planned to complete a new cafeteria for Plant 1. The new construction would expand the seating by two-hundred and assured…*more expeditious service*. Further, it promised to have a modern kitchen with the latest in food serving equipment and…*attractive menu boards*. The company hoped to serve 3,000 factory employees in a three-hour timeframe, and one-thousand six-hundred office employees in a two-hour timeframe (*The Wingfoot Clan - Akron Edition*, December 29, 1943, p. 1).

Company nutritionists and dieticians often wrote articles for the newsletter: **Let's Take Our Job Of Food Preparation Seriously, As Our Nutritionist Suggests, Thus Aiding Uncle Sam In Winning War**. Clearly berating in its tone, women were asked to keep their kitchen tools clean and tidy and to prepare…*nutritious meals that contain the basic food elements…and make sure the lunch you carry from home meets the standards that are set by nutrition experts* (*The Wingfoot Clan*, January 19, 1944, p. 4). Perhaps the nutritionist was concerned about reducing the spread of diseases.

By January 1944, food rationing at production plants made creating menus a challenge. **Carter Tells Of Problem Plant Cafeterias Have: Says Visits To Ration Point**

Cupboard Often Finds It Bare; Hope For Change (*The Wingfoot Clan*, January 5, 1944, p. 1). There were frequent sugarless days and two meatless days and butter-less days each week. Employees were asked for meal suggestions.

I found this article amusing, if not puzzling, given the problems in serving large numbers of workers: ***Aircraft Surplus Store Announces Tableware Sale: Other Items Available At Very Low Prices If Purchased in Dozen Lots***. For sale were…*an ample supply of household goods at special bargain prices…knives, forks, and spoons…picnic supplies, photographic equipment and supplies, and paint* (*The Wingfoot Clan*, August 2, 1944, p. 6). After years of deprivation, workers must have met this announcement with joy, if not surprise that there was a surplus.

Meatless Menus At Times in Our Cafeterias: Late Rulings by Office of Price Administration Make It Difficult To Have Ample Supplies to Meet Demands of Employees. These headlines spoke directly to the continued rationing of meat with a twenty percent reduction imposed by the Federal Office of Price Administration (*The Wingfoot Clan*, March 21, 1945, p. 2).

Victory Gardens: Essential to Improved Nutrition

Commercial crops were diverted to the military, food rationing was introduced in spring 1942, so Americans had great incentive to grow their own food, then preserve it by canning or drying. Not only did this practice safe-guard against food shortages, the practice of gardening boosted morale and allowed everyday Americans to be a part of the war effort. In 1942, about fifteen million gardens were planted, and by 1944, roughly twenty million were planted. These became part of a community-based food security system.

Conversations about demands on food supply within the national food chain again came to the fore in late March 2020. Both the *Duluth News Tribune* and *The New York Times* ran articles about a resurgence of interest in American Victory Gardens.

The Supply Chain…As Disruption Sows Fear, Victory Gardens Return headlined a summary about the history of Victory Gardens in the United States during World War I and World War II. *People seem to be preparing for some serious disruptions in the food supply* stated a co-founder of the Experimental Farm Network (*The New York Times*, March 27, 2020, p. A13).

The *Duluth News Tribune* mirrored the instructions for purchasing and planting with its article: ***A New Season of 'Victory Gardens'*** provided specific information and instructions for northern Minnesota gardeners (*Duluth News Tribune*, March 28, 2020, p. B5).

Erie Proving Ground

I found no articles about Victory Gardens in the *EPG Echo* for 1943.

Bell Aircraft

I found scant information about Bell employees' Victory Gardens, or about Victory Gardens in general in the newsletter. In **Bellorama**, a stock column filled with newsy information about employees, there was a brief account of one male office worker who placed a capital "V" in his garden of vegetables and watermelons (*Bell Aircraft News*, August 6, 1943, p. 2). Another employee told of her children finding a rabbit's nest as they cleared a space for their Victory Garden, and their subsequent care of the displaced baby bunnies (*Bell Aircraft News*, August 13, 1943, p. 2). Finally, in early 1944, I read a seven-panel cartoon depicting the **7 *Steps To Your Victory Garden***. The steps were self-explanatory, and the cartoon character's actions were animated and amusing (*Bell Aircraft News*, March 25, 1944, p. 2).

Goodyear Aircraft

To supplement the food served at mealtime and to address food shortages and rationing, home front workers were encouraged – admonished, really – to sign up for a plot in the plant's Victory Garden or to pledge to create such a garden at their home. The company also offered a $25 War Bond as a prize for the best weeded and cultivated garden. This seemed to be a push particularly in the spring 1943.

More Than 1,500 Have Applied For Plots In Goodyear Victory Garden headlined an article about the company's two-hundred-fifty acres designed for the creation of individual employee Victory Gardens. In addition, employees were asked to pledge their own back yards as space for Victory Gardens (*The Wingfoot Clan*, March 17, 1943, p. 1).

This article provided specific reasons for planting. ***Victory Gardens: Some Of The Reasons Victory Gardens Should Be Planted Are As Follows:*** *1. The demand for food is increasing faster than production, and shortages of farm labor will limit crop expansion; 2. Transportation difficulties will cut the normal shipment of fresh and seasonal fruits and vegetables; 3. Point rationing will place a premium upon home production of food to supplement ration-restricted diets; 4. Home-grown vegetables and fruits, in addition to supplementing diets, will make budgets stretch farther; and 5. Home gardening provides healthful out-of-doors exercise. The victory garden presents a challenge to us all to perform a vital community and national service.*

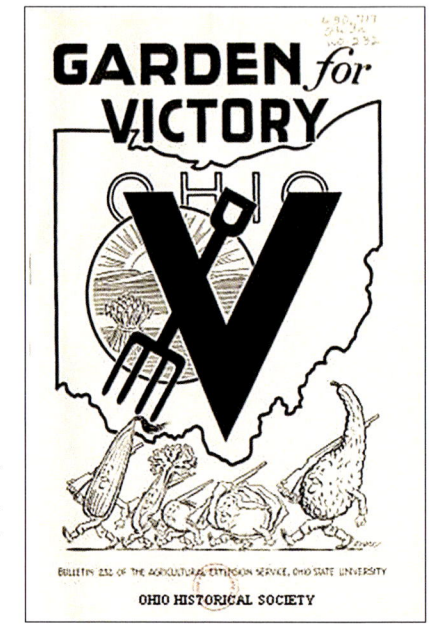

This strongly worded article suggested what types of vegetable to grow and followed up by urging workers to can or dry food to preserve them. While seeming to provide opportunity and healthful suggestions, I know how much work gardening and canning can be. I wondered just how much time and energy workers had to do these things after working a nine-hour shift (*The Wingfoot Clan*, March 24, 1943, p. 2).

In early June 1943, another headline was encouraging but a bit deceiving: ***Victory Garden Plots Assigned to Nearly 1,100***. Goodyear assigned plots, but heavy rains delayed plowing and planting. This had to have been very discouraging to workers who faced food shortages and rationing (*The Wingfoot Clan*, June 9, 1943, p. 2).

There were many articles about Victory Gardens with suggestions for planting and harvesting. One article, however, I thought was potentially inflammatory: a photograph of a woman holding her two children – her husband worked in the plant – was described as not able to have a Victory Garden that year because her neighbor would not let them use his lot. Then their address was printed. The article was clearly designed to suggest that a reduction in family nourishment may be the result of this neighbor's stinginess (*The Wingfoot Clan*, July 14, 1943, p. 2).

Another example of how planting Victory Gardens related to the war was in a caption over a cartoon showing a booted foot using a pitchfork to dig in a Victory Garden: ***Every Dig In Your Victory Garden Is Another Thorn In The Axis Side!*** (*The Wingfoot Clan*, July 14, 1943, p. 5).

The push for employees to continue their Victory Garden work went through 1944 and into 1945. Gas rationing was in full swing nationwide but those with Victory Gardens to attend were offered a break: ***Victory Garden Gas Regulations Just Announced: Special Fuel Permitted Those Traveling To Their Tracts This Season.*** Offered by the national Office of Price Administration, gardeners tending at least 1,500 square feet could receive up to three-hundred miles of travel in gasoline (*The Wingfoot Clan*, April 12, 1944, p. 3).

Finally, in May 1944, the newsletter let readers know ***Plowing Of All Victory Garden Plots Finished: Now Ready For Goodyearites To Begin Planting Seeds For Harvest of 1944*** (*The Wingfoot Clan*, May 3, 1944, p. 3).

Campaigns for Cigarettes to Servicemen

Smoking cigarettes was an accepted part of adult life in the United States; many of my family members smoked at the time, but gave it up during World War II when cigarettes became scarce and money was needed for food. Aunt Monnie and Uncle Al both smoked.

Graduate students in the Department of History, California State University, Los Angeles, looked at cigarette use by the military and published an article for *Perspectives: A Journal of Historical Inquiry*. They found cigarettes became standard issue with K-rations (and C-rations), along with meat, cheese products, crackers, a powdered juice to be added to water, and something sweet, like chocolate. Each ration would contain a four-pack of cigarettes.

Erie Proving Ground

I found no information about cigarette campaigns at this army installation.

Bell Aircraft

I did not find information about campaigns at Bell to send cigarettes to servicemen. Many Americans smoked at this time and negative health effects were either not known or not publicized. ***Prices Reduced On Cigarettes*** was a welcome front page article when it announced that the cafeteria would sell single packs at seventeen cents/ two for thirty-three cents. Due to a shortage of supplies, however, Camels and Phillip Morris packs would be limited two per person (*Bell Aircraft News,* June 3, 1944, p. 1).

Cigarettes were prized by Bell employees, who were shown how to ***Roll Your Own*** in two photographs…*what the boys and girls around the plant are doing to cope with the cigarette shortage.* Four were rolling tobacco and a fifth, a woman, was shown smoking a pipe… *in one of the hobbies enjoyed by her and her husband* (*Bell Aircraft News*, December 2, 1944, p. 7).

A sternly written article under a bold headline about the rationing of cigarettes appeared in March 1945: ***CIGARETTES TO BE RATIONED STARTING MONDAY: Every Employe*** {sic} ***To Be Allotted One Package***. Only one package per week would be distributed for sale to individual employees. *Confidential payroll and Army Air Forces civilian and military personnel will be issued cards which will be punched each week just as check stubs will be.* Employees were asked not to rush the cigarette counters and they were informed that purchases could be made during all working hours, and during every shift. Bell wanted to offer these sales using a system that would… *work here to be best interest of everyone* (*Bell Aircraft News*, March 16, 1945, p. 1). The deleterious physical effects of smoking had not yet been fully examined, and, at the time, smoking was believed to reduce tension.

Goodyear Aircraft

One of the numerous contests held for employees was to donate funds to send cigarettes to servicemen: ***Will Send 7,500,000 Cigarettes To Men Overseas: Aircrafters Start Drive for 'Smokes.'*** Goodyear pledged to send cartons with personal messages in them from the employee who made the donation of fifty-cents per carton (*The Wingfoot Clan*, April 14, 1943, p. 1). Cigarettes were purchased from the P. Lorillard Tobacco Company, the oldest tobacco company in the United States, founded in 1760, and headquartered in Greensboro, North Carolina.

By the end of April 1943, Goodyear touted its campaign as successful because: ***Aircrafters Have About $14,000 In Fund To Buy Cigarettes for Soldiers*** (*The Wingfoot Clan*, April 28, 1943, p. 1). Name-brand cigarettes were sent to soldiers while home front workers had to smoke "off brands."

Then by early May, the donation had increased: *Seven Million Cigarettes Soon On Way To "Our Boys" As Result Of Contribution of $14,740 By Aircraft Employes* {sic}. Employees decided on this disbursement: *10% of total to Alaskan front; 10% to European area; 40% to North Africa; and 40% to South Pacific* (*The Wingfoot Clan*, May 5, 1943, p. 1). Gifts of cigarettes were part of the Christmas gift packages prepared by plant employees and shipped to servicemen who had been employees.

Comes Personally To Say Thanks For "Smokes" Sent His Outfit In Pacific was the headline over a large photo of a sergeant showing a Plant C woman how the cigarettes in one package had been individually signed by his shipmates in a B-17 *Flying Fortress*. Each also signed his name in a small booklet to thank the employees who had made the contribution (*The Wingfoot Clan*, April 19, 1944, p. 3). This is just one of the hundreds of ways that the newsletter linked individuals serving on the battle line to individuals working on the production line.

Still a shortage of cigarettes in February 1945, one woman was photographed smoking a pipe. *No Cigarettes, So "Cookie" Sturm Says She'll Smoke Pipe.* She said she found it just as satisfying as a cigarette (*The Wingfoot Clan*, February 28, 1945, p. 4).

Transportation to Work: Gas and Tire Rationing

Erie Proving Ground

I found no information about transportation to and from the trailer camps or Erie Gardens.

Bell Aircraft

Marietta was fewer than twenty miles from Atlanta and within bus service of several smaller towns. *Second Shift Car Service* announced extended trolley car (*i.e.*, street car) service from the Bell plant to Atlanta, to serve second shift workers. Bell Aircraft had a department that addressed the problems of employee transportation and parking (*Bell Aircraft News*, September 10, 1943, p. 1).

The company campus was large and consisted of several building widely spaced out. *Automobile Service Handles Traffic Between Buildings* announced that this service was available to employees who needed to get to…*main buildings within the industrial fence*. There was a prescribed route that made about four trips per hour. Scooters were also available for employees' use, on an honor system (*Bell Aircraft News*, October 3, 1943, p. 1).

By the end of October 1943, additional bus service was established to transport plant workers from outlying areas. The posted time assured workers and Bell Aircraft that the employees would arrive at the plant twenty minutes before clocking in and leave twenty minutes after the shift change, thereby reducing tardiness or "jumping the clock" (*Bell Aircraft News*, October 22, 1943, p. 1).

By mid-November 1943, other bus lines were expanded so that employees' transportation needs from all three shifts could be met. The bus lines were privately operated, not city bus lines (*Bell Aircraft News*, November 12, 1943, p. 1). Efforts to arrange for increasing bus service continued throughout 1943 and well into 1945. Gas and tire rationing were not mentioned, those restrictions were nationwide.

Finally, ***Bomber Plant-South Atlanta Highway Ready for Travel*** brought welcome news to those living in southwest Atlanta, and who needed a quicker and more direct route that did not contribute to downtown Atlanta traffic. This was the third road that connected the plant, Marietta, and Atlanta (*Bell Aircraft News*, December 3, 1943, p. 1).

A share-a-ride system was in place at Bell and employees were asked to register vacant automobile seats with the transportation office. A renewed appeal went out to employees after a change in shift times occurred plant-wide: ***Drivers Are Urged to Register Car Seats***. The transportation office would match employees with vacant car seats with those employees who needed rides to work (*Bell Aircraft News*, October 14, 1944, p. 1).

Goodyear Aircraft

Of the three sets of newsletters I reviewed, the transportation problems described, analyzed, reviewed, and resolved by Goodyear far outstripped issues faced by the other two facilities. Likely the sheer number of employees working in three shifts under war conditions contributed greatly to Goodyear's transportation problems.

There were shortages in gasoline, rubber, and tires. There was a national push for all citizens to conserve resources, reuse materials, and donate metal and paper scrap for the war effort. Shortages affected employees' ability to get to work or get to work on time.

War production workers thought they would receive tires and replacements, for example, because of the nature of their work. Transportation to production plants became a major issue, especially for Goodyear workers who numbered in the tens of thousands. Newsletter headlines covering the war years are illustrative.

To emphasize the need for thrift and cooperative driving among employees, they read: ***Goodyear Folk Held By Wily Japs***. These were employees of Goodyear rubber plantations located in Southeast Asia, which were taken over by Japanese forces early in 1942, cutting off supplies of rubber needed for military and civilian use (*The Wingfoot Clan*, April 1, 1942, p. 1). The employees were incarcerated in camps. Knowledge of their being captured was personal.

Early on, Goodyear devised a grid/zone map of Akron so that employees who lived near one another could share rides (*The Wingfoot Clan*, April 15, 1942, p. 8). A full page version of the map appeared in a subsequent issue. Employees were asked to study the map with its numbered zones, and return a questionnaire to the Personnel Department, Transportation Division (*The Wingfoot Clan*, April 222, 1942, p. 7).

By the end of April, it was apparent that employees were not ride sharing. Employees' *Response To Plan For Pooling Rides, NOT Up To Committee's Expectations.* Again, employees wrongly assumed they could have their tires recapped when worn out. However, the…*tire rationing board doesn't permit recapping of tires if transportation is available to car owner.* The Joint Labor-Management Transportation Committee planned to continue its push for ride-sharing until the majority of employees complied (*The Wingfoot Clan*, April 29, 1942, p. 2).

Goodyear was at the Municipal Airport and traffic in and out of the plant during shift changes caused considerable problems. Service roads were opened and one-way driving was instituted along with expanded parking. Goodyear worked with the City of Akron on a solution to a growing problem (*The Wingfoot Clan*, May 6, 1942, p. 2).

Many Active In "Doubling Up" Riding Program: Five Thousand Names Included In List Committee Has Under Consideration (*The Wingfoot Clan*, May 27, 1942, p. 2) and *Transportation Issue Being Resolved* (*The Wingfoot Clan*, June 10, 1942, p. 1).

Just when I thought the ride-share program was a success, I read the following alarming headlines: *Will Close Airport Service Road If Workers Do Not Respect Rules* (*The Wingfoot Clan*, July 1, 1942, p. 6). The road was to be used only at shift changes, not all day. *Better Get Busy Immediately On Share-Ride Plan: Just Remember That Tires On Your Car Will Not Be Running Always.* The article admonished employees to ride-share because gas rationing was likely to be imposed and getting new tires was not likely (*The Wingfoot Clan*, July 8, 1942, p. 1).

A new approach was tried by Goodyear when it labeled cars carrying as many passengers as comfortable…*Victory Loads.* The article noted an uptick in the share-ride program since its inception. But, just in case more encouragement was needed, there was this: *But the man who is driving alone really isn't alone. He is riding with the evil ghosts of Hitler, Hirohito and Mussolini. And he is taunted by these ghosts at every turn of the tire-wearing wheels. Do what you can to put a Victory Load in your car. How foolish to be driving alone, permitting your axles to aid the Axis* (*The Wingfoot Clan*, July 8, 1942, p. 5). Ostensibly to remind people to conserve, the choice of words promotes feelings of fear and guilt.

To alleviate continued traffic problems, employees were assigned to specific roads in a newly devised system of traffic control: *Traffic Setup To Eliminate 'Bottle Neck'* (*The Wingfoot Clan*, November 4, 1942, p. 1).

By August 1943, the Akron City Bus Service was curtailed which meant Goodyear had to assist their employees in getting to work. They created city-wide share-a-ride depots, which employees could use to fill their vehicles to capacity. Goodyear had to take quick and decisive action because the curtailed bus service increased plant absenteeism by and alarming fifty percent (*The Wingfoot Clan*, August 8, 1943, p. 1).

One clever woman was cited as a full share-a-ride user: *Mary's 'At Home' On A Motorcycle* (The Wingfoot Clan, August 18, 1943, p. 4). She carried one other with her on the motorcycle. She installed doors on the K-ships (blimps), was an experienced semi-truck driver, and really wanted to work on engines.

By November 1943, the transportation issue burgeoned. ***Must Have More 'Car Pools' Soon Or Situation Will Be Very Serious: Share-Ride Plan Shows Weak Spots!*** This headline on the front page was shared by this: ***Ten Army Buses Will Help Ease Transportation Setup For Employes*** {sic} ***At Aircraft.*** General Motors was slated to deliver the buses after January 1, 1944 (*The Wingfoot Clan*, November 10, 1943, p. 1). Gas and tire rationing negatively impacted employees; twenty-three thousand participated in the share-ride program.

In April 1944, an article again admonished employees to carry a full load of passengers. It pointed out that it was…*imperative that employees do so if they wanted to be… eligible to get the few of the No. 1 grade tires available*. ***Warning Is Again Given Drivers To Carry Sufficient Passengers: Must Abide By Rules Or 'No Tires'*** (*The Wingfoot Clan*, April 12, 1944, p. 1).

Finally, the focused effort of company management and the great cooperation of its employees paid off. ***Aircraft Cited For Having Model Share-Ride System. First War Plant In This Section To Get Citation.*** The award was presented by the Office of Price Administration (*The Wingfoot Clan*, June 27, 1945, p. 1).

Employee Newsletters: Depicting Women at EPG and in Defense Plants

The *Bell Aircraft News* specified the type of news it wanted the employees to submit for weekly publication: vital statistics (births, marriages, engagements, deaths, including the name and department s/he worked in); personals (illness, operations, parties, showers, visitors, and name the people involved if they were plant employees); ***Bellorama*** (this was a stock column and included brief general interest vignettes; military news (anything that happened to the service people related to plant employees – *letters, promotions, citations, and decorations are swell)*; hobbies (unique hobbies that could include a photo of an employee at that avocation); and promotions, transfers, and appointments (welcome new employees, and submissions had to be approved by the department head). The newsletter served as a central feature in the culture that developed in each defense plant.

Of particular interest to me as a feminist - because the events of World War II impacted the post-war second wave feminist movement - and as a writer of the experiences of family members who worked on the home front, I focused on articles for or about women. How women were depicted in the newsletters evolved as they made a greater impact on war production the longer the war lasted. Cheesecake photos were popular throughout, as was the use of the term "girls" to describe women, but those depictions were later accompanied by a greater number of articles about women in the military – those who shifted from production work to war service.

Many college-educated or older women gave up their dreams of becoming an artist, musician, sculptor, office worker, or teacher while many younger high school educated women who had low wage jobs before the war, looked to a production job as a way to learn skills that could be used after the war's end. Women were praised for working hard and learning their jobs, honored for the loss of loved ones, and objectified as sex symbols, or referred to as "feminine" or the "gentler sex." Often these depictions appeared in different articles within the same newsletter.

Whatever each did before the war started and whatever each was asked to do at the plant, women were perceived as wanting news about "normal" things. There were special "Women's Pages" with different titles: *The Personal Line* (Erie Proving Ground); *This Page Of General Interest But News Is Of Special Interest To Women* (Goodyear); *Mostly About Women and Girls At Aircraft* (Goodyear); and *Strictly for the Belles* (Bell Aircraft). The woman's page at Goodyear in 1944 was called *Mostly About Women and Girls at Aircraft*, and gossip was always a part of the column. They contained vignettes about female employees referred to as "The Real Miss America" (old or young, married or single), advice about fashion, admonitions about apparel and makeup at work, nutrition and how to address food shortages, household hints, cleaning hints, and encouragement to write to the men in the armed forces. In the vignettes, Blue Star Mothers (women with a child in the armed forces), Gold Star Mothers (women whose child had been killed in action), women who had relatives or friends in the armed forces, who wrote to soldiers, who gave blood, and who purchased War Bonds were particularly cited. There was a gossip column in each issue – tidbits of information about employees and their lives. Routine notices were written for upcoming marriages, engagements, births, funerals, transfers to the military or to other departments - the type of home town information that keeps employees tied to one another.

Women were trained to do a "man's job" but were reminded about the importance of remaining a...*traditional girl*. Women received mixed messages about how they were to conduct their private lives and comport themselves at work and in public. I realized as I worked through the newsletters that "women's news" created a necessary balance to the increasingly overwhelming news about war and the corollary push for all employees to work harder and faster. People needed to be reminded that some sense of "normal" could be strived for in the worst of times and news for and about women helped.

Women were placed in defense plant departments doing work that would not be at all necessary in today's world with computing systems. Small groups of women office workers completed tasks in hours or days that would take only minutes today. They carried the mail between departments and buildings, hand-operated ditto machines to make multiple copies of documents, delivered employee pay checks to department supervisors, calculated time clock data, hand drafted production plans, and so forth.

As time progressed and the United States moved from defensive tactics to offensive tactics in Europe and the South Pacific, more men and women were tapped for military service putting an enormous strain on home front production. Women's status in war industries moved from being initially fascinating or unique to valuable and productive to desperately needed.

I had to remind myself that World War II was about two decades before the second wave feminist movement in the United States. Even though women war workers provided valuable and essential skills, and were praised for their productivity, many newsletter articles and cartoons depictions would be considered silly or sexist in the 21st Century. The following titles (in bold) or wording within articles (in italics) about/ for women are illustrative only. There was a dizzying array of topics to choose from and I chose only a few to give readers a glimpse of life in a World War II production plant.

1941 through 1942: When the "Girls" Were "Unique" to Production

Erie Proving Ground

The chapter on my aunt delineates her job duties and her many promotions. Her story serves as a case study about the level at which women, and their expertise, were accepted as civilian employees in a military installation. (pp.37-57)

Bell Aircraft

Bell Aircraft News was not published until May 1943.

Goodyear Aircraft

Production manufacturers needed to train their newly hired female workers. **Women's Class Begins Studying Aircraft Terminology Symbols: Goodyear Group Pioneers In An Important Field: Experiment To Be Tried As Men Are Called To Armed Forces**. Twelve young women were enrolled in a special drafting class through Goodyear Industrial University along with twenty-eight men. To qualify for the class, students had to have…*a high school education, exceptional ability in math, especially algebra and geometry*. It was noted that if they pass…*the girls will become the pioneers in another field of endeavor formerly regarded a strictly masculine occupation*. The women were recruited because the company foresaw…*an imminent shortage of manpower, now that the government has begun calling more and more able-bodied men to the colors*. The accompanying photo highlighted the latest in technology: the woman student carried engineering books, blueprints, a T-square, and rulers. Tools of the trade in 1942 (*The Wingfoot Clan*, February 4, 1942, p. 1).

Women Operate Huge Machines As Men Heed Call To Arms was the caption over a double photograph of one woman operating a sander, while the other operated a drill press. At this time, neither was wearing eye protection or work gloves (*The Wingfoot Clan*, February 11, 1942, p. 1).

Sheet metal work was open to women as well: **Women Fit Selves For Places On Aircraft Production Lines**. A series of photographs showed women working in the sheet metal division, with polished nails, no work gloves, wearing jewelry, and having loose hair (*The Wingfoot Clan*, March 11, 1942, p. 1). Later, about one-thousand three-hundred students, of whom three-hundred were women, were trained in sheet metal work: **Thousand Students In Sheet Metal School** (*The Wingfoot Clan*, April 22, 1942, p. 3).

By May 1942, the inclusion of women in war production was of interest to the national press. **Women Writers Visit Goodyear Akron Factories: Intense Interest Shown In Tour Under Auspices of War Department** described in some detail what the six female reporters could observe in their quest to learn the role of women in war production. While the tour lasted all day, a press room was set up for the reporters to type their articles, so their writing could be cleared for publication by army military personnel. Although the number of female employees had increased one-hundred percent in one year, there was still only a small percentage of employees who were women…*but might increase depending on how long the war lasted* (*The Wingfoot Clan*, May 6, 1942, p. 2).

A front-page article, **Machine Shop, Once Held As Man's Castle, Invaded By Woman**, contained a large photo of women operating milling machines to…*do their share in the program to 'Rub Out The Axis'* (*The Wingfoot Clan*, August 19, 1942, p. 1).

World War II aircraft often depicted "Pin-Up Girls" painted on the fuselage. Many books have been written about this art form, and does not need elaboration here. However, there were other ways women were referred to when aircraft were discussed. In August 1942, Lt. General Harry "Hap" Arnold sent a telegram to Goodyear employees thanking them for their effort in building the B-26 *Marauder*, a medium bomber that was used by American pilots in the New Guinea Campaign from January 23, 1945 through August 1945. It was one of the most successful medium bombers produced. He summarized: *You are building planes that can dish out what the Axis cannot take* (*The Wingfoot Clan*, August 26, 1942, p. 1). One plane was used in the European Theater and flew more than two-hundred missions over Germany, the highest number survived by any United States Army Air Forces aircraft. Its nickname in this theater was *Flack-Bait*.

I read the telegram to R. Michael Busch, Busch Aero Works, who replied that I should research the trials and tribulations of the *Marauder*. Although the B-26 was very fast, it was referred to as *"The Baltimore Whore"* (or The Flying Prostitute) because it had no visible means of support"; that is, the wings were so short, the aircraft appeared to have no support for the engines and would have trouble developing lift. The bomber was made by the Maryland-based Martin Company, with Goodyear parts. The reference is unfortunate, to say the least.

Eighteen interested journalists sponsored by the National Manufacturers Association, the army and the navy came to Goodyear in late August as part of a two-week nation-wide tour to war industries: **18 Women News Writers To Visit Goodyear Plants.** Clearly, women on the home front continued to be newsworthy (*The Wingfoot Clan*, August 26, 1942, p. 6).

Older women were singled out for their contribution as in ***Mabel On The Job For Duration.*** The vignette introduced a former comedienne from vaudeville who said she did not need the job, but wanted to do her part as a riveter (*The Wingfoot Clan*, December 2, 1942, p. 2).

1943: Midway through the War When the "Girls" Applied Their Skills

Erie Proving Ground

Specific jobs held by women ordnance workers at EPG included civilian gunner, making A-jacks to block guns, crate-makers, checker, mechanic, sweeper, varityper, crane operator, cannon pressure gage assembler, ammunition belt assembler, and chronograph operator. The latter woman used a count-chronograph to…*write a record of the time or speed of a bullet in flight as it travels from the muzzle of the gun toward the armor plate…All of the operators are girls, three of them college trained, and most of them have a close friend or relative in the service* (*EPG Echo*, July 15, 1943, p. 8).

One issue summarized a…*realistic survey*…about women at EPG. ***Ordnance 'Knows' Women*** starts with the statement: *Army Ordnance is learning a lot about women it never knew before.* The article went on to say:

> Women are replacing men called to the Armed Forces or shipped overseas. They are helping to relieve the manpower shortage. They are working side by side with soldiers and older, draft exempt men in the service establishments of the Ordnance Department, Army Service Forces.
>
> A realistic survey of female employment has been made available to Lt. Col. N. H. Strickland, Commanding Officer of EPG, which employs a large number of women. Here is what battle-tough Army Ordnance personnel experts discovered:
>
> Women have greater finger dexterity than men; greater patience; greater enthusiasm.
> Women will accept 99 percent responsibility, but they always like to receive a final OK on their work from a man.
> Women want their jobs glamourized for them.
> Women do not mind getting their hands and faces dirty, but the lack of beauty shops in the community will cause a serious personnel problem.
> Women take instructions and directions in a far more personal manner than men.
> Women are patriotic without cynicism.
>
> *EPG Echo,* July 15, 1943, p. 8

The survey is clearly a product of its time and fed into stereotypes about women and their attitudes and abilities within the workforce. The EPG personnel orientation booklet described how women needed to comport themselves in industry.

A July issue had more revealing information about women in industry in…***16 Hour Shuttle Service Given By EPG On Tank Armament***. The article discussed the need to move armament from production into service. Nineteen women were listed by name and by their jobs on the production line. *At the firing line an all girl gun crew tests the guns…thirteen women were identified along with their male proof directors* (*EPG Echo*, July 29, 1943, p. 3).

Five Women on EPG's Guard Force Are Capable Assistants led an article about the women who replaced men who were needed…*for more active guard duty at various places on the Post*. The women were trained to clear people through the gates, they were armed, and they operated the radio between the guard house and the patrol cars (*EPG Echo*, July 29, 1943, p. 8).

Bell Aircraft

Accompanying seven women identified in a photo was this caption: ***Escorts in Green*** *– Be it a visitor or new employe* {sic}, *these lovely girls are the "Guiding Stars" of Bell, without which life would be most complicated. Like their supervisor…they all radiate personality and friendliness. However long the trek, it's always a pleasure with the Girl in the Green Uniform. They each have many amusing experiences which they say are all in a day's work* (*Bell Aircraft News*, May 21, 1943, p. 3).

Stamina Girls *–That's what they've dubbed this group of pretties who cover a mile-long route seven times a day with a mail pouch almost as big as a regular postman's. They have little time for conversation but you can lay odds they'll arrive on schedule*. Their names were listed (*Bell Aircraft News*, May 21, 1943, p. 3).

In a third photo listing nine women posing with a bicycle, the caption reads: ***Courier Girls*** *– Under tutelage of "Dotsie" Short these girls have proven there is nothing short about their service except the name of their superior. If you have marveled at their efficiency, it is the result of "Dotsie's" ingenious methods of training, which include: typing classes, round table discussions, and their own Quiz Program – You may rest assured they have all the answer* {sic} *to the $64 question* (*Bell Aircraft News*, May 21, 1943, p. 3).

In the May 28, 1943, issue, a poem and a photograph of a woman in working garb, with safety glasses, reads: ***Miss America, 1943 Model***. The excerpted poem lauds the need to meet safety standards for women: *A kerchief, cap or snood she'll wear…From whirring wheels to save her hair…Her sleeves are short. This dainty doll's…Encased in close-fit coveralls…Her leather shoes are far from ugly…Although the heels she wears are low…And there is no protruding toe…That Miss America is dressed…To kill the hopes of Axis Pest… She's dressed for work – and not for dinner – But you'll agree we've picked a winner*. The photograph reinforces the poetic message: hair pulled back, no jewelry that could be caught in a machine, low heeled shoes, goggles, and short-sleeved coveralls. In the caption, the woman is praised for being an attractive model.

On page three of the June 4, 1943, issue is this photograph caption describing the activity of four women having lunch on the steps outside their building: *Sun Tan Crew – Weather news is restricted but you don't need a weatherman to tell you summer's here when these gals stream out from behind typewriters and file cabinets to find their place in the sun. This sample cluster of bomber-dears getting a lead on Vitamin D straight from headquarters includes…* Their names were listed.

One woman was praised for her excellent skills as a clerk working ten hours a day, six to seven days a week. Her husband was a soldier and she grew her own vegetables, gathered scrap metal, saved kitchen grease, and bought War Bonds. This article exemplified the patriotic fervor surrounding the push to buy Bonds. *She…put down $700 cash on the barrel head for War Bonds. "I thought it might help," she explains, "so I went down to the bank and drew it out of the savings account."* She reassured the readers that her husband would be pleased as…*He sends back every penny he can for bonds…* The article concluded that she…*doesn't even weigh enough to be a blood donor, but she's able to do a woman-sized job of fighting Uncle Sam's war on the home front* (*Bell Aircraft News*, June 4, 1943, p. 3). Most articles or photographs of women workers included a factual physical description, especially of the younger workers - size, hair/eye color, age - along with a subjective description - tidy, small, pint-sized, comely, and so forth.

Five Capable Grandmothers Are Janitorial Supervisors headlined an article talking about the great number of grandmothers working for Bell. The women in the janitorial service were praised for their supervision of the maids…*with quiet dignity.* One woman was the company's only forewoman. A poem, written by the newsletter's staff writer, refers to these woman as "Glamor Gals." The first lines are: *Listen, grandchildren, and you shall hear…How Grandmother labored to make it clear…To Axis Aggressors that all's not play…For "Glamor Gals" in the U.S.A* (*Bell Aircraft News*, July 2, 1943, p. 3).

I had forgotten about ditto machines, which I used early in my career, and which my elementary and secondary teachers used to create classroom handouts. The sheets of paper smelled nice, as I recall, but teachers and secretaries groused about the mess the ink left on their hands. One photograph in the newsletter showed four women, nicely attired in dresses and saddle shoes, operating ditto machines. The caption read: **They Were Not "Born To The Purple,"** *these four queens of the Ditto Room: but their hands and arms acquire a purple hue after they have worked with ditto papers in Department 11. It may sound like a paradox, but their business seems to be everybody's business. Their four machines turn out dittoed directives, memos, reports, training tests, cards and form. The bulletin boards carry neat samples of the work of these "Ditto Damsels."* Their names were listed with this caption: *You say you like their evident devotion to duty? We say ditto* (*Bell Aircraft News*, July 9, 1943, p. 1).

In one article I recalled similar "training" early in my career when I was a secretary at the University of Michigan. **Stenographers In Flying Squadron Hit In Pinches** is a lengthy article about the Stenographic and Typing Section of Department 11... *a stenographic pool better known as 'The Flying Squadron'*...The job these women undertook was...*to pinch-hit and uncork bottlenecks wherever and whenever they may arise, so that production in any department may be increased.* It appeared that this group's skills were loaned out to help other departments catch up on their work, facilitate production, and to trouble-shoot. They might serve in any one department for hours to weeks at a time. Those who did well may have been requisitioned to remain in a department permanently.

The description of their training is telling: *In this pool they are carefully taught all Bell Aircraft's requirements, such as Bell procedure in letter-writing, poise, the art of adaptability, and the prime necessity of a cheerful attitude and appreciation of the opportunity gives them in carrying on their share of the war effort.* Hmmmm (*Bell Aircaft News*, July 9, 1943, p.3).

A woman from Department 11 (Office Manager) won a CDS Award for her design of a...*leveling device for the support of drill presses that will improve the quality of work*. A second woman from Department 35, service...*suggested the numbering of clearance slips to enable quicker disposition of tool clearance forms* (*Bell Aircraft News*, July 23, 1943, p. 3).

The caption of a photo of one Stenographic Pool member referred to the woman as a pilot, with twenty-five flying hours, who soloed after eight and one-half hours. She could...*not use her flying experience against the enemy on account of military regulations, but she can help beat the Axis by working here at Bell Aircraft.* The caption mentioned her husband who was training to be a navy pilot and her four brothers in military service. The woman stated she thought flying was very exciting; the war interfered with her adding more flying time (*Bell Aircraft News*, July 23, 1943, p. 3).

Not exactly a pin-up girl, but a photo of a female employee in her two-piece bathing suit had this caption: **June in July** – *Pre-flight's June Smith beats the heat in this outfit at Atlanta Woman's Club pool where many Bell Aircraft workers spend off hours. Ensemble also has a grass skirt* (*Bell Aircraft News*, July 30, 1943, p. 1).

The October 8, 1943, issue printed a short editorial, **A War Worker Now**, to introduce new female employees to the previously mostly male industry. The message below is mixed.

> "You're about to buck rivets, weld seams, assemble or inspect parts. Embark on a new adventure. It's not like flying to Ireland or sailing to Africa. But it does take a little preparation." Thus begins "You're a War Worker Now," a handy pamphlet prepared by Louise M. Snyder, chief counsellor for women of the Industrial Relations division, for feminine newcomers to the Bell Aircraft fold at Marietta.
>
> The booklet, attractively illustrated by Manager E. M. Lusink, Silas Snodgrass and H. L. Kinsman of the art department, is full of helpful suggestions for women whose war work will throw them into an entirely new environment and way of living.

> An excerpt from the work says, with respect to industrial etiquette:
> "Men don't pick up your dropped rivets or blow torches (if they did, they'd be using their job time to do yours).
> "Men who are efficient in their work don't want to be distracted by feminine wiles during work hours. (They prefer to enjoy their femininity in larger doses in their homes, at social affairs or public entertainment centers).
> "Successful foremen don't appreciate attempts to substitute gushing or apple polishing for accurate inspection, correct template cutting or doing any job correctly.
> "Sub-foremen aren't pleasant and helpful because they want you for an intimate friend. But because they want you to like your job, turn out a maximum of work, up their department's production record."
>
> *Bell Aircraft News,* October 8, 1943, p. 2

A Bell policewoman was highlighted in: ***Husband and Son of Bell Policewoman Hour Apart in War Zone, Haven't Met***. Her SeaBee husband was recuperating in New Guinea while one of her two sons was an hour away serving as a navy pilot in the Pacific Theatre. The article about this woman's family made the efforts of military service personnel real (*Bell Aircraft News*, February 5, 1944, p. 3).

A photograph of a woman from Department 15 announced she had been chosen for membership in the American Society of Tool Engineers, an international organization started in January 1932. She was one of ten women in the United States who garnered that honor. The Society assisted in converting American industries into primary military suppliers for the Allied war effort, what President Roosevelt labeled an "Arsenal of Democracy," to shore up the Allies prior to the United States' entry into the war. The Society of Women Engineers was founded in 1950 (*Bell Aircraft News*, August 13, 1943, p. 1).

Another woman's professional credentials were lauded in ***Assistant to Office Manager Is Exponent of Womanpower*** when the article stated she...*proved by her own attention to duty that womanpower is also important in war industry*. The article talked about her association with the Business and Professional Women's Club of Atlanta and her leadership in establishing the Vocational Counselors' Center...*to advise women on how to find essential jobs and get information of types of jobs available. This enterprise is being conducted in cooperation with the U. S. Employment Service and the War Manpower Commission in an effort to tap all available sources of womanpower* (*Bell Aircraft News*, September 24, 1943, p. 1/ p. 4).

Woman Crane Driver, Unafraid of Altitude, Worries Over Grounded Mate's Welfare told the story of an self-described "tomboy" who wanted this dangerous job because there was no man to do it, and most other women, she reasoned, would not want to climb the heights (*Bell Aircraft News*, November 5, 1943, p. 3).

Six women took advantage of opportunities for flight instruction. **Belle Pilots Form Beginners' Club** allowed women to practice flying on Sundays, when weather permitted it (*Bell Aircraft News*, November 5, 1943, p. 3).

Goodyear Aircraft

By April 1943, **Aircraft Plans To Employ 3,500 More Workers By First Of June: Mostly Women for Plant D To Build FG-1 Ships: Demand For More Production Has Necessitated Big Increase In Labor Personnel**. The FG-1 *Corsair* fighters were built for the navy, and 13,000 women were already at Aircraft, forty-six percent of the total employment. The company wanted to have a total of 34,000 employees and stated: *Skilled men are hard to get, but we believe that we can recruit a large number of women who are over 18 and in good physical condition* (*The Wingfoot Clan*, April 28, 1943, p. 1/ p. 3). Women played an increasingly important role in producing weapons of war.

On page five of the same issue, **Helen Staley First Girl At Aircraft To Become 'Official' Truck Operator**. She was shown in a photo operating an electric truck for Dept. 227, Transportation (*The Wingfoot Clan*, April 28, 1943, p. 5).

With an increase in the number of men called into the military, production plants opened up more classes to train women to do the work: **Engineering Course Open to Girls – Board, Room, Tuition Paid By Aircraft**. The enrollees had to have...*completed college algebra, plain and solid geometry*...and be at least eighteen years old. Students had to have above average intelligence and be able to...*assimilate this concentrated training*...in six months to become a junior engineer. The company acknowledged there was a shortage of qualified men and remarked: *This was an unusual opportunity for girls who can qualify* (*The Wingfoot Clan*, May 5, 1943, p. 1).

By mid-1943 there were an increasing number of women at Goodyear cited as... *the first to*...**Six Feet Tall, Weighs 185 Pounds, Does Man's Work At Aircraft, Pleased With Job**. This caption appeared over a photograph of a woman wearing acceptable safety garb and operating a router machine – the first woman to do this (*The Wingfoot Clan*, June 23, 1943, p. 7). The newsletter writers remained fascinated with the physical attributes of the company's female employees.

Young Woman Is An Engineer In Big War Effort introduced a woman who had been a hospital secretary, had attended two colleges and a secretarial school, but who came from a family background in construction. She had taken a course in machine shop and drafting (*The Wingfoot Clan*, August 11, 1943, p. 3).

Women became Blue Star Mothers when their children entered the military. Sadly, women became Gold Star Mothers when a child was killed in action. Goodyear noted these losses and allowed co-workers to publicly grieve with the mothers. **Tears Mingle With Prayer As Associates Present Gold Star Pin To Mother Whose Son Died In Japanese Concentration Camp**. The poignancy with which this news was presented, along with a long editorial in the same newsletter, brought tears to my eyes. A mother who worked on blimp assembly learned that her twenty-year-old son had died of fever while in a Japanese prisoner of war camp. He had been taken prisoner at the Battle of Corregidor {May 5-6, 1942} and she learned of his death in July 1943. Her coworkers took up a collection to buy the Gold Star Pin, a U.S. Army chaplain delivered a sermon and prayer in the department where she had worked for nearly a year. She reportedly would take a brief vacation to help her get over the shock (*The Wingfoot Clan*, July 7, 1943, p. 4). The loss of a child and the support of this mother illustrated the heavy losses women on the home front faced. Her co-workers' actions were very personal and brought the distant war home in a poignant manner.

An editorial in the same issue elaborated on the…*tight bond of sympathy and love, which makes us one big family…***The Tie That Binds Us Into One Big Family.** *Certainly the shock to Mrs. Goldner is great but the death of her boy is just another entry in the casualty list that brings the war closer to home…Mrs. Goldner can proudly wear the pin, which designates her as a Gold Star Mother in honor of her heroic son, and in remembrance of a sincere devotion that came from the hearts of her associates at Goodyear* (*The Wingfoot Clan*, July 7, 1943, p. 2). While the writer of the editorial may have had the best of intentions, I thought the writing was preachy and smarmy. Among those servicemen reported to be missing, captured, or killed in action, this one story made me think that, perhaps, the woman would rather scream for her loss than wear a pin.

Some of the best workers were women over the age of sixty: ***Alice Lillibridge, 60, With Interesting Career Enjoys Work At Goodyear Aircraft.*** She was an experienced business woman, who worked in food prep in the cafeteria. She said she…*likes to work…and is taking a hotel management course, bookkeeping and all* (*The Wingfoot Clan*, August 11, 1943, p. 6).

The newsletter's stock column, **The Real Miss America**, featured a fifty year-old woman who was a thirteen-month employee in assembly. She was touted as having two Victory Gardens at her home, and came from a long line of men serving in the military (*The Wingfoot Clan*, August 18, 1943, p. 3). Articles always mentioned family members in the military, and often described outside activities participated in by the woman, and were sure to mention their purchase of War Bonds.

By November 1943, Goodyear was desperate to hire more workers as so many young men had been called to the armed forces. ***Girls 16-17 To Be Hired In Factory.*** For the first time in factory history, girls were hired to meet the labor shortages. There were caveats: each girl could work only on approved factory operations, the company had to follow state laws concerning female and child labor, and the girls could work only between the hours of 6 A.M. and 10 P.M. A second, shorter announcement, stated: **Jobs! Boys, Girls Jobs in Mail Service** were open to boys age 15 and girls age 16 and 17 (*The Wingfoot Clan*, November 17, 1943, p. 1).

1944: When The "Girls" Became Women Essential to Production

Erie Proving Ground

There was no data available because the *EPG Echo* was no longer printed. Local newspapers from the time are on microfiche at the Ida Rupp Library, Port Clinton, Ohio, and were not available through inter-library loan at the time of publication.

Bell Aircraft

There was a vignette about a nineteen-year-old employee in the welding department: ***Welding Has Its Beauty Aids, Says Pretty 'Torchbearer.'*** She was the only female welder on first shift and one of only two female welders in the plant. She had been in tooling, storage and expediting but said she wanted to do more. Despite her taking on this important new job, she was described this way: *A slim, brown-eyed, brown-haired, freckle-faced, 19-year-old girl is holding down one of the toughest jobs on the Bell production line. She's a welder.* She was quoted as saying she needs clothes that were designed for a woman, and not the men's overalls, men's gloves, and men's shirts. To put more femininity into her required garb, she painted a cute face on her helmet (*Bell Aircraft News*, January 29, 1944, p. 3).

The writers of the newsletters often expressed surprise at a woman's ability to do a "man's job." ***Traffic Chauffeurette 'Manhandles' Jeep To Amazement of Hardened Army Sarge*** described the abilities of one of three "chauffeurettes" employed by Bell. Her qualifications as a driver exceeded those needed for a chauffeur; at Moody Field, near Valdosta, Georgia, she moved tuggers (aircraft tug) and twin-engine bombers. She was licensed by the government to drive passenger cars, one-ton to one-half ton cargo trucks, and two-ton and larger cargo trucks. None of the three women had had an accident (*Bell Aircraft News*, March 25, 1944, p. 3).

Former Cake Icer Takes Up Rivet Gun At Plant described the…*10,000th trainee to go to war on the Bell Bomber production line.* The woman's husband was in the military and her brother worked in the navy yards in Pearl Harbor. She…*checks her powder and paint in the locker rooms of Dept. 38-2 each morning, and then for the next eight hours, or more, she is in there sparring with the rest of the gang for victory* (*Bell Aircraft News*, June 3, 1944, p. 3).

By September 1944, women were a common sight at the plant. Several women, described as "amazing," were highlighted in ***Women At Work --- At Home And At Bell***. Each was praised for her work at Bell, the long distances each traveled from home to the plant, and talked about their household responsibilities. However, one woman had a maid who cooked dinner although the employee supervised the cooking (*Bell Aircraft News*, September 23, 1944, p. 1).

Amid the many articles about Family Day, held at the plant on August 12, the message was clear that the focal point of the day's events would be viewing the B-29 in its stages of assembly. For security reasons, family members had not been able to see the aircraft prior to this. Photographs of family groups accompanied the article. One-hundred thousand people attended Family Day.

Women who were portrayed in the November edition seemed superhuman in their work ethic. **Their Time seems Anybody's Except Their Own**: *Six days a week for nine hours they build oxygen panels for B-29s at Bell. Five nights a week for three hours they study nurses' aide work at the Marietta hospital. Every Friday night they attend Civil Air Patrol meetings as cadets. And in their spare time they write letters to servicemen scattered all over the world*. They passed their nurse's training and began to work at the hospital two nights a week, and were asked to teach a course in aircraft instruments to the local Civil Air Patrol cadets (*Bell Aircraft News*, November 4, 1944, p. 1). The women and their busy schedules were not uncommon at the plant.

Just before Thanksgiving in 1944, the commandant of the U.S. Coast Guard visited the plant and said that operations in the Pacific were being held up because of a shortage of planes and ships. In **Superfort Is Weapon For Defeat of Japan, Says Admiral: Pacific Success Hinges on Ship, Bomber Output**, he said it is…*almost criminal to lay down on the job these days*. He went on to praise Bell workers after a tour of the assembly line for the B-29s (*Bell Aircraft News*, November 18, 1944, p. 6). Few articles simply praised workers; most were written with a warning or, quite simply, a verbal guilt trip, if they did not work harder.

Goodyear Aircraft

Nineteen women completed a company-sponsored six-month course in engineering at the University of Akron. Under a large photo of the women, the courses were described as…*aerodynamics, mathematics, stresses, mechanics, drafting, design and descriptive geometry*. The women, **Nineteen Girls Receive Their Diplomas As Engineers**, would be assigned to various areas within Aircraft (*The Wingfoot Clan*, February 2, 1944, p. 2).

In the February 4, 1942, newsletter, Goodyear Industrial University announced a drafting class for women, and noted this was an experimental idea. **First Woman On Airship Drafting Work** described an employee who immigrated from Scotland who said that drafting had been…*a recognized field for women for years* (*The Wingfoot Clan*, February 16, 1944, p. 4).

On May 31, 1944, the newsletter reported that twenty-thousand men from Goodyear had been called to service, and that was why the company needed to employ more women (*The Wingfoot Clan*, p. 1).

In May 1944, one woman was heralded as: **Typical American Heroine: I'll Keep On Working For My Other Boy in Army, Says Mother Advised One Son Has Been Killed In Action.** The early heartfelt quotes given by this grieving mother were in contrast to the last paragraph in which she purportedly appealed to coworkers to stop complaining about gas rationing and to purchase War Bonds. "KEEP 'EM FLYING." (*The Wingfoot Clan*, May 10, 1944, p. 2). Some articles were hard to read; this was one.

When the Allied D-Day Invasion of June 6, 1944, was announced to Goodyear employees, a very emotional article appeared in the newsletter, accompanied by a photograph of workers in prayer (*The Wingfoot Clan*, June 14, 1944, p. 1). Some workers thought the end of the war was at hand, but newsletter articles throughout the summer urged workers to stay on the job as there would be much fighting ahead. They were admonished to keep working (*The Wingfoot Clan*, August 2, 1944, p. 1).

Again in August 1944, one headline seemed a desperate plea: ***More Workers Needed On Plane Jobs At Aircraft: Places Open For Several Thousand Persons At Once.*** Needed were two-thousand five-hundred to three-thousand more workers to fulfill the needs of an increased number of contracts for parts for other aircraft and to meet the needs of an accelerated production schedule for current aircraft. Goodyear had contracts for the P-38 *Lightning*, and accelerated production of parts for the B-29 *Superfortress*, the P-61 *Black Widow*, and the Goodyear *Corsair*. Workers were asked to refer friends and relatives to Aircraft (*The Wingfoot Clan*, August 16, 1944, p. 1).

Famous aircraft that Goodyear took part in building were: K-Ships, GA-1 *Corsair*, Boeing B-29 *Superfortress*, Lockheed P-38 *Lightning*, Martin B-26 *Marauder*, F6F Grumman *Hellcat*, Northrup P-61 *Black Widow*, Sikorsky Helicopter R-4, and Consolidated B-24 *Liberator* (*The Wingfoot Clan*, August 23, 1944, p. 2).

Older men, and women were encouraged to apply for work; there were hundreds of separate tasks in building aircraft (*The Wingfoot Clan*, August 30, 1944, p. 1). A late September headline pleaded with housewives: ***Campaign To Induce Housewives To Accept Aircraft Jobs Is Intensified: Plenty of Women Available In City Says U.S. Survey*** (*The Wingfoot Clan*, September 27, 1944, p. 1). In this one headline, women had evolved from their being a novelty as a production worker in 1941 to that of a valuable and desperately needed worker in late 1944. Many former full-time female employees thought the war was over, so they went home. Women were urged to return to work part-time so that they could complete their own household chores and were praised for coming to work part-time (*The Wingfoot Clan*, October 4, 1944, p. 5).

Mighty Shout Goes Up At News Of Bombing Of Tokyo was a photo caption showing mostly women workers cheering at the news that a B-29 *Superfortress* had bombed Tokyo on November 24, just one day after Thanksgiving 1944. This marked the first time Tokyo had been attacked since Doolittle's Raid on April 16, 1942 (*The Wingfoot Clan*, November 29, 1944, p. 1).

By December 1944, Goodyear's management and employees knew the war was winding down, despite predicted hard battles to come. Goodyear published its company policy regarding male employees who left the company to enter the armed forces. Categorically, each was returned to his former job with this caveat…*his progress and position will depend upon merit, as in the past.* No mention was made of the impact the headline must have made on female employees: ***Company Policy Regarding Men Returning From Service Of Their Country*** (*The Wingfoot Clan*, December 6, 1944, p. 1). This meant that some women would be losing their jobs.

In the column, *The Real Miss America*, one of the few women in the nation…*who manipulates the big Farnham rolls of aluminum or steel in Dept. 951, sheet metal machine shop, Plant C*…was praised for her work. It had taken her eighteen months to learn the job, which she had for one year as chief operator (*The Wingfoot Clan*, December 13, 1944, p. 6).

The B-29 *Superfortress* at Bell

The Boeing-designed B-29 was built in four locations in the United States: Boeing, Seattle and Renton, Washington; Glenn L. Martin, Wichita, Kansas; and Bell Aircraft, Marietta, Georgia. The impact of the B-29 *Superfortress* Bomber cannot be overstated in its service during World War II, especially in the Pacific Theater. I have included articles specific to this aircraft because Bell employees' total focus was on assembling an aircraft that would bring their loved ones back to them. Bell employees were kept abreast of military action by the B-29s, especially those built in Marietta. News about the aircraft, its crew, its combat mission successes, and it importance were central to the newsletter from June 1944 through August 1945. Photographs of the aircraft in assembly, in flight, and in battle were prevalent. Women workers were essential to the successful assembly and flight of one B-29 per day. Articles are noted as their personal nature and impact on company morale was central to the company's culture.

Intermixed with the praise-worthy articles about the B-29 were short announcements about a brother who was missing in action, a brother home for a short visit, another brother returning to duty, fathers or husbands who were awarded a Purple Heart (sometimes posthumously), announcements of sons' combat missions, women who were called into the military, sons recently released from prison camps (especially Japanese camps), and the never-ending lists of those killed or missing in action. The emotional impact on readers can only have been dizzying, and with the push to continue producing aircraft, it seems little time could be spent in mourning.

Workers Cheer As Reports On B-29s Come In noted that this long-awaited news went through the plant…*like wildfire…and was received with an enthusiasm unseen here before…First news that "their" bomber was blasting the Japs came in the form of a United Press bulletin telephoned to Bell public relations office by Fred Moon, city editor of the Atlanta Journal…Washington, June 15 (UP) B-29 Superfortress American plane today bombed Japan, the War Department announced. The targets attacked were not revealed.* Employees were described as feeling that they had at last begun to really participate in the war (*Bell Aircraft News*, June 17, 1944, p. 1/ p. 3).

General Henry H. 'Hap' Arnold told Bell Aircraft management they were awarded a contract to build the B-29 on December 22, 1941. The company began production of the B-29 in December 1943 and concluded with the production of six-hundred thirty-eight aircraft by fall 1945. The first ones arrived at airfields in India and China in April 1944. In November and December 1944, B-29s began operating against Japan from the islands of Saipan, Guam, and Tinian. Eventually, as many as one-thousand Superfortresses at a time bombed Tokyo destroying large parts of the city.

Larry Bell. President of the company, wrote and signed a thank you to the employees; it appeared on the front page on June 17. 1944.

> **'I Know You're Proud,' Says Bell**. This news from the War Department today telling of a raid by B-29 Superfortresses on Japan will, I am sure, be joyous news to the workers in the Bell Bomber Plant. The unceasing, round-the-clock effort of you workers in the production of B-29s has aided and will continue to aid greatly in the final destruction of the enemy. I know that you are proud to be part of this great new offensive action; one that will carry the fight directly to the enemy's homeland.
>
> The outstanding job which has been and will continue to be done by the workers of Atlanta, Marietta, and other parts of the south in producing this super mechanical marvel, the B-29, will, I am sure, be reported as one of the outstanding achievements of the war. What has been accomplished by you workers in this short period of time, is, in my estimation, an industrial miracle.
>
> I am sure that the Bell Bomber Plant workers will carry on with renewed vigor, proud of their assignment to produce more and more bombers to deal the enemy more and more decisive blows.
>
> *Larry Bell*

The story of the B-29 was viewed from many angles as expressed in these headlines: *Aviation Writer Tells of B-29's Flying Qualities*; *B-29 Proves Mettle Against Jap Fighters*; and *Japan Bombing Boosts Sales To $440,000* (War Bonds) (*Bell Aircraft News*, June 17, 1944, p. 1).

Japan and Return was written by a *Time Magazine* correspondent and reprinted in the newsletter. The plane flew out of bases in China and headed for Kyushu Island, the location of Japanese iron and steel plants. The author identified the plane's crew by name, age, and duty, then described the bombing run in some detail. It read like an adventure story, especially the tricky landing just ninety miles short of the enemy line. The attack by Japanese planes and the ultimate destruction of the B-29 was vivid. The crew hid and escaped. The story was designed to engage its readers in the most personal way as each employee could imagine that one of her/his brothers could have been a member of the crew (*Bell Aircraft News*, July 1, 1944, p. 1/ p. 3).

Other impactful articles in the July issues included: B-29 *Dedicated to Lost Airman; Employes,* {sic} *Company Buy Three B-29s* (War Bond purchases); and *Bell-Built Georgia Peach Hits Japan* (print of a detailed letter written by a local man to his parents whose plane participated in the June 15 Yawata raid over Japan; his plane was named "Georgia Peach"). The bombing of Yawata's Imperial Iron and Steel Works was the first air raid of the Japanese home islands by the United States Army Air Forces.

Between August and December 1944, reports/articles about the B-29 increased and became a vehicle for engaging readers in a more personal manner. The progress of the war easily can be followed by reading the newsletters, although later historical records would add details not quoted in real time during the war. ***Georgia Peach Pilot Spikes Jap Story of House Bombing*** quoted the Marietta pilot's denial that B-29s bombed residential areas in Japan cities. *We hit factories and I know it said the square-jawed former athlete who flew General Eisenhower's African invasion plans to Washington and completed several other important missions before the Japan assignment* (*Bell Aircraft News*, August 12, 1944, p. 1). To date, he had flown three of four assaults on Japan. The article brought to employees the exploits of a "local boy" and assured them that only the Japanese military people were targeted/dying.

A large photo of a B-29, built at another facility, landed in Marietta in August 1944: ***Bomber Builders Welcome Kin*** is the headline over the photo caption *A Dragon-fly Returns*. The caption under the photo was quick to point out that Bell-built B-29s had already participated in raids on Japan (*Bell Aircraft News*, August 13, 1944, p. 1).

Other August articles about the B-29 included praise for the thousands of Chinese "coolies" who met the deadlines to build air bases to accommodate the Superfortress – Chinese Built B-29 Strips the Hard Way. The final sentence was telling in its dismissiveness: Families were broken up (to provide construction labor), crops were lost (the laborers were largely farmers), the work was harder than they had done before (few mechanized tools) and incomes dropped almost to the vanishing point in China's spiraling inflation. But the farmers of Air Base Province responded to the need with patience and good humor (Bell Aircraft News, August 19, 1944, p. 1/ p. 8). I'll bet not.

The Allies used the Chinese-built air bases as jumping off points for their bombing runs on Japan. Superforts Served As Own Supply Line Over Orient was a telling bit of news from Headquarters XX Bomber Command in India. The B-29s had to import supplies and fuel from India to forward bases in China and had to fly over the Himalayas as there was no overland route from India to China. This article pointed to a second use for the large aircraft - supply flights so that the war could be brought closer to Japan (Bell Aircraft News, August 19, 1944, p. 1/ p. 8).

The bombing of Yawata was brought to readers' attention in late August when Yank Correspondent Describes B-29 Ride Over Japan, a front page story by a Yank Staff Correspondent. The story is gripping in its description of the flight, the attack, and the return to base (Bell Aircraft News, August 26, 1944, p. 1/ p. 8). Again, the telling was designed to bring the lesson home to the aircraft assemblers - your workmatters.

B-29s Pulverize Formosan Goals In Daring Raids headlined a story designed to elicit pride in the company's workers when they learned that the raids were on...*vital repair and staging center for the Japanese air force…After today, Formosa should no longer be a target for the Twentieth Air Force. We knocked hell out of them…for the first time we have* *completely destroyed a target…It was the third such raid within 72 hours and the destruction was described as terrific. Not a single one of the Superfortresses was lost. In the three daring raids on this Japanese stronghold only one plane is reported missing* (*Bell Aircraft News*, October 21, 1944, p. 3). Formosa is now modern-day Taiwan, the Republic of China.

The push to continue assembling the B-29s remained unabated, even with the announcement of victories in the Pacific Theater. With V-E Day (Victory in Europe) on the horizon, Bell workers were admonished on the front page: **PEAK B-29 OUTPUT TO CONTINUE AFTER VE-DAY; B-29 Urgently Needed in New Japan Thrusts**. The Army Air Force called for continued peak production of the aircraft even after victory of Germany was achieved. *VE-Day schedules…call for no let-down in production at the Marietta plant. And we ask that there be no let-down by workers turning out the B-29. Every man and woman is needed. Every ounce of their energy and skill, every minute of their working hours is needed. They are turning out the Army Air Forces' most important offensive weapon* (*Bell Aircraft News*, October 28, 1944, p. 1).

The above article was on the same page as a renewed push for employees to give to the Sixth War Loan Drive, which showed satisfactory gains. The editorial, **Make Victory Certain**, stated that victory was near, that Allied aircraft were…*pounding Germany*, and that the B-29s were…*smashing Japan*. The editorial said it was not enough to work hard, but each employee needed to invest in War Bonds. The combined effort would end the war sooner (*Bell Aircraft News*, October 28, 1944, p.2).

One page away was a report on B-29s attacking Kyushu…*one of the main islands of the Japanese homeland…at the southern tip of the archipelago…***Kyushu Blasted By Superforts** (*Bell Aircraft News*, October 28, 1944, p. 3). The article did not measure the success of the attack.

Telling was a request from the United States Navy directed to employees: **Navy Requests Photos of Japan**. *If you have snapshots or photographs taken on the Japanese mainland or on islands of Japan's war empire, please send them immediately to the nearest Naval Intelligence office. You may thus help shorten the Pacific war.* The photographs were needed by the military to formulate strategies for an eventual invasion of Japan. Ground level photos would be used to augment those taken by air. Then the article said: *The intelligence officers would like to interview all persons with first-hand knowledge of these areas* (*Bell Aircraft News*, October 28, 1944, p. 6).

I was appalled by the editorial below purporting to give Bell workers reasons for giving thanks at Thanksgiving. It appeared on page two in the same issue on which the front page held an article entitled **Tokyo Blasted By First Raid Of Superforts** (*Bell Aircraft News*, November 25, 1944, p. 1). Surely, workers understood that their war work created the horror that they were reminded they were lucky not to have happen to them. The juxtaposition of these articles, and articles like them, is dizzying to comprehend.

> **Reason for Thanks**
>
> Just consider for a moment what it is like to be awakened by air raid sirens in the middle of the night and to dash out into a ditch in your backyard. There to listen to the angry roar of thousands of bombers overhead and to hear the whistle of bombs coming down out of the darkness. You might hold your breath as the shattering crashes came closer. And, when all was still and the bombers gone, you stumble out to see the smoldering and smashed wreck that was once your home. Your children would look up at you with faces aged beyond their years and you would hold them close so that their undernourished bodies would not tremble too much in the cold.
>
> Idle imagination? No! You know such a happening has been a common thing in many parts of the world during these war years. On this Thanksgiving Day let us give thanks to God that it has not happened here to our families, our homes, our America!
>
> Bell Aircraft News, November 25, 1944, p. 2

The Christmas issue brought articles about goals exceeded in the blood drive, lockers available for all employees not just a select few, visits by a Georgia senator and a marine veteran, an announcement of bonuses that went to twenty-five thousand plant workers, transient wounded remembered by airport crews, war bond sales, dinner-dances, and a large photo layout of workers attending training classes.

There was a special holiday message from the Georgia Division Manager, James V. Carmichael. The last sentence is unfortunate in its admonishing tone – a tone that was all too common throughout the newsletters at Goodyear and at Bell.

> **A Message**
>
> I wish to extend to every worker in the Georgia Division my very best wishes for a Happy Christmas. The past year has been a hard one. Many misfortunes have beset us; notwithstanding this, you have done a magnificent job for the war effort. December will be the biggest month in the history of the Georgia division. We will deliver more combat planes than we have ever delivered in any previous month. The possibilities are that in January we will beat our December record. This has been possible only through the untiring work and loyalty of each person employed in the Georgia division. In wishing for you a Merry Christmas, I also extend to each of you my sincere gratitude for the wonderful job you have done. I am confident that you will not let the holidays interfere with your continuing to do what the boys in the Pacific are expecting of you.
>
> Bell Aircraft News, December 23, 1944, p. 1

Two final editorials for 1944 appeared on page two of the December 30 edition. The first discussed the successes of the B-29s: *Tokyo Blasted; Fleet of B-29s Returns Intact…B-29s Blast Tokyo Again; Jap Capital Left Aflame.* This was followed by a third bold statement: **B-29s SMASH TWO NIP WAR PLANTS**. *Every day you work you may be working on the ship that will break the back of Japan…there is no time to lose… no single wire can remain unconnected; no single rivet can remain undriven because YOU were not there on the job!* The editorial led the workers to understand that their efforts could engender this future headline: **B-29s LED WAY TO VICTORY OVER JAPAN, GENERAL SAYS.**

This was followed by a second editorial, **No Time For Absenteeism**, reprinted from the *Atlanta Constitution* talking about the…*vexing problem of absenteeism. An…intelligent effort is currently under way to study and analyze the evil*…of a reported five percent absenteeism on a good day to twelve percent on bad days. Representatives from labor, industry, the ministry, government, and civic leaders were meeting to discuss ways to combat absenteeism. The editor believed…*absenteeism was inexcusable and incongruous in times like these* (*Bell Aircraft News*, December 30, 1944, p. 2).

Designed to encourage workers to greater productivity, this article appeared in January 1945: **Bell-Built B-29s Plaster Japan Nearly Every Day, Says Wolfe**. A smiling Major General Kenneth Bonner Wolfe had been stationed at Bell as director of plans and technical training, was later commander of the 20th Bomber Command, the first to bomb Japan. His current assignment was at Wright Field in Georgia. He had predicted that a miracle would be needed to defeat Japan, and was gratified to state: *The miracle has come to pass and almost every day Bell-built bombers are carrying that miracle to the homeland of the Japanese.* He went on to state how proud he was of workers from Georgia and the South (*Bell Aircraft News*, January 6, 1945, p. 1). His comments spoke directly to the workers' feelings of pride.

Combat stories written by soldiers to their families often appeared in newsletters. A member of an ordnance unit in the Philippines wrote about his combat with Japanese paratroopers as the unit fought to protect an advanced airstrip. **Jap Paratroops Join Ancestor – Thanks to U.S. Ordnance Men** told a harrowing story of four ordnance men who fought an all-night battle. They were joined the following morning by an American fighting unit that…*annihilated the attackers.* The final sentence pulled the reader back to the B-29s: *John writes that men out there have nothing but good to say of the B-29s, which are appearing more and more frequently in the Pacific skies* (*Bell Aircraft News*, January 13, 1945, p. 1).

Wolfe Urges Triple Output Of B-29s in '45 headlined the general's comments to the Aviation Writers Association. He predicted more aircraft would be needed as American troops closed the gap on Japan…*to carry a decisive air war to her homeland, cripple her industries, divert her air power to home defense and carry on successful integrated operations with the navy against Japan's forces in the field and against the heart of her empire* (*Bell Aircraft News*, January 20, 1945, p. 4).

Marietta workers rose to the occasion, as announced on the front page of the February 2, 1945, edition. *PLANT PRODUCTION RECORDS ARE AGAIN BROKEN: Teamwork Held Responsible; Warns Against Optimism*. Plant workers were praised by Jimmy Carmichael, the general manager, for their teamwork, and he predicted that Bell could meet any schedule set by the Army Air Force. However, true to his style of communication that gave both praise and warnings, he said: *It's easy to get smug and over-optimistic when things are going good. Let's avoid that pitfall at all costs*

On March 3, 1945, Bell management thanked employees in an open letter from Jimmy Carmichael, manager, and Larry Bell, president of the company. This time the praise was warm and was not followed by admonitions to do better:

TO ALL EMPLOYES {sic}

February was the shortest month of the year. We had fewer flying days in February than in any other month during the year. Notwithstanding this, you exceeded our schedule of fly-away deliveries to the army during this month and exceeded the schedule of planes out of the factory and through final modifications for the month. This is the fourth consecutive month that you have broken the record. My sincere thanks and heartiest congratulations to every employe {sic} of the Georgia division. Without the united efforts of you and the army personnel stationed at this facility, such an outstanding record would not be possible. James V. Carmichael, Manager, Georgia Division.

Congratulations to your gang and the army bunch for beating the February production schedule of B-29s. This is a grand showing and I appreciate everybody's interest, cooperation and hard work.

Larry Bell

Bell Aircraft News, March 3, 1945, p. 1

Employees began to get good news about the war in Europe in mid-spring 1945. Bell management needed its workers to understand that *Our War Is Not Over* even if Germany surrendered unconditionally. *But not one piece of equipment built at this place is being used in Europe. Our production gun sights are trained on Japan, and no matter how enthusiastic we may feel about the Continental victories, we still have plenty of producing to do before the Japanese rats are rooted from their holes. Machinery and parts used here will still be needed for B-29 production. Yes, the news is good, but for us the war is NOT over. Nor will it be until final victory over Japan is achieved* (*Bell Aircraft News*, March 30, 1945, p. 1).

An adjacent article reinforced the editorial comments in: *Arnold Indicates 1,000 -A-Day B-29 Raids for Japs By Fall*. General H. H. Arnold stated that…*300-plane raids were already being carried out*…and predicted that raids of one-thousand planes are in the planning stages (*Bell Aircraft News*, March 30, 1945, p. 1/ p. 5).

A medical officer, and war hero from the battles on Java, spoke to management and members of the war bond committee: **More Superforts Needed for Job, Says Java Hero**. He praised the work of the Seabees, navy, and marines, but emphasized that… *But unless they've got an umbrella on top they can't do but one of two things—get in a hole or run* (Bell Aircraft News, April 7, 1945, p. 5). His visit was used to inspire greater efforts among employees.

A large four-photo collage appeared in the April 13 edition: **TO TOKYO AND BACK** with a detailed caption that showed a B-29 at a 20th Bomber Command base, its 500-pound bombs…*which later fell on Jap air installations at Okayama*. Details of bombing runs in and out of a base on Saipan included the crash of a B-29 on base. *All planes that "don't make it" must be replaced from an unfailing supply built by us at the Bell Bomber Plant…An infinite amount of planning, materiel and men are required to make these raids successful. A maximum effort must be put forth and both industry and the army must continue to work as a team so that final victory against Japan is assured. Even though the battle against Germany has approached a conclusion the war will not be won until menace of Japan is stilled* (Bell Aircraft News, April 13, 1945, p. 3).

To boost the pride of Bell employees, a visiting colonel offered this: **Bell-Built B-29 Outruns Others Thornhill Says**. He stated the Bell-built aircraft…*flew five to eight miles an hour faster—a great advantage when a Jap in on your tail* (Bell Aircraft News, May 5, 1945, p. 1). A second article ran adjacent: **Quotas Beaten For 6th Month** thanked employees for exceeding production schedules…*but stressed urgent need for conservation of parts and staying on the job…we cannot quit with the job only half done!* (Bell Aircraft News, May 5, 1945, p. 1/ p. 4). Employees had begun to resign as they assumed the war in Japan would be over soon.

In the same issue, Radio Tokyo was quoted in a boxed-in and bolded announcement: **Superfort Most Effective Weapon of War – Tokyo**. The three paragraphs read: *Radio Tokyo has termed the American B-29 as the most effective weapon of the war against Japan. The enemy broadcast revealed that more than 3,000,000 Japanese have been made homeless by Superfortress bombings that have destroyed 770,000 homes in Tokyo, Osaka, Kobe and Nagoya. The broadcast admitted that Japan will not be able to stop the Americans. Tokyo says -- and we quote -- "Nothing now seems possible to stop the enemy raids." The Jap radio says the Americans seem bent on extermination of the Japanese nation* (Bell Aircraft News, May 5, 1945, p. 6). The newsletter was printed just three days before the Allied Victory in Europe, May 8. With the successes in Europe and the statistics given in this article, it is understandable that many Bell employees thought the war was near its end.

President Harry S. Truman broadcast a proclamation officially terminating the war in Europe, but Bell Aircraft management wanted to emphasize to its employees that the job was not done. Employees were lauded for their work and reminded of their duty…*This action of yours is convincing evidence of your patriotic devotion and understanding of the tremendous job still ahead of us in the Pacific. You were saying to the boys on Okinawa: "We will not forget you! We will not let you down! We will do our bit to bring you home!"*

I salute you! James V. Carmichael, Vice President, Manager, Georgia Div. (*Bell Aircraft News*, May 11, 1945, p. 1).

The longest and most impactful article was printed on May 11, 1945. It covered the entire page: **WRITER LOGS SUPERFORTRESS RAID OVER TOKYO**. It was written by Bell former public relations director who was, at the time of the writing, a correspondent for the *Washington Evening Star*. He was aboard a B-29 on its bombing run from an airbase in Guam to Tokyo, a total of three-thousand three-hundred miles, a trip and return which took from 7 P.M. to 9:05 A.M. The pilot was twenty-five and the tail gunner was nineteen. A night flight, early morning bombing of Tokyo (between 1:28 A.M. and 2:05 A.M.), evasive action to avoid searchlights and flak, flying out of range of enemy fighters, an engine on fire, drinking the beverages they brought along, joking with each other, and landing…*I touch my hand on the ground. How good the solid earth feels* (*Bell Aircraft News*, May 11, 1945, p. 7). The article was rich in detail, emotive, and gave the home front workers a real taste of what the B-29 crews endured.

To drive home the importance of the B-29, a former prisoner in a Japanese internment camp was quoted: **Superfort 'Magnificent Ship,' Says Ex-Japanese Prisoner**. The captain had survived the Bataan Death March (April 9, 1942, sixty-five miles, brutal conditions, thousands American and Filipino soldiers perished) and had been a prisoner for more than three years. In a visit to the plant, he described the reaction of the five-thousand prisoners when they saw the aircraft overhead; morale increased dramatically as they awaited final delivery by American army rangers (*Bell Aircraft News*, June 16, 1945, p. 4). The article brought home the horror faced by one individual. These articles, about individuals and not about complete missions, made the war real for employees. Readers could grasp the horror faced by a person directly speaking to them more readily than by reading descriptions of the actions of military units. War is personal.

DOOLITTLE CHOOSES BELL-BUILT B-29 FOR OWN headlined Lt. General James H. Doolittle's personal choice of aircraft #42-63731 to be his plane when he rejoined his redeployed Eighth Air Force in the Pacific Theater. He chose one assembled at the Boeing-Wichita plant, but he praised all B-29 assemblers. He encouraged workers to keep on the job. **War Half Won, General Tells B-29 Builders**…*The boys out there in the Pacific are doing their job and they are counting on you here to continue to do yours. I know you will deliver the goods* (*Bell Aircraft News*, July 6, 1945, p. 1/ p. 6). Doolittle's Raiders were the first to attack Japan in April 1942, so he had come full circle, returning from his duties in Europe to rejoin the fight in Japan.

Atomic Laden B-29s Smash Two Jap Cities. The article was printed on page four, not on the front page of this issue, as I would have expected. The last three paragraphs, part of Lt. General Jimmy Doolittle's announcement, are telling: *Hiroshima, the first city to feel the tremendous impact of this elemental bomb, was razed by the one 400-pound explosion…Another atomic strike came Wednesday, this time on Nagasaki, Japan's largest naval base. It, likewise, was demolished by one bomb…Borne by the masterful Superfortresses, the* *atomic bomb and the plane together probably will be recorded in history as the greatest single factor in bringing the Jap war to a victorious end* (Bell Aircraft News, August 10, 1945, p. 4).

The August 17, 1945, issue featured a large photograph of several B-29s dropping clusters of fire bombs on Yokohama, Japan. The caption described the process in detail: **When Bombs Rained On Yokohama**. Below the photograph was a lengthy article, accompanied by three photographs of employees cheering the news about the end of the war: **War Over, Workers Celebrate Briefly, Then Return to Work**. Celebration was loud, although some employees still worried about relatives incarcerated in Japanese internment camps or grieved over the loss of family members in other battles (Bell Aircraft News, August 17, 1945, p. 1/ p. 4).

Finally, there was this news about a Bell-built B-29 assembled in Marietta, Georgia: **Bell-Built B-29 Flew World's Longest Combat Mission**. The aircraft had no name, but flew twenty hours and thirty-four minutes on a mining mission from India to Singapore; it had also completed nineteen combat missions. The crew was understandably proud, even if a bit tongue in cheek…*she's unusually fast and is always running away from other B-29s* (Bell Aircraft News, August 24, 1945, p. 1).

1945: Bringing the War to a Close

Erie Proving Ground

Proof firing continued and environmental concerns were not raised for decades. However, civilian workers were exposed to the chemicals used to proof-fire ordnance: asbestos, chlorine, and other hazardous materials. That Monnie was exposed to hazardous chemicals is assumed, but any long-term effect on her health is unknown. Van Keuran's book has a more thorough exploration of this emerging problem.

Bell Aircraft

Over a photograph of a woman in a crane it stated: **Woman Crane Jockey Surveys Most of Plant From High Perch**. *Frances, by way of explanation, is one of the prettiest overhead crane operators in the plant…she required only one week of instruction before taking over a double-bridge crane alone, and now handles jobs operators with much more experience might be called upon to do* (Bell Aircraft News, January 20, 1945, p. 3). It is noteworthy that she was referred to as a woman, and not a girl, in this article.

The newsletter posed a question to five women employees in mid-spring 1945: **From Your First Wage Earning Experience Would You Like To Continue Working After the War?** Three indicated they would like to continue working outside the home. One was a mother of eight children, lived on a farm, and said about her job as an assembler: *It's entirely different from housework and not half as bad*. The wife of the editor of a local newspaper worked as a production clerk said her responsibilities at home were few, found her work at Bell fascinating, and hoped to set aside funds during the war to build a little bungalow. The third woman, an assembler, wanted to continue working to save money to buy a small farm (*Bell Aircraft News*, March 3, 1945, p. 6).

Five women were asked…***If You Had Been a Man What Career Would You Have Chosen?*** The question was posed in March 1945. The answers were: professional baseball (Material Clerk), chemical engineer (Intermediate Clerk), physician (Store Keeper), aerial photographer (Expediter), and pilot a fighter plane (Junior Inspector). There was no mention of pursuing other careers when they left Bell (*Bell Aircraft News*, March 30, 1945, p. 7).

Goodyear Aircraft

Twenty-Five Women Engineers Graduate, Take Jobs At Aircraft. I believe this is one of the first articles in the newsletter that used the word "women" in a headline; the article continued the use of the term "girls," however. This marked the third class of…*girl engineers* (*The Wingfoot Clan*, January 10, 1945, p. 5).

The Goodyear Flying Squadron was started in 1914. World War II workers who belonged to the group learned practical knowledge and had classroom instruction on various phases of aircraft production. ***102 Women Among 165 Graduates: First Time Since Squadron Was Organized Has Honor Gone To "Gentler Sex."*** One woman received an Award of Merit for being an outstanding woman student (*The Wingfoot Clan*, January 31, 1945, p. 4). When I read this article, I thought the honor was overdue; women had been in aircraft production for four years.

The depiction of women continued to be sexually charged. ***Instructor Puts Group of Pilots Though Acid Test In Handling Of Mae Wests, As Well As Rubber Rafts*** (*The Wingfoot Clan*, February 2, 1945, p. 3). "Mae Wests" are inflatable personal life vests, named after an actress – a national sex symbol - whose bust line was of ample proportions. I assume, given her bawdy comedic acts, that she was flattered to have her name attached to the device.

Women were still valued employees and, along with others, were offered on-the-job training in the skills needed to perform their work: ***Nineteen Girls Receive Their Diplomas As Engineers***. The caption under the group photo said the women had completed a six-month course at the University of Akron, where they studied…*aerodynamics, math, stresses, mechanics, drafting, design, and descriptive geometry* (*The Wingfoot Clan*, March 21, 1945, p. 2).

Aircraft's Force of Policewomen As Fine As Found Anywhere said there were thirty-one police officers and depicted them wearing quasi-military uniforms with Army-style hats. They received training in general factory rules, military courtesy, discipline, interior guard duty, and judo (*The Wingfoot Clan*, May 12, 1945, p. 7).

In the final issue of *The Wingfoot Clan*, August 22, 1945, several women were interviewed and expressed their happiness at the war's conclusion and looked forward to returning home. ***Women Happy To Discontinue War Work And Return To Normal***

Life In Their Homes may not have been true for every woman worker. Much literature and research on American women workers since World War II indicates that many women liked working outside the home and wanted to keep their jobs. Many did, but the majority were forced out of the industrial plants because men returned from the battlefront to resume working at what had been perceived as "a man's job" (p. 5).

Another Way for Women to Serve

From the National World War II Museum and the Navy History and Heritage Command, I pulled basic enlistment statistics pertaining to women serving in the military during World War II. About three-hundred fifty-thousand American women served in uniform overseas and on the home front. They volunteered to serve with the Women's Army Auxiliary Corps (WAAC), Navy Women's Reserve (WAVE), the Marine Corps Women's Reserve, the Coast Guard Women's Reserve (Semper Paratus, Always Ready - SPAR), the Women's Airforce Service Pilots (WASP), the Army Nurses Corps, and the Navy Nurse Corps. Between July 1, 1941, and December 1945, the greatest number of female enlistees occurred during 1943 and 1944. Others could volunteer to serve at service-related canteens or sell War Bonds through the American Red Cross or the Office of Civilian Defense.

Erie Proving Ground

A smiling woman was photographed behind her desk in Mail and Records. She was Ottawa County's first member of the Marines: *EPG Clerk Joins Marines*. A second woman from Civilian Personnel was awaiting her acceptance into the marines as well (*EPG Echo*, June 3, 1943, p. 5). A third woman was feted with a dinner given by friends as she waited for her call to active duty in the marines (*EPG Echo*, June 17, 1943, p. 5).

One employee, cited in *Serving In Uniform*, reported for active duty in the WAVE on June 28, 1943 (*EPG Echo*, July 1, 1943, p. 4). A fifth woman, who worked in Stores and later in the Anti-Aircraft Unit of Proof, joined the WAVE, and attended the United States boot camp at Hunter College in the Bronx on June 14, 1943 (*EPG Echo*, June 17, 1943, p. 4). About ninety-thousand women went through six weeks of basic training. The Welfare Department housed "morale counselors" with whom employees could consult about personal problems. Although not specified what those problems might be, it seems reasonable that some young women might have sought counseling before they transitioned into military life.

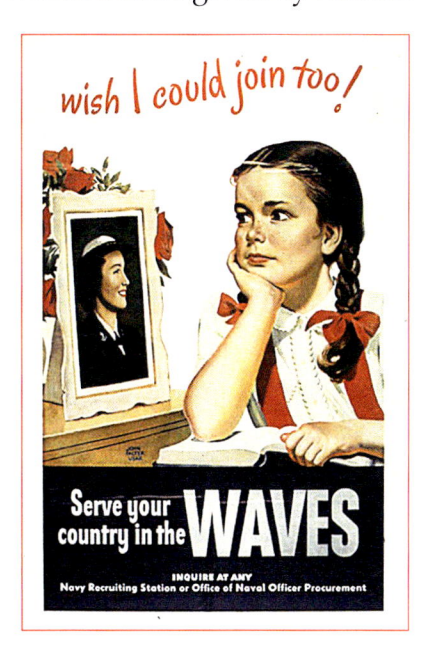

Bell Aircraft

Many articles focused on the serious efforts of women to do their part during World War II. For example, ***One War Effort Leads to Another, Panama Beckons to "Jimmie" James***. She worked in the Traffic Department and...*mastered the intricacies of train and plane schedules to become a sort of one-man information bureau.* She was headed for a stint in Panama with the United States Army Air Force: *Her work will be concerned with reports and other data* (*Bell Aircraft News,* June 25, 1943, p. 3). In September 1943, "Jimmie," now in the Army Air Corps, wrote to a former co-worker to describe working conditions in the Panama Canal Zone; eight-hour days, seven days a week in hot, wet weather. She reported being...*made an honorary charter member of a fighter squadron* (*Bell Aircraft News,* September 17, 1943, p. 1).

In The Service was a regular newsletter column, and the September 10, 1943, issue announced one female employee's enlistment as a U.S. Cadet, Nurse's Corps (p. 3).

Another service veteran, a woman who had been injured during WAC maneuvers, joined the Bell Aircraft production line as described in: ***WAC Joins Ranks of Veterans Taking Up Airplane Building***. She wanted to return to the military, but since her injury might prevent that, she considered her job as an inspector to be equally important (*Bell Aircraft News,* January 29, 1944, p. 2).

Age Discovered by WAVES, Geneva Signs As War Worker was the headline of a front page article about a young woman who lied about her age to enlist in the WAVE. When it was discovered that she was only eighteen, she was given an honorable discharge. *It is the story of a dark-haired, dark-eyed Georgia lass who was riding high with the Waves until they discovered she had upped her age...Everyone hated to see Geneva leave the Waves,* {sic} *for she had the stuff it takes to make a sailorette, but regulations are regulations... Since Geneva was training as a machinist's mate, it is expected by the training center that her experience will come in handy on her job as an inspector* (*Bell Aircraft News,* January 15, 1944, p. 1/ p. 3).

One of the plant's...*two girl welders*...joined the WACS in ***Jeanne Fox, Welder, Gives Up Welding Torch For Army Duty.*** As soon as she celebrated her twentieth birthday in February, she resigned her position at Bell on April 1. She hoped ...*to get as close to the war front as possible* (*Bell Aircraft News,* April 1, 1944, p. 1).

In the column, ***Bellorama***, there was a brief announcement that a woman who worked as a wage analyst joined the WACS the same day her husband was inducted into the navy (*Bell Aircraft News,* April 29, 1944, p. 2). In May, a woman expediter... *scored one of the highest entrance marks every made in Atlanta, on her exam for the WACs.* She wanted to serve overseas (*Bell Aircraft News,* May 6, 1944, p. 2).

Ex-Beauty Queen Visits was the caption over a photo of a WAC private, and former "Miss Bell Bomber" as she stood under the nose of a B-29. She was visiting former co-workers in the photographic department, and had recently completed a medic course (*Bell Aircraft News,* April 21, 1945, p. 6). ***Visitor*** appeared over a photo of a

WAC private and former Bell employee in tool control. She was a clerk at the Miami Army Air Base, and the article's author quipped… *And her big smile and natty appearance are proof enough that Air Wacs {sic} are indeed Uncle's most favored nieces* (*Bell Aircraft News*, May 5, 1945, p. 3).

A woman chemist in the functional test lab at Bell Aircraft was lauded for her ability to fly an aircraft. ***Ex-WASP Flier In Functional Test Has 2,000 Hours Without Mishap*** spoke generously about Ruby Mullins…*Bell's birdwoman chemist.* She left college her junior year, got her civilian pilot's license, then joined WASP when it was organized by Jacqueline Cochran in Sweetwater, Texas. After training, Ruby was… *stationed with the Sixth and Twenty-First Ferrying groups at Long Beach and Palm Springs, Calif…She was first pilot* {pilot in command} *on huge C-47 and C-49 cargo planes and B-25 Mitchell bombers. She co-piloted Flying Forts, Liberators and Douglas C54s…but her own special favorites are the tiny speedsters – fast little trainers, Dauntless dive bombers, and the fighters: Kingcobra, Airacobras, Mustangs and Thunderbolts* (*Bell Aircraft News*, July 6, 1945, p. 4).

After the war ended in the Pacific, a brief announcement was printed about a former Bell stenographer: ***Ex-Belle Now Sergeant***. She left the company in November 1943, and served as supply secretary at the Cherry Point (North Carolina) Marine Air Base (*Bell Aircraft News*, August 17, 1945, p. 4).

Goodyear Aircraft

First Aircraft Girl To Join WAAC worked for the chief inspector for Plant C. She graduated high school in 1939. She was headed to Ft. Des Moines, Iowa, for training - the first in her family to serve in the military. She wanted more war activity than she was contributing on the home front (*The Wingfoot Clan*, September 30, 1942, p. 1).

Lillian Krummel Proves That She's Busy Girl In War: She Completes Several Courses; Now Seeks Enlistment in WAAC. This is another example of a woman, who was praised for being the *first girl welder* at Aircraft, who wanted to serve her country in another way (*The Wingfoot Clan*, December 16, 1942, p. 6). In 1943, more women who joined the military were highlighted. The company's first girl welder did join the WAACS in January 1943 (*The Wingfoot Clan*, January 27, 1943, p. 4).

In the column ***For and About Women***, a photograph of a woman in a WAVE uniform was highlighted in ***Now At Aircraft***. She had a doctorate in chemistry from New York University, further training at Massachusetts Institute of Technology, with other aerological research completed at the Guggenheim Institute (*The Wingfoot Clan*, September 22, 1943, p. 4).

In November 1943, in ***Now At Aircraft*** the newsletter highlighted the credentials of one WAVE Ensign who completed officer's training at Smith College, and held a master's degree from Monmouth Academy. The other WAVE officer training school was at Mt. Holyoke located in South Hadley, Massachusetts (*The Wingfoot Clan*,

November 10, 1943, p. 4.). Readers are encouraged to review Mundy's excellent coverage of code girls who were recruited from several of the Seven Sisters private colleges in the United States.

In March 1945, the newsletter published a photo of a woman employee who became an...*air WAC in the army intelligence office*... (*The Wingfoot Clan*, March 21, 1945, p. 6).

Virginia Clawson Member Of Exclusive Marine Corps Band praised this cornet player for her membership in the Women's Reserve Band. She enlisted in April 1943 after working at Aircraft in office services (*The Wingfoot Clan*, May 23, 1945, p. 4).

Employee Newsletters: Especially for Women

Safety Garb and Office Attire

When women first obtained factory jobs, they worked in the clothes they brought from home. They used makeup and nail polish, they wore jewelry, and their hair was often long and not pulled back or covered. Special articles and cartoons were created to address these uniquely female issues. Women in production were encouraged to work safely as were all workers but to purchase slack suits that were designed for them, to wear hair nets/ scarves (headdresses)/ snoods, and to leave their jewelry at home. This specialized safety campaign was needed because long hair, loose clothing, and jewelry could be caught in machinery causing significant injury. Safety protocols and reminders were printed in the newsletters throughout the war.

Sobering national safety statistics were printed by Goodyear in 1944 and served as a reminder to employees about the need for safety. ***War Front Safer Than Home Front Since Pearl Harbor***. The source for the data was the Office of War Industry (OWI):

> o Armed Forces: 25,389 dead; 35,805 injured; 32,951 MIA; 26,820 POW.
> o Home Front: 88,000 dead (workers); and 8,200,000 injured.

It was calculated that home front accidents were equivalent to seven-hundred fifty million losses in man-days. This equaled the time required to build thirty-five thousand bombers or one-hundred-eight battleships (*The Wingfoot Clan*, March 15, 1944, p. 3).

Erie Proving Ground

Safety Organization Hopes To Make EPG One Of The Safest Ordnance Posts In U.S. The push for safety at EPG was centralized...*in accordance with Ordnance Department regulations*. Safety committees were organized by department: Proof, Stores, Service and Inspection, and Erie Ordnance Depot. The committee reviewed the frequency and severity of accidents that occurred in the previous year. The committee was made up of officers and civilian men (*EPG Echo*, July 1, 1943, p. 3).

Below the article was a large photo of two Women Ordnance Workers (WOWs) demonstrating the proper manner in which to lift a heavy box. It was pointed out that *…both girls are wearing slacks and short sleeved blouses…{although}…coveralls and overalls are equally satisfactory. Dresses and smocks are suitable only for women engaged in office work. Both girls have procured special safety shoes…and wear them consistently* (*EPG Echo*, July 1, 1943, p. 3).

Bell Aircraft

By February 1944, more reasonable work attire was made available for female employees. **Slack Suit** was the caption over a photograph of a woman worker wearing a one-piece jump suit and turban. They were available for sale in the Employes' {sic} Service Store in blue or green for $3.95 and 35 cents respectively (*Bell Aircraft News*, March 4, 1944, p. 4)

At the time, in both the United States and in Europe, there was much discussion about the perceived lack of morals of any woman who opted to wear slacks in public. The emphasis on women's safety in the workplace, then, had to be reiterated so that women would feel comfortable in slacks as they worked.

Spring, Summer Fashions headlined an article about what…*a tastefully-dressed woman war worker will wear this spring and summer.* The accompanying photo showed a woman who wore a hairnet that completely covered her head, a one-piece pants suit, low-heeled substantial shoes, goggles, and she wore no jewelry. I found it interesting that even by 1944, women production workers had to be reminded to wear safety clothing (*Bell Aircraft News*, April 15, 1944, p. 2).

A four-panel cartoon in one Bell newsletter illustrated what a female worker should do and not do with her long hair while working around machinery. The first panel showed the cartoon woman catching her loose hair in a machine; second panel showed her with a head scarf but loose hair got caught in an electric drill; and the third panel showed one end of the "kerchief" getting caught in a machine and pulling her face into it. The final panel showed her "kerchief" properly wrapped around her head, no hair showing, with the ends of the scarf tucked in. The caption read: *Here are all the hair safety features to insure post-war beauty* (*Bell Aircraft News*, April 22, 1944, p. 2).

Goodyear Aircraft

She Is A Very Careful Worker read the headline about a woman lathe operator who was...*chosen to help introduce the use of approved safety garb among women workers*. In the photo, this older, widowed, woman wore one of five-thousand new safety uniforms ordered by the company for female workers (*The Wingfoot Clan*, February 17, 1943, p. 2).

Production workers eventually were given specially designed clothing that looked like the uniforms worn by a WAVE: a one-piece pantsuit with short sleeves and a *GAC* (Goodyear Aircraft Corporation) insignia on the left sleeve, with a cap that was military in style. For safety, the pantsuits were important, but another message was conveyed: these uniforms gave the appearance of a united force and allowed women production workers to visually stand apart from other women employees. Their garb was more like what male employees wore.

Apparent Competition among Women

There was an apparent dichotomy between office workers and production workers at Goodyear, not only in the skills they brought to their jobs, but in the greater publicity focused on women who worked on assembly lines, in the paint department, in the tool crib, or who handled large pieces of ordnance or aircraft production tools or who operated machinery.

In addition, employees' work apparel, described above for the women, created a visual difference between workers. For example, this was apparent at Erie Proving Ground in an article on safety cited above when employees were educated about the differences between clothing that was acceptable in an office as differentiated from the safety garb worn by women ordnance workers.

As I worked my way through the myriad depictions of women over the course of their employment, I began to see a disturbing differentiation along socio-economic lines. This is apart from the segregation of workers by race, or the mention of age when describing a worker. Instead, the pattern I saw was an apparent dichotomy between the overall better educated (some college) office workers and those less well educated (high school or less), and between older local "club women" and younger women who may have come from anywhere in the country, or from local rural areas, to work in war production.

My observation became relevant when one office worker seemed to complain that female production workers got all the attention. Indeed, it was unusual for women to be on a production line, as any number of historical works written about "Rosie the Riveter" will attest. The content of the regularly printed **Real Miss Americas** column apparently stuck in the craw of one Goodyear office worker. Featured in the column, this woman was quoted as saying: *She expressed the view of many Aircraft Secretaries when she explained that girls in the offices are doing constructive war work as well as the girls wearing slacks in the factory.* The column appear within **This Page Of Interest To All**

Aircrafters, Especially Women (*The Wingfoot Clan*, March 3, 1943, p. 4).

The emphasis on women working in production is evident in this news piece: **Mostly Women For Plant To Build FG-1 Ships**. The FG-1 *Corsair*, was a fighter flown by American navy and marine servicemen largely in the Pacific Theater. The article went on to say that by June 1, 1943, the company would have…*3,500 more workers, mostly women. In fact, Goodyear employed…13,000 women, 46% of the total employment, which was the highest in the entire aircraft industry* (*The Wingfoot Clan,* April 28, 1943, p. 1). In a numbers game, it is understandable that more press attention might be paid to production workers over office workers

Production workers did get a lot of attention and were kept abreast of the victories they helped achieve. **Aircrafters Cheer When They Hear Corsairs, Planes Like They Build, Downed 16 of 17 Jap Zero Fighters.** The large group photograph had about fourteen women cheering with their male coworkers. The battle action referred to was west of Guadalcanal and the FG-1 *Corsair…was hailed by pilots as the fastest plane on the firing line today* (*The Wingfoot Clan*, May 26, 1943, p. 1). It is understandable, given this type of publicity and the moniker "Soldiers of Production," that filing paperwork might seem less glamorous or less worthwhile. Japanese fighters referred to the *Corsair* as *Whistling Death* because of the peculiar sound it made at higher airspeeds.

In addition to the need for production workers to wear clothing appropriate for working around machinery, for assembling parts, or for climbing on ladders, and to crawl into aircraft to finish their tasks, Goodyear Aircraft outfitted many production workers in uniforms, including a cap, that were designed very much like those worn by WACs. **Uniforms For Women Workers Designed To Promote Aircraft's Safety Program** described a short-sleeved pants suit, with a *GAC* insignia on the sleeve worn with a cap. The outfits were navy in color and seen as slenderizing. The photo showed three women standing smartly, almost at attention. The uniforms, recommended by management and labor…*will give us assurance that we can work safely, dress attractively and be comfortable at our tasks*. Office workers did not have this distinctive garb (*The Wingfoot Clan*, June 30, 1943, p. 3).

When I read **College Club Sends Gifts Overseas**, with its accompanying photo of six women from Aircraft's College Club, I sensed a pattern of distinct socio-economic lines among employees. There were thirty-five members of the Club, each…*with two plus years of accredited college training*…who were photographed sending care packages to former employees serving overseas (*The Wingfoot Clan*, October 25, 1944, p. 1).

In January 1943, Goodyear Aircraft needed more workers especially to collect and analyze statistics. **Clubwomen On Job At Aircraft To Aid In Solving Problem of Help Shortage** described the work of twenty-four women who were hired for "white collar jobs" in the Department of Selective Service Statistics. When the company realized what skills were needed it…*turned to Akron's social register when a desperate need developed for a group of women to do office detail work in compiling information for a perpetual inventory of manpower*. These women had been doing charity work in the community and the company management believed…*the usual sources of employees {was} close to the saturation point, industry must now look to those who have never before worked to fill the rapidly developing jobs in office detail which is a national result of increased production* (*The Wingfoot Clan*, January 27, 1943, p. 1). Upper class women, presumably well-educated, were given these jobs because other women were needed on the production line

Women Production Workers and Childcare

Erie Proving Ground

The Welfare Section of the Civilian Personnel Branch of EPG met with Port Clinton officials to consider the need for a child care program for Port Clinton mothers engaged in defense work. Such a program would…*promote the employment of women with children and would reduce absenteeism among women in war industries*. The article suggested such a program would be organized by the local superintendent of schools, be available for children up to age fourteen, and could be paid for with federal funds. The idea was to promote the employment of mothers and reduce instances of absenteeism for women who had small children (**Port Clinton May Sponsor Child-Care Program**, *EPG Echo*, July 15, 1943, p. 6).

Bell Aircraft

In consideration of the needs of working mothers, nursery schools in the area surrounding the defense plants stated: **Nursery Schools Will Care for Children of Working Parent** -- *Preference to mothers in war industry is given at the schools operated with the assistance of state and federal funds*…(*Bell Aircraft News*, June 18, 1943, p. 1).

One nursery school needed to register fifteen children and Bell urged working mothers to enroll them: **More Children Needed To Open DeKalb County Nursery School**. The school cost $2.00 per week per child and was open from 6:30 AM to 7 PM, and children up to age fourteen could be cared for after school hours. It was to the benefit of the war production plants to encourage these enrollments because women workers were increasingly needed (*Bell Aircraft News*, July 23, 1943, p. 1).

Child Care Center Is Opened For Kiddies of Bell Workers. This front page headline had to come as a relief to many workers. Financed by federal funds and operated under the public school system…*fifteen children who had been vaccinated and who had secured health certification were in attendance*. There were forty more children who would be admitted as soon as they met the health requirements (*i.e.*, no communicable diseases, and vaccinated for smallpox and antitoxin for diphtheria). First preference is given to working mothers whose children would be cared for all day, given a hot lunch, naps, with isolation being offered to children with colds. This cost per week per child was $2.50 (*Bell Aircraft News*, Friday, October 29, 1943, p. 1). A second, then a third child care center were opened in late 1943 in Cobb County, Georgia, all geared to assist war workers. Later, the child care unit offered 24-hour care to assist the night shift workers (*Bell Aircraft News*, December 18, 1943, p. 1).

By February 1944, the child care needs of shift workers and night workers needed to be addressed again. ***All-Night Care For Marietta Children*** was announced to accommodate second and third shift workers as well as those working overtime. Children ages two through ten could be left in the late afternoon and picked up between seven and eight-thirty in the morning. Charges for the service per week, per child, fit the needs of the parent: $2.50 without a meal; $3.00 with supper; and $3.50 with supper and breakfast (*Bell Aircraft News*, February 26, 1944, p. 1).

Another fifteen-student nursery school was announced - ***New Nursery School Planned*** - to be opened as soon as the requisite number of children were enrolled. Women workers were encouraged to meet with their personnel counselor to sign an agreement (*Bell Aircraft News*, April 15, 1944, p.3).

As late as November 1944, more nursery schools were established to accommodate plant workers. ***New Nursery School Opened Near Marietta*** offered a cottage atmosphere, with…*competent teachers*…who would be in charge of the children. Hours of care included 6 AM to 6 PM for children ages two and six (*Bell Aircraft News*, November 18, 1944, p. 7). Bell Aircraft needed its female workers to stay on the job so providing their children with a safe environment for twelve hours per day was appealing.

Another nursery opened in November 1944 to accommodate employees from the night shift. ***Child Care Unit For 2nd Shift Opens Monday*** provided care for children ages two and fourteen from 4:30 P.M. to 7:30 A.M. Supervised by the Marietta school system, children would be given one meal for $3.00, two meals for $3.50, or $2.50 a week for children who did not require a meal. Again…*competent teachers will be in charge of the night center, it was stated* (*Bell Aircraft News*, November 11, 1944, p. 1). This arrangement would have appealed to female workers who, at this time in the United States, were largely in charge of child care in their families.

Even in 1945, when the war seemed to be winding down, child care facilities were added in the Atlanta/Marietta geographical area. Night care was particularly needed when women worked the second shift: ***Night Nursery Care Available***. Children from two to twelve years could be cared for from 5 P.M. to 8 A.M. at one of two new locations in Cobb County (*Bell Aircraft News*, January 27, 1945, p. 6). Adjacent Fulton County nurseries announced vacancies for Bell workers' children at two locations during the day, six days a week: ***Nursery Units Have Vacancies*** (*Bell Aircraft News*, March 24, 1945, p. 7).

As long as women worked outside the home, there was a need for child care, especially at night: ***Nursery Opens At Pine Forest***. A new facility provided night care…*answers a long standing need…and would relieve crowded condition at*… another nursery. For varying prices, the children were served chocolate milk, a vegetable dinner, and fruit juice (*Bell Aircraft News*, April 7, 1945, p. 1). Other similar announcements of newly opened child care facilities occurred regularly through July 1945.

Goodyear Aircraft

There were only one or two articles or announcements about available childcare.

Employee Newsletters: Especially for Men
Women in Beauty Contests as Morale-Builders

There were regular features about...*lovely, comely, pretty or feminine girls*...individual women workers or groups of women from a single office, and there were regular feature articles about women production workers (*e.g.*, **The Real Miss America** from Goodyear's *The Wingfoot Clan*). Each was accompanied by a photograph with captions that emphasized what was considered feminine or beautiful. Women were often described by their height, weight, and hair/ eye color, long/ shapely legs, make up, or by their apparel.

Beauty contests have been part of American culture for decades. There was an apparent desire/ need for those events to continue within the microcosm of the home front culture. Contests were held throughout the war by departments or divisions, by shift, or in honor of a met quota, or held to represent the entire company. Dances chose queens. Office workers and production workers were eligible. Women were nominated over the course of five or six weeks, typically, and chosen for their...*looks, production performance, personality, and presentation*. Several headlines, generally printed on the front page of a newsletter, illustrate the importance of, or at least, the popularity of, these events to the workers.

Erie Proving Ground

Hi, Soldier, Here She Is – An EPG Pin-Up Girl includes a photograph of a smiling young blond woman seated on a table, wearing sandals, a very short shirt (knees pulled up so that her legs are fully exposed), and a V-neck sweater. The caption reads: **AND SHE'S TALENTED**...*Mary Yaraco, 20 and single, was chosen by Lt. Daun E. Yeagley to start the series of "pin-up" girls. Mary is from Toledo and works the night shift as a proof director out at Armor Plate, Bldg. 94, and she helps support younger brothers and sisters. She is a blonde and pretty (as if we needed to tell you) and plays the piano and accordion. She also has a lovely singing voice. And by the way she is five fee-three inches tall and weighs an even one-hundred pounds* (*EPG Echo*, July 15, 1943, p. 5).

Bell Aircraft

Beauty Contest To Be Sept. 11 Dance Feature was a brief announcement about the *Welcome South* dance billed as the best of the season to be held at the Atlanta Municipal Auditorium. All Bell departments were urged to enter a contestant. Trophies would be awarded to the winner and runner-up. The next Miss Bomber Plant was anticipated (*Bell Aircraft News*, August 27, 1943, p. 1).

Predictably, this article appeared: ***"Miss B-29" Will Be Chosen From Plant Beauties.*** Each department at Bell was…*expected to sponsor a candidate…asking that they enter their most beautiful girl employee…* The contest was held at the Shrine Mosque, the *Welcome South Dance*, which the governor and his wife would attend. The winner would receive prizes from leading Atlanta businesses and the winner and runner-up would receive a trophy (*Bell Aircraft News*, September 3, 1943, p. 1).

Similarly, ***Miss Bell Bomber Awaits Coronation*** presented the names of ***Fifty Beauties to Compete in Dance Affair.*** This is the same event as the one described above, so I am unsure it the name of the title changed or if there were two contests. Contestants were both single and married women. The judges, all male, carried interesting credentials: internationally known photographer and lecturer; artist famed for his depiction of feminine charms; editor of the *Atlanta Constitution*; a United States Army Air Force intelligence officer; and company officers (*Bell Aircraft News*, September 10, 1943, p. 4).

Two group photographs of contestants presented in an article for the ***2nd Miss Bell Contest Series Opens Tonight.*** The winner of the contest would become "Miss Bell Aircraft" (*Bell Aircraft News*, April 29, 1944, p. 2). ***Crown 'Miss Bell Aircraft' Tonight: 20 To Complete In Auditorium Beauty Finals*** (Bell Aircraft News, May 13, 1944) There had been over 100 applicants.

The "pin-up" girl photos continued unabated in the newsletter. ***Oh You Kid!*** was the caption over a photo of the winner of a costume contest at annual BRC kid party in Atlanta. The woman, standing coyly, is wearing a plaid pinafore, a ribbon in her hair, and bobby sox with saddle shoes (*Bell Aircraft New*, December 9, 1944, p. 5).

Goodyear Aircraft

"Quota Queen" To Be Chosen From Among Women Employed In Plant D; Goodyear Aircraft's *Corsair* production employees chose a woman to christen February's *Victory Ship* which she named *Victory Queen*. Also she was given a $25 War Bond. The company had produced one-thousand *Corsairs* in less than one year (*The Wingfoot Clan*, January 26, 1944, p. 1). The contest winner was a married Blue Star Mother, and a Red Cross volunteer who had given blood five times. She had worked at Aircraft for four years (*The Wingfoot Clan*, March 1, 1944, p. 2).

Who Is Production Queen? This bold question was posed for a contest *open to… office girls and production workers*. The article emphasized that beauty was not the greater factor and that this was not a popularity contest. Those eligible would be judged on productivity, attendance, safety and good housekeeping, qualities of leadership, dependability, and cooperation in the war effort. The contest would be held by plant, then an overall winner would be chosen (*The Wingfoot Clan*, November 8, 1944, p. 1).

Goodyear's nominating blank captured requisite data:

Nominating Blank

I nominate _____

    Dept. No. _____   Clock Card No. _____

    For Production Queen at Plant _____

Her Supervisor is _____

    _____   _____

         Name   Dept. No.

Younger Girls At Aircraft Challenge Mothers In Spirited Campaign for "Production Queen" said that the younger women had husbands and brothers in the service, and the older workers, Blue Star and Gold Star Mothers, had sons in the service or had lost sons to the war (*The Wingfoot Clan*, November 22, 1944, p. 1). Of the thirty-four nominees, there were four finalists: one unmarried younger woman, one married younger woman, and two older married women with children (*The Wingfoot Clan*, December 20, 1944, p. 1). The winner was the same woman chosen as the Quota Queen the previous spring, a married, *Corsair* production worker with children in the service: ***Aircraft "Production Queen" Honor Bestowed Upon Mrs. Ada Phillips*** (*The Wingfoot Clan*, January 1, 1945, p. 1).

Reports from War Zones

Reports from the battlefronts were heavily censored, to be sure, but the number of articles about servicemen killed in action, placed in prison camps, or wounded and recovering, along with general information about battles won and lost created an emotional soup for employees to experience. Likely, there were many war-related actions or events that were not talked about in complete detail. In 2020, researchers still do not have a complete picture of what happened in all areas of World War II. War-related newsletter articles were inspiring, terrifying, motivating, informing – all designed to cement the employees' resolve to keep going on with their production work.

Goodyear had not yet heard if the FG-1 *Corsair* was effective in battle, then this article appeared: ***FG-1 Superb Fighter Plane, Says Navy Bureau of Aeronautics Chief***. Admiral D. C. Ramsey said…*To every employee who helped send such a superb fighter against the Japs we say: "Well done. Keep them coming"* (*The Wingfoot Clan*, December 15, 1943, p. 2). The first FG-1 rolled of the assembly line in February 1943.

Big Flock of Corsairs Leaves Aircraft For Fighting Fronts: Most Intensive Air Activity Ever Seen At Akron Airport: Largest Delivery of Craft To Uncle Sam's Navy In Singe Day Since First Plant Left Nine Months Ago (April 1943) (*The Wingfoot Clan*, January 12, 1944, p. 1).

The joy of delivering large numbers of aircraft was mirrored in *"Eight Ball" Squadron Is Marine Fighter Unit*, a caption over a large photo of a twenty-seven man squadron taken at Munda Field, a captured Japanese base…*this squadron has shot down twenty-eight Jap planes* (*The Wingfoot Clan*, January 12, 1944, p. 3). Munda Field, also known as Munda Point Airfield, was located on the southern coast of New Georgia Island in Western Province, the Solomon Islands. The battle was fought for six months, ending with Allied occupation in August 1943.

In January 1945, Goodyear printed sobering statistics about the realities of waging war: *629,000 casualties, 134,000 KIA, 64,000 POWs, 75,000MIA, and 356,000 wounded.* Under the headline *"At This Time We Must Produce More, and Quickly" Says H. E. Blythe* (VP and General Manager) (*The Wingfoot Clan*, January 17, 1945, p. 1).

The author summarized the production of armament:
- Airplanes: 253,286
- Tanks: 75,000
- Trucks: 3,500,000
- Machine guns: 2,422,000
- Rifles/ Small Arms Ammunition: 37 billion rounds
- Army Artillery (22 mm +): 393,500

Men in Service:
1939   352,500
1944 11,900,000

Reports about war zones often included stories of American civilian and military prisoners of war. Several Goodyear employees were incarcerated by the Japanese when Imperial Forces overran the rubber plantations in the South Pacific. *Goodyear Man Home After Being Held Three Long Years By Japanese Fiends: Harry Lundberg, Rubber Plantation Executive, Tells of Confinement In Philippines Camp, Where Filth, Disease, Abuse Hold Sway, While Wretches Of Nippon Deliberately Strive To Starve Prisoners To Death.* He detailed the horror of life in the camp while wearing sun glasses to protect his vision, which had been impaired by a meager prison-based diet. He reported that when prisoners appealed to their captors for better treatment, citing the Geneva rules of war…*the Jap's cold-blooded reply was: "As far as you are concerned there is no international law."* Seventeen Goodyear employees made it back from the camp, three died in the Philippines at Santo Thomas, which was liberated on February 3, 1945 (*The Wingfoot Clan*, April 11, 1945, p. 1). The blaring headline on the front page brought the war home in a most personal manner to civilian employees.

More articles like the one above, written by other Goodyear employees, reiterated in detail the horrors within the Japanese prisoner of war camps. *Another Goodyear Family Freed From Clutches Of Jap Fanatics: Hubers Arrive In Akron After Long Period In Prison: Rice-Water Diet Supplied By Nips But Neither Medicine Nor Clothing Given.* The family, included the Huber's wife and three children, suffered from starvation resulting in severe weight loss, developed cataracts, and suffered from beriberi, a common ailment from a vitamin B-1 deficiency (*The Wingfoot Clan*, May 2, 1945, p. 2). Any reader of this news article could easily imagine him/herself in that camp.

Recreation for Employees

Erie Proving Ground

The *EPG Echo* contained scant information about organized recreational activities for employees. There were news items about dances, bond parties, suppers, stag parties, picnics, and wedding showers. In one of Aunt Monnie's background checks, it indicated she attended USO dances with co-workers. The Italian and German POWs, incarcerated at the adjacent Camp Perry, played sports and had a number of other recreational activities, but it is unlikely that they played sports with civilian or military employees.

A small article asked: **Want A Team, Girls?** It introduced the idea of an indoor baseball team for…*girls in offices, and warehouses of different division…This would be an ideal sport, and create an interest between the different division employees. If this sounds favorable, write in your suggestions to the EPG Echo* (*EPG Echo*, May 20, 1943, p. 3).

In the June 3, 1943, issue, the front page suggested: **Civilian Club of Post Will Be "Reactivated"** by the Welfare Branch of the Civilian Personnel Division. The military was in charge of activities. The club was to promote recreational and social facilities for employees. However…*Official military sponsorship and assistance will be given the planning of picnics, summer outings, dances, and other pastimes and amusements…The Welfare Branch will be prepared to furnish lists of suitable locations, entertainment features available at the suggested places, and will give assistance in transportation problems.*

Bell Aircraft

Newsletters talked about recreational activities available to employees at military installations and manufacturing plants. At Bell, a sport/ recreation section covered at least one page per issue. Employees participated in horseshoe pitching, table tennis, archery, choir, holiday plays, volleyball, basketball, boxing, golf, baseball/softball, bowling, fencing, touch football, rod and gun clubs, dances, drama club, and so forth. Some recreational facilities were lighted so that the night shift could have some recreational time during their midnight lunch hour (*Bell Aircraft News*, September 17, 1943, p.2).

An acapella group of first shift singers – a quartet at first, then up to two-hundred individuals – sang during lunchtime to entertain other employees. Some listeners stated that listening to the old time tunes – many hymns – took the place of attending church; others said they just like to sing. The article, ***Noonday Singers Find Rest, Comfort in Song***, cited the many positive effects of this spontaneous group including a boost in morale, employees meeting more of their co-workers and creating lasting friendships, and just a more positive feeling in the plant (*Bell Aircraft News*, September 17, 1943, p. 1).

Not to be outdone, the second shift organized a group of singers as well and challenged the first shift singers: ***Second Shift Choir Challenges Noonday Church Hymn Singers*** (*Bell Aircraft News*, October 8, 1943, p. 1).

By March 1944, ***Stairway Singers Seek All-Woman Choral Group*** announced an application to the Bell Recreation Club to form a female chorus. Women were encouraged to send an AVO (Avoid Verbal Orders) written request to the welfare office (*Bell Aircraft News,* March 11, 1944, p. 4). This was an all-white women's group.

Recreation and time away from work for its employees was important to Bell management, but the announcement of time for holiday shopping came with a warning. ***PLANT TO CLOSE DEC. 16 FOR CHRISTMAS SHOPPERS: Move To Allow Employes*** {sic} ***Time To Buy Gifts*** was a front page headline in the Saturday issue just after Thanksgiving. Bell management said it…*truly appreciates…its workers' efforts and wanted to provide time for them to shop. It* (management) *also is done with the conviction that Bell employes* {sic} *will take advantage of the holiday and not be absent from work on other days when vital production of B-29s for the Pacific War is so vitally needed* (*Bell Aircraft News,* November 25, 1944, p. 1).

Bell expanded its recreation program in 1945 to include a large building to house a variety of indoor sports (*Bell Aircraft News,* February 24, 1945, p. 1).

I found one final article about women's recreational interests very humorous. ***Women's Recreation Interests Are Sought*** printed a check-off questionnaire for female employees to answer and return to the recreation office by intra-plant mail. My favorite is Ouija Board (*Bell Aircraft News,* July 13, 1945, p. 3).

> Women's Recreation Questionnaire
>
> Archery   Bridge   Croquet   Dancing   Darts
> Horseshoe   Ouija Board   Table Tennis   Shuffleboard
> Swimming   Tennis   Other activities

Goodyear Aircraft

The company created the position of director of recreation whose job it was to give everyone a chance to participate in some sport to keep physically fit so that they could do their job (*The Wingfoot Clan,* April 15, 1942, p. 8). Recreational activities required varying degrees of physical participation. Aircraft sponsored leagues in baseball, hockey, basketball, bowling, hard ball, horse shoe tossing, golf tournaments, and sponsored soap box derbies. Individuals were highlighted for horseback riding, ice skating, swimming, ping-pong, and personal hobbies. Art club and choruses were open to employees. Aircraft and its employees were involved in company-sponsored Boy Scouts, and Aircraft started the first Air Scout Troop in the nation. Most recreational activities were segregated by gender and ethnicity.

Women employees were allowed to attend Happy Days Camp in Virginia's Kendall Park: ***Weekly Camping Program for Aircraft Girls: Promises Unusually Fine Treat.*** At a cost of $3.00 those who applied could participate in this weekend camping program. Each would leave at 5 P.M. on a Saturday and return late Sunday, in time to return to work on Monday. The camp was open from July 11 to the end of August and offered…*nature walks, swimming, excellent food, and comfortable sleeping accommodations* (*The Wingfoot Clan*, June 16, 1943, p. 6).

Employee Newsletters: Diversity within the Workforce
Veteran Production Workers

I can only imagine the emotional impact on production workers as they stood next to or had lunch with a man who may have been in combat just a few months before becoming an employee himself. The range of emotions can only be surmised. I assume the stories added to the stress of a nation at war, and to the stress felt by each person working on the production line.

At Erie Proving Ground, ***EPG Chief Inspector Was Rifle Champion*** led into a long article about a World War I veteran who was a former First Lieutenant in the Ordnance Department, 2nd Army Corps, and who had substantial experience overseeing another proving ground. His expertise in rifle marksmanship was central to his many personal and professional credentials (*EPG Echo*, July 15, 1943, p. 6).

Bell Aircraft recognized the need to hire veterans from World War I and World War II and the corresponding need to retrain many who had been severely wounded in battle or, too old to fight, and needed skills retraining to work in a production facility.

Under-Age Veteran Now At Bell Tells of War In the Pacific Area quoted a young marine corporal who joined in 1941 when he was only sixteen years old. He had been in heavy combat against the Japanese. The article stated…*They (Allies) have learned to kill with all the cold-blooded cruelty which the Nips themselves made infamous, and they're doing it with gusto…*The corporal told a particularly gruesome story about how he killed a Japanese soldier who was stealing food (*Bell Aircraft News*, June 25, 1943, p. 1/ p. 3). I was surprised at the specific, and horrific, details included in this article. It read like a short horror story, and must have made an unforgettable impression on the readers. It certainly did for me.

A plant policeman recalled his horror of the Japanese attack on Pearl Harbor (December 7, 1941) in ***Survivor of Jap Raid Carries Vivid Memory of Pearl Harbor***. He was wounded while…*stationed with an air squadron at the time of the raids…*He and other wounded were found two days later…*they had survived on their emergency rations of hard tack, sardines and a half a canteen of water.* He was released from medical care including care for his severe shock, after eight and a half months. He joined Bell in May 1943 (*Bell Aircraft News*, October 22, 1943, p. 3).

Front Line to Production Line described those who…*for reasons of age and disability, have laid down their arms and taken up tools in the vital war production which sooner or later is expected to turn Axis dreams into nightmares.* The plant created a rehabilitation program to…*prepare and place them on jobs for which they are best fitted.* The company moved four or five veterans per day into production, most having come directly from their care in a hospital; no one was rejected (*Bell Aircraft News*, December 18, 1943, p. 1).

Right away the company announced that one World War I and World War II veteran Chief Petty Officer left the navy to lead Bell's police force (*Bell Aircraft News,* December 24, 1943, p. 3).

Three more examples of military veterans working in production are illustrative of their determination to continue to serve their country.

One marine corps veteran enlisted in 1940 and was honorably discharged…*for disabilities incurred in the Pacific area*…He was assigned to the aircraft carrier, USS *Hornet*, a ship that went down near Guadalcanal in the Pacific Theater (Battle of Guadalcanal was fought between August 7, 1942 and February 2, 1943). **Modification Worker Saw Doolittle's Men Take Off**, and described…*a swarm of birds flying toward the rising sun*…was an allusion to the Rising Sun logo of the Imperial Japanese Forces. The young serviceman witnessed Doolittle's Raiders take off from the *Hornet – the Tokyo express (April 1942)* (*Bell Aircraft News*, January 1, 1944, p. 3).

In early February 1944, two veterans – one from the Battle of Guadalcanal (Pacific) and the other from the Attu Campaign (Aleutian Islands) – were students at Bell's Training Center studying aircraft inspection. The marine who saw combat in the Pacific said he…*was sent to a New Zealand hospital with malaria, stomach trouble, and battle-shattered nerves*.

The ranger described the hard combat he faced in freezing conditions at Attu. In a 24-hour rest – after 11 days and nights in the snow – both his feet and hands were frozen. Each man had a message for their new co-workers about the need to continue buying War Bonds…*'Back the attack by buying bonds' aren't so many words. They're flesh and blood*…(*Bell Aircraft News,* February 5, 1944, p. 1).

The Battle of Attu was one of the deadliest in the war, second only to the battles at Iwo Jima. Attu Island is part of the Aleutian Islands off the coast of the Alaska. Twelve-thousand five-hundred U.S. soldiers battled to retake the island from the Japanese who had overrun the area from June 3-7, 1942. The battle took nineteen days, from May 11 to May 30, 1943, and claimed five-hundred forty-nine dead, one-thousand one-hundred forty-eight wounded, and one-thousand two-hundred severe cold injuries. The weather was responsible for more casualties than was enemy fire.

By February 1944, it was reported that a veterans' organization was being established to include any employee honorably discharged from any branch of service. It was estimated that Bell Aircraft employed several hundred ex-servicemen who might be interested in being…*developed into a potent force for the furtherance of civic and patriotic activities in this area* (*Bell Aircraft News,* February 12, 1944, p. 3).

Target, Rumania! was the headline over a photograph of a former master sergeant gunner on a B-24 *Liberator*. The front page headline, **Vet of 26 Bombing Missions Now Helping in Production,** told the story of a man who completed those missions in over one year of combat duty aboard the *Boomerang*. The brief article just touched on the successes of this one *Liberator*. At Bell, he worked as…*a preflight senior inspector in wings installation*…When in service, his military outfit bombed the oil refineries in

Ploesti, Romania. He joined Bell in mid-March 1944, after the Army stated he was too old (age 39) to continue with combat flying (*Bell Aircraft News,* April 22, 1944, p. 3).

One more example illustrates the publicly acknowledged horrors of war on individual Bell employees. A former air force tail gunner, who worked servicing and testing machine guns, told of his bailing out of *Sweet Adeline*, a B-17 *Flying Fortress* that caught fire while over the Mediterranean Sea. He spent fifty-four hours afloat with two other crewmembers. The tail gunner told of having nightmares in which he sees a German *Messerschmitt* (ME-Bf109) attack him as he is parachuting to safety. Four times the (dream) plane headed for him with its…*Nazi pilot in his impersonal oxygen mask, like a robot…*The Nazi pilot repeatedly waved off and did not fire on the tail gunner.

Apparently the nightmare was his reliving what actually happened as his plane, part of the last squadron to bomb the steel works at Terni, near Rome, headed for base in North Africa. They were attacked by fifteen ME-Bf109s. When he hit the water, the tail gunner, who could not swim, inflated his "Mae West" and was joined my one other crewmember for their hours together. Sick from all the salt water, a leg injury, and…*the emotional experience that he underwent coming down…*he was hospitalized until December 23, 1943. He joined Bell in January 1944 (*Bell Aircraft News*, March 11, 1944, p. 1/ p. 3).

The B-17 *Flying Fortress*, a four-engine heavy bomber, was given its name by a news reporter amazed at the number of machine guns on the plane. The B-17 dropped more bombs than any other aircraft during World War II.

On the front page of the January 1945 newsletter, a disabled four-year veteran technical sergeant from a B-17 *Flying Fortress* was taking electrical training, having injuries so severe from the final combat run of the bomber that he could not continue in the military. **Hero of 'Yankee Doodle' Crew Is 20,000th Trainee Inducted** summarized the man's heroic efforts: *he was a radioman/gunner for General Doolittle when the famed leader was first to bomb Rome…He has three Nazi planes to his credit – one Focke-Wulf 190 and two Messerschmidt 109s…He wears the Distinguished Flying Cross and the Air Medal with nine Oak Leaf Clusters.* His description of the final flight from Sicily back to base was graphic and detailed (*Bell Aircraft News,* January 27, 1945, p. 1).

At Goodyear, similar stories abound. In late spring 1945, an Army Air Force sergeant served as a ball turret gunner on a B-24 *Liberator*. He was wounded twice, and had been a POW in an internment camp in Romania. The headline, **Went Through Some Tough Experiences; Happy To Be Back**, says it all (*The Wingfoot Clan*, May 30, 1945, p. 3).

African American Production Workers

African Americans worked in defense plants across the nation, especially after President Franklin D. Roosevelt signed Executive Order 88022. It prohibited discrimination within the job sector. Discrimination occurred in defense plants and in the military nonetheless, by segregating employees by department or unit. Articles about

African Americans were quick to label them as "Negro" or "colored" to differentiate them and their work from other employees.

Erie Proving Ground

I found one article about an African American employee in the *EPG Echo* (July 15, 1943, p. 2), along with only five other brief references. In a column asking selected employees *What Shall I Do When the War is Won?*, one man, a former porter on the railroad, operated a tractor crane in Building 160. His son was a corporal stationed in Louisiana. This employee stated he would simply rejoice at the end of the war. A photograph of each employee who answered the question was attached.

Officers And Committees of EPG Civilian Clubs Plan Events was a short article with five group photos of local club officers. The Toledo Club's president and vice-president were African Americans (*EPG Echo*, July 29, 1943, p. 7).

A question about vacation plans and gas rationing was posed to a small, random group of seven employees including one male African American janitor (*EPG Echo*, July 1, 1943, p. 2). Another question-answer column asked employees about their pet peeves. Eight responded including an African American woman who drove a tractor crane for the 75 mm pack howitzer and assembled guns (*EPG Echo*, July 29, 1943, p. 2).

There were no feature articles about African American employees, although a head shot photograph accompanied the interview statements discussed above. The employees names were listed.

Bell Aircraft

Bell's Oldest Janitor Takes First Sick Leave told of an eight-year employee, who at age eighty-three, needed to take two weeks' sick leave. He claimed to be Bell's oldest employee and said…*my legs are not so strong…He needed to rest. He owned a small farm… and invests in war bonds through the payroll deduction plan* (*Bell Aircraft News*, July 23, 1943, p. 3). Based on other data, I assume this janitor was an African American.

There was apparent confusion as to the location of first aid stations and the recommended protocol for reporting to them to seek aid: get a permission slip from the supervisor and report directly to the aid station. An editorial, ***First Aid And Where To Get It***, specified the location of twelve first aid stations. They were placed close to where employees worked, near elevators or stairwells, in the plant hospital, and there was one for office workers (*Bell Aircraft News*, August 27, 1943, p. 2). The editorial emphasized the need for workers to use these services to avoid the occurrence of more complex illnesses (*i.e.*, infections).

Presumably, the first aid station for African Americans was placed close to where they worked, but the article did not specify. Although Bell Aircraft hired African Americans, their lower status among workers was revealed in a brief notice: ***First Aid Station For Colored Employees.*** The chief of the medical department announced the opening and its location in…*Tunnel No. 3, B-1 building*. He went on to state that…*competent Negro registered nurses will be in charge of this new station* (*Bell Aircraft News*, September 3, 1943, p. 3). The tunnel system constructed between buildings within the Bell campus was used to transport food from a main kitchen to a cafeteria or to use by employees who needed to go to another building.

In another article, singled out for special recognition were eighteen women employees in the…*Negro unit of the finishing department.* **Negro Employes** {sic} **Give War Bond** described the actions of a group who gave a $25 War Bond to the Carrie Steele-Pitts Home for Negro Children after…*passing the hat around last payday* (*Bell Aircraft News*, December 11, 1943, p. 3).

Among the many articles about the cafeteria at Bell Aircraft, this small one, **B-1 Cafeterias to Begin Staggered Plan Monday,** mentioned that the four cafeterias in the B-1 building would start a staggered eating plan so that there was ample food for everyone. Passes were issued to all employees. *To bring them nearer centers of activity, tunnel cafeterias will be operated in B-2, B-4, B-5 and <u>B-6, the latter for colored workers</u>* {author's emphasis} (*Bell Aircraft News,* September 17, 1943, p.2).

In one November 1943 issue, a series of three photographs of African-American workers appeared on page three. ***It Goes In Here and It Comes Out There*** showed workers feeding scrap metal into a baling machine. Processing turned salvage in to 68-pound briquettes which were shipped to another location for reworking and use again in war production…*against the Axis*. The workers in each photo are African-American (*Bell Aircraft News*, November 5, 1943, p. 3). Three digitized photographs provided by Kennesaw State University depict African-American men involved in waste removal, collecting scrap to be shredded, and shredding scrap at Bell.

A photograph of a uniformed Joshua Watson, Seaman 2nd Class and a former Aircrafter in final assembly, Plant C, appeared with this caption: ***At Camp Peary***. His sister worked as a janitor and his father was employed in Plant 1, although the brief announcement did not say what he did (*The Wingfoot Clan*, February 2, 1944, p. 6).

A photo of an adorable seven-year-old African American girl appeared with this caption: ***Singer-Dancer***. Her mother worked in…*Dept. 836, janitors' service, Plant C*. She was clearly proud of her child (*The Wingfoot Clan*, February 9, 1944, p. 3).

Negro Workers Continue Fine Presentee {sic} ***Records in Plant*** was an editorial in on July 22, 1944 (*Bell Aircraft News*, p. 2). *Two Negro workers are pointing the way for their fellows in the janitorial department by building up enviable presentee* {sic} *records*. On the job every day for fifteen months, this female employee's sons served in the war; one was a fighter pilot in the U.S. Army Air Force, the other in the marines. After praising her employment record as a maid in the hangar building, Emma O'Neal was quoted as saying…*I get a real kick out of making things comfortable for the people I serve…first, because they are such fine people, and second, because I feel that in serving them I am helping to win the war*.

In August, an article delineated the skills and contributions provided by African

American workers. ***Negroes Show Skill In Plant*** said about one-thousand three-hundred "Negroes" were employed at Bell, of whom...*250 men and women area actively engaged in metal fabrication...Many of the women have acquired skill in stack drilling and routing, while others have proved adept in handling parts to be heat treated.* Later the article said there were two-hundred thirty-one...*Negro janitors and 307 maids...cleaning nearly 100 acres of floor space and 39 miles of cat-walks. Also they...separate metal and standard parts from sweepings and put them into salvage barrels, and to put aside all waste paper that can be baled and sold for reclamation.* These employees were praised for their...*record for being punctual at work is very satisfactory and the Negro employes {sic} have participated 100 percent in all War Bond campaigns* (Bell Aircraft News, August 13, 1944, p. 4).

Routine contests were established between departments to rank groups of employees in War Bond purchases. Overall purchases by employees were touted in other articles. That the African Americans were singled out by ethnicity in addition to their jobs in the janitorial department is telling of a time in this country when other employees needed to be assured that hiring diverse individuals was acceptable. From mid-summer 1944 through 1945, camera crews photographed workers at their machines to create photo collages that revealed more about assembly work than previous issues had done. ***Lens-Eye View of Bell's Training Program*** included ten group photographs of employees learning more skills. Photo *10* shows at least twenty African American company trainees, both male and female, being instructed at Booker T. Washington High School in Atlanta (Bell Aircraft News, December 23, 1944, p. 8). Established in 1924, it was the first public high school for African American students in Georgia and within the Atlanta Public School system.

Negro Sports, Song Programs Are Expanded stated in the first line: *Negro employes {sic} of the Georgia division are expanding their recreation program.* The chorus worked under the direction of the director of music from Booker T. Washington High School. Both male and female (*girls*) employees made up the teams from the first and second shifts; they played at the...*colored Y.M.C.A., Atlanta.* The players were identified by name and indicated many had played in high school and college (Bell Aircraft News, January 20, 1945, p. 6). Negro spirituals were often sung by white-only choruses.

Another example of the racial segregation of employees was found in ***Cafeteria Kitchen Scenes*** a collage of nine photographs showing kitchen workers and diners. Each employee was identified by name and task. Photo *6* shows African American women alongside white females assembling various types of salad. In photo *7*, nine African American women preparing vegetables for cooking are supervised by a white woman (Bell Aircraft News, March 10, 1945, p. 8).

The Negro Chorus of Department 86, first shift, was credited with opening a program...*with several songs*...that lauded the workers for exceeding their production schedule in ***Quotas Beaten for Sixth Month***. *At the conclusion of their well-received recital, Carmichael* (General Manager, James Vinson Carmichael) *announced that their department had bought 226 per cent of its quota in the early stages of the Seventh War Loan drive* (Bell Aircraft News, May 5, 1945, p. 1/ p. 4).

Family Day was a huge event for the aircraft workers and their family members in 1945 as this was the first time families could see the B-29 up close (seventeen thousand family members attended). *Family Day Scenes* was a collage of ten photographs showing parents and children visiting various areas in the aircraft production complex. Photographs *9* and *10* depicted African American families and photo *10* named the worker, his twin daughters, and his wife as they smiled and posed below the nose of a B-29 (*Bell Aircraft News*, July 20, 1945, p. 4).

Goodyear Aircraft

Of the hundreds of articles about Goodyear Aircraft workers, only a smattering of those were about, or depicted in a photo, employees who were African Americans. Only six percent of all employees in the aircraft industry were African Americans. The need for workers temporarily broke down some racial barriers in defense plants, although discrimination against African Americans in general continued.

Tosses First Ball From Top of Dock was the caption over a photograph of Stan Junius, a star halfback for Central, University of Akron and the South Akron Awnings for twelve years. This African American opened the Aircraft softball season (*The Wingfoot Clan*, June 18, 1941, p. 4). Later in September, Junius was applauded for wining a special 50-yard dash in competition with another employee (*The Wingfoot Clan*, September 3, 1941, p. 4). The company sponsored a baseball team throughout the war.

Two janitors were cited as ***Two Negro Workers Happy At Tennis***…*on the colored championship tennis team*…One was a member of the Akron colored team, and one would return to Akron University in the fall (*The Wingfoot Clan*, August 6, 1941, p. 4).

A photograph of the twelve-man Aircraft softball team included two African Americans. Each member of the team was identified by name: ***These Lads Brought Home the Bacon*** (*The Wingfoot Clan*, September 17, 1941, p. 4).

Two smiling African American men, who were identified by name, were commanders of Commando units, part of the Emergency Defense Corps at Aircraft: ***Commandos? Yes, Sir, At Aircraft*** (*The Wingfoot Clan*, September 23, 1942, p. 4).

Over the photograph of a smiling two-year-old African American girl was this caption: ***She's Greeter***. She was the daughter of G. M. Walker, a Goodyear Aircraft chauffer (*The Wingfoot Clan,* December 2, 1942, p. 2).

Ninety-three percent of Aircraft employees participated in the 1942 War Bond Drive. ***$500 War Bond Is Beasley's Gift To Nine-Year-Old Son: "Will Come In Handy For Son's Education, Says Father."*** This African American had been employed for one year as a driver of an interplant bus…*There's no better investment than one of Uncle Sam's War Bonds*…he said (*The Wingfoot Clan*, December 23, 1942, p. 11).

The award-winning basketball team was feted at a banquet in their honor at a local hotel. A photo at the top of the page was captioned ***Awards Made To Champion Basketball Team***. Included in those identified was Tommy Field, manager of the Aircraft Aces, an African American man, and Bonnie Spring, a captain of the ***Wonder***

Gals of Plant C girls' champions (*The Wingfoot Clan*, April 28, 1943, p. 8).

Later in my research when I went back through the newsletters, I found **Five Capable Grandmothers Are Janitorial Supervisors** who supervised the work of the maids in the plant and were lauded for their role as grandmothers; none was African American (*The Wingfoot Clan*, July 2, 1943, p. 3).

A large photo of the men's softball team all identified by name - sixteen men, three of whom were African American - won the Aircraft softball championship. The photo's caption stated: **General Stores Team Takes Championship** (*The Wingfoot Clan*, September 1, 1943, p. 8).

Gossip was part of each issue of the newsletter in a column called **More News Gathered While Roaming Over Plant D**. Of note in early October was **Three Negro Girls Simply Await "Day"** that talked about the wedding dreams of three women who worked in Dept. 670, pre-assembly, Plant D3. *Occasionally they strike up a song and their co-workers say the three make a fine trio.* One of the three was quoted: *We all like it here. Folks are fine, work isn't hard and we are make some money with which to buy War Bonds* (*The Wingfoot Clan*, October 6, 1943, p. 7).

That issue carried more news: **Lawdy, I'll Be Glad When I Get T-Bone** declared Roy Roland, janitor, who had just had all his teeth removed and was living on soft foods and liquids. A one-and-a-half year employee in Plant D3, he said he longed for pork shops and steaks (*The Wingfoot Clan*, October 6, 1943, p. 7).

One of the first articles I found about African Americans working at Goodyear was in an October 1943 issue. It highlighted a female employee who had three sons in the military: army tank division, the navy, and the air corps. There was a photograph of each of the servicemen. She worked in Plant D as a janitor. She received a letter containing significant praise from the navy about her son; the letter was printed in total. Briefly, it praised his leadership ability, his academics, and…*considers him an inspiration to his shipmates* (*The Wingfoot Clan*, October 13, 1943, p. 6).

A photo of a seven-year-old African American girl was in February 9, 1944, with a short article describing the child as…*a graceful dancer and a good singer.* Her mother worked in janitorial services (*The Wingfoot Clan*, February 9, 1944, p.3).

Increase Pledge was the caption over a photograph of an African American woman janitor who increased her War Bond purchase during the Fourth War Loan drive. Her daughter also worked at the plant, while her husband was in the armed forces (*The Wingfoot Clan*, February 16, 1944, p. 3).

Articles or letters from servicemen were published in the newsletters. In 1944, the Allies were making headway over the Japanese in the South Pacific, and one serviceman sent a photo of himself seated below a carved depiction of a woman wearing a halter top and short shirt. He had carved the statue from a palm tree and decorated it with makeup, a bracelet, and painted nails so she would appear as a "lady." He named her *Empress Augusta*, and said he carved her so that he would have someone to talk to. He said…*The 'empress' is the only white 'woman' on the island…* (**Not One Woman On**

Island, Neis Wonger Carves One Out Of Tree "To Talk To", The Wingfoot Clan, March 22, 1944, p. 7). He praised the *Corsairs*, which he called *Whistlin' Willies*.

There was a photograph of one young uniformed African American man, under the caption that read: **"Sam" Is Overseas**. He was a former storeroom employee. Other family members worked at Aircraft: an aunt in the janitorial services, and an uncle in truck transportation (The Wingfoot Clan, May 10, 1944, p. 3).

Child care was provided for defense plant workers: **Child Care Centers Watch Over Children While Mothers Are Busy On Jobs In War Industries**. One of the accompanying photos showed two African American children washing their hands; other photos showed children eating, and playing (The Wingfoot Clan, July 5, 1944, p. 2).

A photograph of a ten-month old African American boy appeared in January 17, 1945, under the caption, **Daddy In France**. The father, Walter M. Hunt, was a corporal in the Quartermaster Corps, his mother was employed in boom assembly, while his grandfather was employed in Dept. 251, janitorial services, Plant A-B (The Wingfoot Clan, January 17, 1945, p. 8).

Sixteen Have Perfect Attendance Record In 1944 Materials Division. Of the sixteen listed, three are women, and two of these are African Americans (The Wingfoot Clan, February 7, 1945, p. 4).

In the March 7, 1945, issue of The Wingfoot Clan was the caption, **On Assembly Line**, over a photograph of a young African American woman. The article stated that she was…*a member of one of the oldest Negro families in Akron, Grace {Carrington} is employed on the assembly line in Dept. 393, pre-assembly Plant B. She has participated in the suggestion program at Aircraft and has collected cash for her efforts*. The article went on to mention her husband who worked in Plant C, her sister in pre-assembly, and two nephews who served in the armed forces. This was the longest article I found about African Americans at Goodyear Aircraft (p. 6).

Traveling minstrels were entertainers in the early half of the 20th Century. **He'll Sing Again** was the headline caption over a photograph of a white man in "black face." He was…*featured as end-man in the minstrel show to be given in Goodyear Theater April 6 and 7* (The Wingfoot Clan, April 4, 1945, p. 3).

Goodyear Aircraft held a company-wide picnic in August 1945. Among the thirty-thousand people attending, one African American family of five was photographed, dressed up with picnic baskets in hand. The man worked in Plant C machine shop (The Wingfoot Clan, August 22, 1945, p. 6).

American Indian Production Workers

Erie Proving Ground

I found no reference to American Indian workers at Erie Proving Ground. However, given the history of tribes from Ohio, I find it difficult to believe that there were no American Indian workers at EPG.

Bell Aircraft

In *Plant Life*, a cartoon series, a caricature of an American Indian man, in traditional regalia, is seen standing in front of his teepee using a garden hose to water his vegetable garden. The sign posted next to the dwelling states: ***Chief Waterspout / Rainmaker / Victory Gardens a Specialty***. Though typical of the time, this depiction is all too tiresome (*Bell Aircraft News*, April 8, 1944, p. 2).

Another article's opening line is: *Cherokee Indians are a peaceable tribute, but they've always known how to get on the warpath when the course of human events makes it necessary.* The article quoted an aircraft assembler who informed his co-workers that two thousand of his tribesmen, noted as legally residing in North Carolina's Cherokee reservation, serve in the armed forces. He went on to say…*you'll find that in every war, Indians have taken part. This country is their home, and they want to help all they can.* At the end of the piece, the writer reminded workers that…*Harris hates like everything to disappoint folks, but he has always spoken English and not an Indian dialect. He does not greet paleface friends by saying "How!" and he does not say "Ugh" at all* (*Bell Aircraft News*, November 18, 1944, p. 4). It must have been a recurring struggle for acceptance by Native American workers.

Goodyear Aircraft

The company acknowledged the presence of American Indian employees with ***Austin Buckles, Sioux Indian Employed at Aircraft, Has Pipe Smoked by Sitting Bull; Booster of Native State, Montana***. The article reported that Aircraft contained a veritable…*melting pot…practically all nationalities are represented*. The employee from Montana went on to educate readers about life in his home state. Clearly, this was an article meant to rid readers of pre-existing notions of life in the "Wild West." The author was sure to emphasize that Buckles was…*a full-blooded Sioux Indian* (*The Wingfoot Clan*, January 21, 1942, p. 1).

A photo of a smiling woman had this headline: ***Choctaw Indian Woman At Aircraft*** was an inspector in B-26 pre-assembly, Plant B. To introduce her to her co-workers, she was identified as…*first of her race at Aircraft…she attended a government boarding school at Chilocco, Okla., and Wheelock Academy, an Indian girls' school at Millerton, Okla.* She also had training as an x-ray technician and had worked as a nurse (*The Wingfoot Clan*, September 9, 1942, p. 7). While the information was very newsy, it decried the destruction of a culture that occurred in boarding schools designed for American Indian children.

An unfortunate article, and one meant to be humorous, was merely derisive in its alluding to American Indians. The story described a social gathering at a bar of a group of employees from one department. The vocabulary used to describe the bar patrons was typical and ethnocentric: chief, wampum, warrior, brave, squaw, papoose, loin cloth, teepee, and pipe of peace (*The Wingfoot Clan*, May 12, 1943, p. 3).

In May 1945 three *Heroes Of Iwo Jima Flag-Raising Visit Aircraft While on Tour Of Bond Rallies* were photographed and identified by name. However, the wrong man in the photo was identified as an American Indian; it should have been Pfc. Ira H. Hayes (Pima Native American), and not Pfc. Rene Gagnon who was labeled… *a full blooded Indian* (*The Wingfoot Clan*, May 23, 1945, p. 2).

Sightless Production Workers

Erie Proving Ground

I found no reference to the employment of blind individuals at EPG.

Bell Aircraft

Typically, riveting is a two-person team effort and a rhythm is established as they work together. The team cannot stop when a rivet is dropped. To this day, dropped rivets are reclaimed at the end of a shift, cleaned, resorted, and put back into stock.

I was surprised when I found articles about the hiring of blind people to work in defense plants; I had not considered this possible. *Sightless Workers Valuable In Sorting Scrambled Rivets* changed my perspective in a long article describing in detail the training of seven sightless men learning a job of sorting rivets by size…*which is one of the countless little jobs that add up to the super-bomber*. Employees who riveted often dropped rivets which were swept up at the end of a shift. These needed to be sorted by size, types, lengths, and materials. The job took three steps and was completed by a team of two brothers, a husband and wife, and three others. Praised by their supervisors for their excellent and patient work, the last line in the article read: *Theirs are 70 more fingers around the Axis' neck* (*Bell Aircraft News*, May 6, 1944, p. 3).

Goodyear Aircraft

Although Blind, They Contribute Their Part To War Effort was the headline showing a photograph of three men and two women workers in the machine shop where they did final hand-finishing (deburring and filing) on machined parts (*The Wingfoot Clan*, September 6, 1944, p. 2).

In a reminder to all employees to purchase War Bonds, blind employees were highlighted: **Blind Men Good Workers; Each Has 25 Percent of Wages Deducted for Bonds**. The men worked in Goodyear's Newark Plant (New Jersey) burring and other operations in the machine shop…*with such rapidity and finesse that they amaze their fellow workers* (*The Wingfoot Clan*, October 20, 1943, p. 7).

"Deaf-Mute" Production Workers

Erie Proving Ground

The archives technician at Gallaudet University indicated there was no sign of any deaf club or organization in Port Clinton, although there was one a few miles away in Toledo. Two deaf Ohioans were active in placing deaf people at Goodyear and elsewhere, but there was no indication that placements occurred at Camp Perry or Erie Proving Ground. Gallaudet cautioned: the absence of evidence is not evidence of absence.

Bell Aircraft

Deaf employees were used in wing assembly at Bell Aircraft. ***Deaf To Assist In Dealing Woe to Hitler, Et Al*** headlined an article that described the employment of between four-hundred and seven-hundred deaf people at the plant. March 1, 1944, was their "day one." Georgia State School for the Deaf estimated there were seven-hundred to eight-hundred deaf persons in Georgia suitable for the work (*Bell Aircraft News*, February 19, 1944, p. 1).

Silent but determined men are beginning to take over some of the noisiest jobs in the whole Bell Bomber Plant was the lead sentence in ***Quiet Men Handle Noisy Tools***. An expanding group of "deaf-mutes" were trained to work in wing assembly where the noise from rivet guns was greatest. They used sign language and lip-reading to communicate. *Our deaf employes {sic} are anxious to learn and eager to work…Nothing seems to distract them from the job in hand* (*Bell Aircraft News*, April 8, 1944, p. 1).

There was a group photograph of six deaf employees receiving an orientation from the plant's Personnel Counselor through a sign language interpreter. ***Group Can't Hear Own Clatter But Japs to Hear From Them*** describes the workers, between seventeen and twenty-one, hired in wing assembly, their first jobs. They were touted by their supervisor: *They are all swell workers…they work hard and conscientiously – every one of them* (*Bell Aircraft News*, July 15, 1944, p. 3). While praising these workers, their difference from other workers, and the need to describe them as good at what they do, seems both to educate hearing workers and to justify their being hired. Bell Aircraft was dedicated to hiring a diverse workforce. The tone of the article is typical of the time, but may seem patronizing to current readers.

Company management wanted greater communication between hearing and hearing impaired workers, so the newsletter printed a series of eight photographs showing a woman signing a few words of everyday expressions such as: wait, good morning, I like you, sweet, thank you, yes/no, and Japs. The caption for the photo ***Sign Language*** provided instructions on how to make the hand signals. The sign for "Japs" was a finger pulling one's eyebrow up and outward. The caption ended with a request…*Mutes would like it if others would learn a few simple signs and the alphabet* (*Bell Aircraft News*, July 29, 1944, p. 3).

Deaf Employes {sic} *Ideally Suited To Wings Work* described the preparation of wing panels and bulkheads completed by deaf employees in an area of the plant that was very noisy. Hearing employees wore earplugs to cut down on the racket of rivet guns. About fifty deaf employees were in this section. *They are envied by their fellow workers and have gained recognition as a most efficient unit in the battalion of Bell bomber builders* (Bell Aircraft News, February 17, 1945, p. 3).

A group of men…*Smiling at the cameraman are some of the deaf-mutes who work unmindful of the terrific din*. Each of the eleven men was identified by name in this collage of nine photographs taken of men and women working together (**Operations in Depts. 38-0, 38-3 and 38-4**, Bell Aircraft News, February 17, 1945, p. 8).

Goodyear Aircraft

Goodyear Aircraft also hired "deaf-mute" employees. **Thirty Members of 'Silents' Group Not To Be Outdone On Production** was the headline over an interesting article about both male and female employees working on the second shift in wing assembly. The production quota for wing assembly was four wings in a shift. The *Silents* made five in one shift and did not brag about it. So, first shift in wing assembly, all hearing employees, did the same thing and bragged about it by posting their work on a bulletin board. Second shift then did six wings, but had to clock out to complete the task, as overtime was not authorized. The supervisor said…*Of course, the Silents have boys in the service, too, same as the rest of us. It's their war, too* (The Wingfoot Clan, February 2, 1944, p. 6). I found the supervisor's comment smarmy.

Silents To Have First Aid Class was a boxed in announcement on the front page letting readers know that a ten-week evening class would be held for employees who could not hear…*and will be composed entirely of silents with a silent instructor* (The Wingfoot Clan, April 21, 1943, p. 1).

The United States Senate became interested in how well "deaf-mute" workers performed in war industries. A Senate investigating committee held a hearing and were told of the work *Silents* did on the B-29 *Superfortress*, P-61 *Black Widow*, and the FG-1 *Corsair*. In **Silent Worker Appears Before Body of Senate**, the writer explained that ninety percent of the *Silents* in the United States were gainfully employed when war came, and this experience made it easy for them to adapt to a new industry (The Wingfoot Clan, September 20, 1944, p. 2).

Mary Merrow Figures Prominently As An Interpreter In Aircraft's Plants. She was a special union steward for the *Silents*, and had been a teacher at the State School of the Deaf. She had deaf parents (The Wingfoot Clan, September 27, 1944, p 2).

A small announcement appeared in the November 15, 1944 issue: **For Silents League** asked to form a *Silents* basketball league (The Wingfoot Clan, p. 6).

Midget Production Workers

Aunt Monnie's home town newspaper, *Osakis Review*, printed a short article about the manner in which midgets were employed by aircraft manufacturers to get into spaces inaccessible to bigger employees (*Osakis Review*, Local News, June 17, 1943).

Erie Proving Ground

I found no mention of midgets being hired at Erie Proving Ground.

Bell Aircraft

There was a special promotion announced in the August 1943 front page: **Four Midgets Sought For Tight Spaces In Plane Production**…*Applicants must be true midgets with slender hips and shoulders enabling them to work in small spaces inaccessible to regular sized aircraft workers. Men are preferred but women will be considered*…The company employment office was canvassing circuses, side-shows, and carnivals looking for recruits…*for this important operation* (*Bell Aircraft News*, August 27, 1943, p. 1).

Signing Up was the caption under a large photograph of the…*first midget to join the bomber plant personnel. Three others are being sought*…to work in final assembly (*Bell Aircraft News*, September 3, 1943, p. 3).

Bell hired at least two midget employees, brothers who worked in final assembly. They were photographed picking cotton, a commodity needed in the production of military apparel and munitions. They picked cotton because so many field hands had joined the military that local farmers put out a call for workers. They would have picked cotton after their shift at the plant. Interestingly, the caption pointed out that… *They have between them 10 children, all standard size* (*Bell Aircraft News*, October 1, 1943, p. 2). I thought the final comment was unnecessary.

Goodyear

Mary Alice Just a Little Short For Clock Card Racks talks about the first woman midget at Aircraft. She and her husband, who was also employed, had been circus performers (*The Wingfoot Clan*, December 2, 1942, p. 2).

"Bobby" Shields Is Little But He Does Get Around was the lead caption over a photograph of a male midget, eighteen and 4'5" tall. A high school educated man with excellent math skills, he worked on K-ships (blimps) getting into spaces too narrow for other workers to reach (*The Wingfoot Clan*, May 19, 1943, p. 2).

Employee Newsletters: Belittling the Enemy
War Department Communicates With Production Workers

High ranking military men and representatives of the War Department often sent telegrams to defense plant employees to thank them for their production efforts. These messages were much touted by the editors of employee newsletters, and the personal wording of each telegram was designed to speak directly to individual workers.

On May 27, 1942, the front-page headlines of *The Wingfoot Clan – Akron Edition* contained a personal message to aircraft employees from Brigadier General James A. Doolittle, who led Doolittle's Raiders on a bombing run over Tokyo on April 18, 1942. The action served as a boost to American morale after the Japanese attack on Pearl Harbor. General Doolittle praised the aircraft workers like this:

"We Bombed Tokio {sic} With Bombers You Helped Build"

So Says Brigadier General JAMES H. DOOLITTLE In Telegram to Goodyear

Following Is Message Daring Flier Sends To Employees Of Our Company

Now it can be told officially: We bombed Tokio {sic} in the North American bombers you helped build. Each plane performed magnificently, racing to its objective just over the housetops, then shooting up a few hundred feet to drop the bombs.

Our planes easily outmaneuvered the Japanese pursuit ships. Every bomb seems to smash into its target. Flames poured from the military and naval installations and one salvo made a direct hit on a new warship under construction.

We flew low enough at times to see the surprised look on faces in Tokio {sic} and other Japanese cities.

Every one of the seventy-nine men on the flight joins me in praising the B-25. The Jap planes couldn't do a thing to stop us. They will never stop us if you keep up your great work.

JAMES H. DOOLITTLE, Brigadier General, U. S. Army Air Force

The Wingfoot Clan – Akron Edition, May 27, 1942, p. 1

This North American B-25 bomber, similar to the type used to bomb Tokyo, has established a unique combat record in several war theaters. Lieutenant General Henry H. Arnold, deputy chief of staff for air, said the B-25 can "go farther, faster, and carry more bombs than the best ships of our enemy"
October 1942
Palmer, Alfred T., photographer
Library of Congress photo

A week later, on June 3, 1942, the date of the Battle of Midway, *The Wingfoot Clan Aircraft Edition's* huge front page banner led into a telegram sent by General Henry H. "Hap" Arnold, Commanding General of the U. S. Army Air Force. It reads:

PRAISES WORK AT AIRCRAFT
"YOU TURN THEM OUT; OUR FLIERS WILL OWN THE AIR."

The Telegram Printed Below Came From the Commander of the Army Air Force, Praising Work Done at Aircraft In Program Designed To Put Japanese Out Of Business

---

Washington, D.C., May 30, 1942

Goodyear Aircraft Corporation
Akron, Ohio

Reports to the Army from the southwest Pacific reveal the definite superiority, over Japanese war planes, of the Martin Bomber you build. The operational commander of one of our advanced northern bombing bases says:

"The Martin Bombers have speed and firing power enough to be self-sufficient and are able to raid over heavily protected enemy territory without fighter protection. The B-26, in large numbers combined with fighter planes, could throw an almost impregnable aerial screen over the southwest Pacific."

Getting those large numbers of B-26 bombers depends on you who make them. You turn out and our fliers will own the air. Together we'll smash the Japanese.

LT. GENERAL ARNOLD
Commanding Army Air Force

Anti-Japanese Rhetoric

Not unusual in a time of war, enemy combatants often were portrayed as not-quite-human, their exploits derided, their battle successes were downplayed, news about them as individuals was negative, and sometimes stories were provided by an employee's son or husband. None of these portrayals was flattering. I found only one article that placed Japanese Americans, *Nesei*, in a flattering light.

One woman, a secretary for two tobacco companies, worked in Japan for twenty-two years. She had been interned at Kobe, Japan. The article quoted her as believing the Japanese were terrified of an aerial bombing. In ***Japs Love of Death Not***

Shown At Home, Says Ex-internee compared the home front Japanese as not having the same courage as their soldiers. The first sentence depicted Japanese fighters in derogatory terms: *The banzai-screaming Japanese warrior, who prefers disembowelment or some other fancy means of self-destruction to the dishonor of capture, has no counterpart in his brothers on the home front* (*Bell Aircraft News*, January 20, 1945, p. 6).

Erie Proving Ground

I found no reference to the Japanese or the Pacific Theater in the *EPG Echo*.

Bell Aircraft

The stock column, ***Bellorama***, contained bits and pieces of news about Bell employees. One American soldier wrote to his wife: *In a bloodstained letter from her overseas husband, Frances Waldron, Final Assembly, received some pictures of a Japanese family. Most of the children were in native dress, but one little girl wore what appeared to be an American sailor's middy. The pictures were taken by Sgt. Waldron from the body of a son of heaven who had gone where all bad Japs go when they die. Waldron hopes to help plenty more get there – he's fighting on Bougainville Island* (*Bell Aircraft News*, January 8, 1944, p. 2).

Goodyear Aircraft

One September newsletter contained a particularly damming editorial with this caption under a large photo of Japanese soldiers marching a group of captured American servicemen: *This photograph came out of Japan by way of neutral countries. Japanese say it was taken at Corregidor. It shows the gaunt, weary heroes of America's defense of the Philippines 'being marched away to captivity after the fall of Corregidor.'* The Battle of Corregidor was on May 5/6, 1942, and was part of the Japanese conquest of the Philippine Islands.

The editorial went on with words that fairly shout at the reader: *Note the smirking Jap soldier on the left! Does it make your blood boil? Does it make you want to do everything within your power to avenge this humility to our boys and our colors?*

The editorial talked about free labor in the United States and its responsibility to keep working hard. However, I can only imagine the greater impact of this photo had there been an American soldier in the picture who was related to a defense plant worker. The trauma of war depicted on the faces of the men in the photo brought the realities of war to the attention of home front workers (*The Wingfoot Clan*, September 2, 1942, p. 5).

By far the most pointed anti-Japanese sentiment was depicted publicly in Goodyear's *The Wingfoot Clan* in late spring 1942, during a six-week contest for employees. A large cartoon showing a Japanese soldier, whose facial features were exaggerated by the cartoonist (*e.g.*, buck teeth, extremely slanted eyes, spikey hair, and thick glasses), was accompanied by an empty "bubble" so that employees could suggest what he might be saying. The ***Nippo-Nazi Say*** contest was initiated on April 15. 1942, and ended on June 30, 1942. It was touted an unbelievable success.

Set in historic context, the first six months of 1942 had already witnessed the initial bombing of Tokyo by Doolittle's Raiders, and battles in the Pacific including the invasion and conquering of the Philippine Islands, Andaman Islands, and Burma, and battles in the central Pacific including the Solomon Islands Campaign, the Battle of Java Sea, the Battle of Coral Sea and the Battle of Midway. Employees had begun to receive information about the take-over of the Goodyear rubber plantations in the East Indies and the imprisonment of company employees/ families in Japanese internment camps, and about battles in which some employees had already lost loved ones. Tension was high, prejudice was rife, and the country as a whole was angry and frightened. The contest suggestions, in microcosm, reflect those national feelings.

In March 1942, one-hundred ten-thousand to one-hundred twenty-thousand Japanese American citizens were removed from their homes and businesses and relocated into ten internment camps in Montana, New Mexico, and North Dakota. The camps were euphemistically referred to as "War Relocation Camps." Canada and Mexico also interned their Japanese residents. Their plight has been much documented by other historians, anthropologists, and psychologists during and since their incarceration. The internment was massive, a result of fear and envy. That the contest described below began the next month cannot be a coincidence, but rather a calculated plan to manipulate feelings of antipathy toward the Japanese by American workers.

Nippo-Nazi Contest For Aircrafters encouraged participation: *Every aircraft employee will want to be in on this Nippo-Nazi Contest! It's novel! It's different!* The article provided guidelines for this six-week contest and said that the newsletter would print accepted phrases and print them on a *Nippo-Nazi* poster (28" x 42") with the name of the author of the winning phrases. The guidelines cautioned that the suggested words needed to be relevant to the employee's department, there was a ten-word maximum, and winners would be announced weekly. A form was printed in the newsletter and later the form was separately printed and placed around the plant.

```
┌ ─  ─  ─  ─  ─  ─  ─  ─  ─  ─  ─  ─  ─  ─ ┐
│              MY NIPPO-NAZI SAYING            │
│  ..........................................................................  │
│   Yes, my saying is original                 │
│  ..........................................................................  │
│   Name                              Dept.    │
│  ..........................................................................  │
│   Clock No                          Shift    │
│  ..........................................................................  │
└ ─  ─  ─  ─  ─  ─  ─  ─  ─  ─  ─  ─  ─  ─ ┘
```

Within one week, on page three of the April 22, 1942, edition, a narrow column's headline read: *Suggestion Contest Arouses Much Interest*. A second contest entry form was printed and five prizes were awarded for the following suggestions:

- o   "Make slippy in Shippy, be happy for Jappy."
- o   "You take nap; it will help Jap."
- o   "Me like haphazard inspection; will lead to Allies' subjection"
- o   "A slacker is my backer."
- o   "Less paint spread, less chance to spread Allied victory."

On April 29, 1942, the page three winning suggestions were:

- o   "Worky pokey – okey dokey."
- o   "Sneak smoke, slow work, maybe burn shop, sank you."
- o   "No drop hammers go, no drop bombs on Tokio" {sic}.
- o   "Work less, talk more; that's what me waiting for."
- o   "Waste time now for Uncle Sam; work someday for me."

On May 6, 1942, the page five headline said: *Workers Turn In 308 Nippo-Nazi Saying In a Week: Poster Show In Various Departments of Plants at Aircraft*. Clearly, there was intense interest in this contest and the wording expresses frustration, heightened fear and tries to encourage greater production efforts. These were the winners:

- o   "More you fool, surer I rule."
- o   "He who works like a sap, works for a Jap."
- o   "Aircraft shirker, Nippo-Nazi worker."
- o   "Men slow pokio, makes greater Tokio" {sic}.
- o   "Today you sleep, tomorrow you weep."
- o   "You work too slow, I come before snow."

By May 13, 1942, the page two headline was: *Those Sayings By Nippo-Nazi Keep Rolling In – Interest Increases Weekly In Contest For Workers At Aircraft.* The selection committee expressed difficulty in sorting out the best five or six entries each week. This third week of the contest awarded prizes for the following suggestions that were printed in upper and lower case:

- o   "Don't Buy Bonds, Wear Ours."
- o   "Me Like Kick In Plants, Thank You."
- o   "You Killee Time, I Killee You."
- o   "Man Who Sits on Fannie Helps Japanie."
- o   "You Go Slow On Job Please; Me Catch Up."

Nippo-Nazi "Sayings" Contest Is Rolling Along With Many Entries was the headline on page four of the May 20, 1942, edition. Nearly five-hundred additional entries had been submitted since the previous week. Employees who won suggested these phrases:

- "So Happy To see You Late Today, My Little Helper."
- "Wear Tires Thin, Help Me Win."
- "Thumb In Buzz Saw Makes Tokio {sic} Ha Ha!"
- "Workmen Loafing While He Can, Pride and Joy of Nippo Man."
- "Everybody Ride Alone, Some Day Fight Alone."
- "Scratches – Scrap – Happy Jap."

In its sixth week the contest headline was printed on page four on May 27, 1942: ***Nippo-Nazi Contest Ends With 650 Sayings Since Wednesday: The Clan Decides To Award Ten Prizes in Final Week of Very Interesting Activity***. The selection committee awarded prizes for these final ten sayings:

- "Break little drill, give me big thrill."
- "He who shirks duty help us get our booty."
- "Ride alone and four Japs ride with you."
- "Slower you fabricate, faster I eradicate."
- "We thrive on mistake; see how many you can make."
- "Leave a big gap, let in Jap."
- "More chips help Nipps."
- "Be a lazy old louse and me sit in White House."
- "Your slip of lip is tip for Nip."

Employees whose sayings were posted could take the posters as souvenirs. The selection committee removed all posters plant-wide between May 31 and June 1 and left them with department supervisors.

This exploration of ethnic hatred was hard to comb through. Just when I thought the last word had been said about these "sayings," a front-page article on June 3, 1942, caught my eye: ***Nippo-Nazi Contest Appeals to Others***. Sadly, the article reported the following:

The Nippo-Nazi Contest at Aircraft aroused much interest in many sections of the country. Inquiries have come from various sources as to how the idea started, what prizes are offered, where approved sayings are posted, and so on.

The Glenn Martin aircraft company thought so well of the idea that it has asked for 500 of the large posters, on which that company will have inscribed many of the sayings submitted by Aircrafters, the posters to be conspicuously displayed in the Martin plants near Baltimore.

The production of the *Corsair* was in full swing by mid-spring 1944 when the 1,000th plane came off the assembly line in less than one year. On this plane, factory workers wrote: ***Ain't I Sweet! And I Can't Be Beat!*** Employees painted a skull and crossbones and the workers autographed the plane (*The Wingfoot Clan*, March 29, 1944, p. 1). The plane may have gone to a U.S. Navy squadron that used the skull and crossbones as an emblem – Fighter Squadron UF103, the *Jolly Rogers*.

The poem accompanying the photo told volumes about workers' sentiments:

The Rising Sun Is Under The Gun
The 1000 Corsair
In Tojo's Hair
1000 Wallops To
Tojo's Chin
More Coming, Sure As Sin

A corporal sent his son a souvenir from the Pacific Theater. **The Jap and His Souvenir** is the caption above a photograph of a boy showing his mother what his father sent to him. The photo caption is telling: *When Cpl. Charles F. Gentry sends home a souvenir he also sends along a picture of the Jap who furnished it. Here son Jerry shows his mother, Receptionist Wyolene Gentry, a sheath knife Daddy made from the bayonet of the Nip whose picture appears on the Japanese army pay book above. He won't need it any more. The corporal was serving on Makin when he made his find* (Bell Aircraft News, April 8, 1944, p. 3).

In March 1944, a letter written by an American-born Japanese man, was included. **American Of Japanese Ancestry, In Armed Forces, Send His Thanks For Cigarettes**. *I received your carton of cigarettes on aboard a ship, while I was coming to Minnesota. I'm an American of Japanese ancestry, born in Hawaii. I'm volunteer and station {sic} at Camp Savage, Minnesota. I just got in army. I volunteer as a {sic} Interpreter and Translator. I'm Japanese boy, born in Hawaii, went to American school, was taught the American way, live in American way. So, I'm serving in service to show my loyalty to the United States. Thanking you for your gift. Best wishes and good luck. Aloha for me. Sincerely yours, PVT Tsugio Simika* (The Wingfoot Clan, March 1, 1944, p. 7). His letter's tone emphasizes his feelings of loyalty to the United States.

Camp Savage was the U.S. Military Intelligence Service Language School (MIS-LS). It moved from its location in California in June 1942 to Minnesota because it was believed that the instructors would face less prejudice in the Minnesota. The school's purpose was to teach the Japanese language to U.S. Army soldiers so they could interview captured Japanese and translate captured documents. The school moved to Ft. Snelling in August 1944.

In an admonition to employees not to miss work, this caption appeared over a drawing of a smiling Japanese officer with exaggerated ethnic facial features: **He Chuckles**. He says: *If you absent yesterday, then thank you so much! You help us attack soldiers and sailors you sent across Pacific ocean {sic} to fight Japanese* (The Wingfoot Clan, December 13, 1944, p. 8).

Anti-Nazi/ Anti-German Rhetoric

As the war progressed, there were several articles in the *Bell Aircraft News*, accompanied by photographs, about souvenirs sent by servicemen to their parents or wives. These included gifts from indigenous craftspeople, but increasingly included war trophies. For example, a photograph of a large Nazi flag was held up for viewing by five Bell Aircraft women. The caption was telling: *For the privilege of trampling a Nazi flag… the women in the photo were rewarded for their large purchases of war bonds. The red, white and black banner bearing Hitler's hated swastika trademark, was taken in Holland by…who is now in Germany with a field artillery outfit in the 30th (Old Hickory) Division. He sent the battle trophy to his wife…* (*Bell Aircraft News*, November 11, 1944, p. 7). The photograph was published on November 11, celebrated as Armistice Day, the end of World War I.

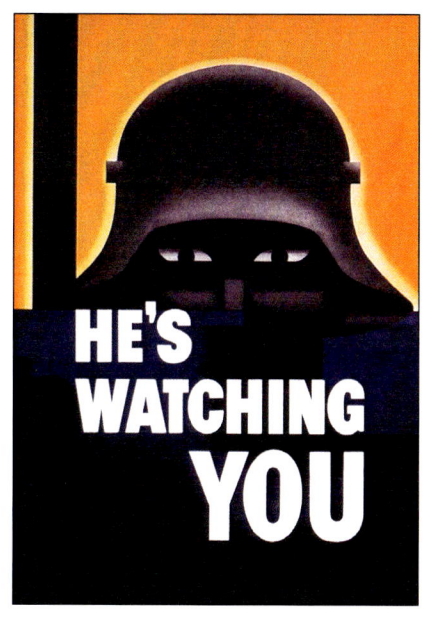

Nazis Shoot At Him When He Bails Out was the story of a technical sergeant, former radio gunner, who was captured after he parachuted from his damaged plane. He reported that the Nazis shot at him all the way to the ground where he was captured and put in a prisoner of war camp for six months (*The Wingfoot Clan*, June 20, 1945, p. 6). Readers would have seen this action as a violation of the Geneva rules of war, and certainly fueled anti-German feelings.

Employee Newsletters: Oddities

Some of the newsletters contained articles that placed me onto truly unusual research paths. One such path was the "Short Snorters." A woman inspector of *Corsair* parts had soloed after just nine hours of flying, and the article mentioned she was a member of this mythical organization (*The Wingfoot Clan*, October 11, 1944, p. 1). This is a bank note signed by people traveling together or gathering at social events. During World War II Short Snorters were signed by flight crews and conveyed good luck.

175

Ending the Research

I ended my research in August 1945, leaving unanswered questions about what my aunt's extended family did after World War II. Those personal stories need to be told by her Palmatier nephews and nieces, not by me.

The war in Europe was over May 8, 1945, and victory in Japan was declared after the bombing of Hiroshima and Nagasaki, August 6 and 9, 1945, respectively with surrender document signed September 2, 1945. Erie Proving Ground continued its operation until the base was decommissioned in the late 1960s. I left untold, also, the detailed history of military installations and home front companies after the war ended. In general, military installations closed or were given new missions, and companies were bought by larger concerns to create new products. Those histories have been summarized by others and did not add to the story about my aunt.

"The conclusion of research is what writers strive for, I think, even though the end may leave the writer searching for another topic." This is what I wrote at the close of my first book. This time, I will not have to search far for another topic. The shear amount of information – historical and cultural – found in home town newspapers, newly released declassified war records, home front companies' newsletters, or military newsletters can inform a myriad number of new books. I truly enjoyed the research and writing this story gave which me greater insight into what family members did during the war, and taught me oddles about the role of women on the home front.

Appendices

1. Ancestry Kinship Diagram for the Palmatier Family

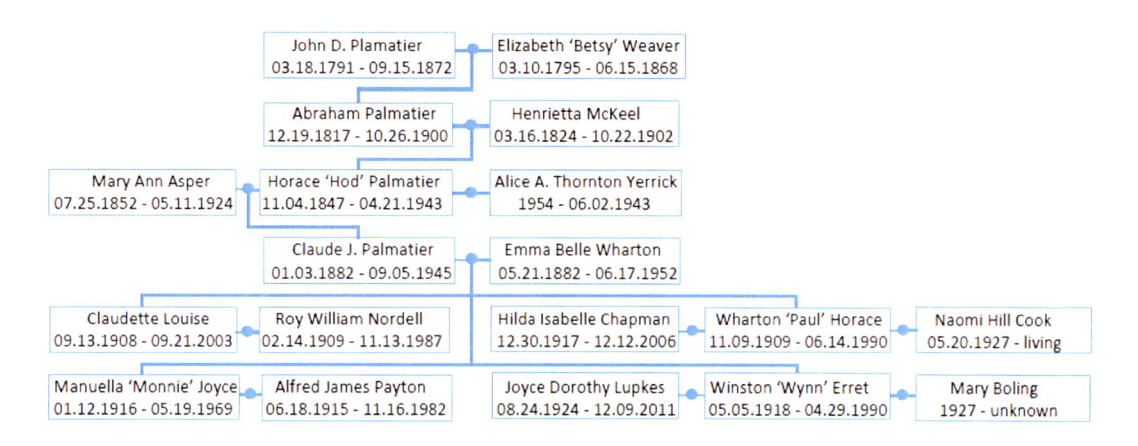

Kinship Diagram for John D. Palmatier and Descendants
Family members descend from settlers in the
Colony of New York, British Colonial America

2. Timeline for Manuella Joyce Palmatier from June 1933 to June 1945

Dates	Location	Activity
June 1933	Osakis, MN	Graduated from Osakis High School.
Fall 1933	Osakis, MN	Still living at parents' home.
1933	Osakis, MN	Typist: The Osakis Review, town newspaper until newspaper was sold. Worked for Clement Horatio Bronson, editor and owner.
November 1933 to April 1934	Osakis, MN	"Library project": Civil Works Administration (CWA). Short term; CWA lasted six months nationally. Supervisor: Dr. L. S. Harbo (perhaps Leif Sverre Harbo, WWI vet – Cpl. Marines).
April 1935 to September 1935	Red Wing, MN	Occupation unknown. Lived there April 1, 1935. Start date unknown.
September 1935 to April 1936	St. Paul, MN	Student: Paul's School of Hairdressing and Cosmetology
April 1936	Alexandria, MN	Student Employee: Lois Beauty Nook. Owner: L.C. Johnson (Lois C. Johnson).
May 1936		Recived Operator License

177

May 1936 to July 1937	Alexandria, MN	Assistant Operator: Lois Beauty Nook. Owner: L.C. Johnson.
July 1937 to August 1939	Long Prairie, MN	Manager: Beauty Salon. Owner: L.C. Johnson. Monnie left because "she wanted to find a job in the city" (i.e., Minneapolis).
September 1939 to November 1939	Minneapolis, MN	Employee: Russel Beauty Salon.
November 1939	Minneapolis, MN	Attended hairdressers' convention.
December 1939 to July 1940	Minneapolis, MN	Employee: Laura's Beauty Shoppe, Bryn Mawr District, Cedar Lake Road. Owner: Laura Paulson. Monnie left for "a better job."
July 1940 to August 1941	Minneapolis, MN	Employee: Curtis Hotel Beauty Parlor. Owner: Mary Ann Martin. Monnie left "because of ill health." She had already applied for work with the War Department.
September 11, 1941	Newcomerstown, OH	Monnie traveled here to visit her elder brother, but expected to go to Texas for training through the War Department. It is unclear if she went to Texas.
October 16, 1941 to June 1945	Port Clinton, OH	Monnie accepted a stenographic position "working for the War Department." Erie Proving Ground. Monnie resigned "to be married" on June 15, 1945.
September 13 1945 Minneapolis,	Osakis, MN	Monnie attended her father's funeral.

Data Excerpts: *Osakis Review* (1933 to 1945), Osakis Area Heritage Center, Osakis, Minnesota; National Personnel Records Center, National Archives and Records Administration, St. Louis, Missouri; Douglas County Historical Society, Alexandria, Minnesota; and the 1940 US Census.

3. Photograph of CCC Company 1721, F-17, Camp Isabella, or Dunnigan, Ely, Minnesota

Company 1721, F-17, Camp Isabella, or Dunnigan, Ely, St. Louis County, Minnesota, December 1933. Civilian Conservation Corps panoramic photograph collection 2008.0082.3752. Minnesota Discovery Center, Chisholm, Minnesota. Al Payton is seventeenth from the right, back row.

Al Payton from the panorama photograph of CCC Company 1721.

In the photograph above, dated December 1933, Al was eighteen and a half years old. As he was very tall, he stood in the back row of this group of camp workers. As I looked at the expressions on the faces of these men, only a scant few smiled; most held serious expressions, and some appeared angry. While the reasons for their expressions cannot be discerned accurately, the men worked extremely hard in all weather, lived in a quasi-military environment, and may have been stressed about the economic straits of their own families.

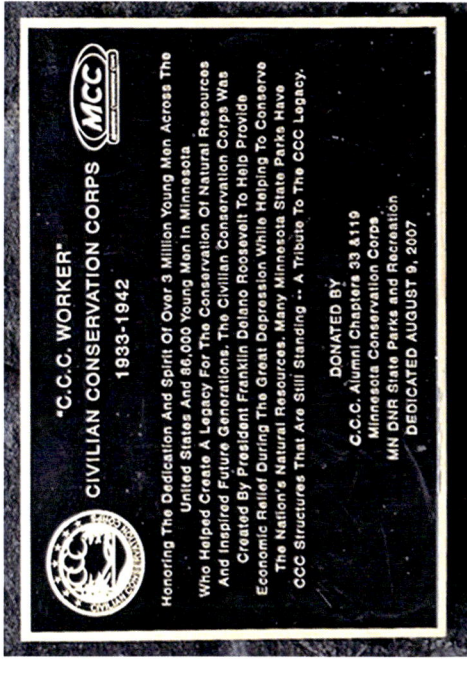

179

4. Timeline of Service to the United States by Alfred James Payton

Date	Place - Name of Ship - Naval Air Station (NAS) - Receiving Station (RS)	Rate	Assigned Duties
Civilian Tour of Duty:			
June 5, 1933 to November 30, 1934	Civilian Conservation Corps - Camp Isabella, Ely, Minnesota	Enrollee	Forestry work. Returned to Fargo, North Dakota.
U.S. Navy Tour of Duty: Interwar			
May 14, 1935 to September 7, 1935	Naval Training Station, San Diego, California		Enlisted: May 14, 1935 from Minneapolis, Minnesota.
September 7, 1935	USS Arizona (BB-39) Philadelphia-class "super dreadnaught."	AS	Aviation Support Equipment Technician.
May 12, 1939			Mustered out: May 12, 1939.
U.S. Navy Tour of Duty: World War II			
September 9, 1940		Sea1c	Enlisted: September 9, 1940 from Minneapolis, Minnesota. Lived in Fargo, North Dakota.
September 11, 1940			Naval Recruiting Station (NRS) Minneapolis, MN
September 30, 1940	Receiving Station, NOB Norfolk, Virginia	Sea1c	Norfolk, Virginia – no records Records Not Received
October 31, 1940 to December 31, 1940	USS *Wyoming* Norfolk Receiving Station	Sea1c	USS *Wyoming* was the lead ship of her Dreadnaught-class of battleships.
April 28, 1941	USS *Pokomoke* (AV-9) *Pokomoke*-class sea-plane tender.	SC3c	Received on board Ordinary Commission No sailing designation given
May 1, 1941	**Change of Rating (CR) CR(ADV): Sea1c to SC3c	SC3c	Auth: BN ltr. Nav-631-Wg/ P17to2/17 of 25 April 1941.

Date	Ship/Location	Rank	Notes
May 31, 1941	USS *Pokomoke* (AV-9)	SC3c	Ship's Cook, Third Class Petty Officer.
September 30 to November 30, 1941	USS *Pokomoke* (AV-9)	SC3c	Auth: BuNav ltr. Nav-631-Wg of 24 Oct 1941.
November 30, 1941	USS Pokomoke (AV-9)	P3c	Sailed from Naval Station Argentia Bay, Newfoundland. **CR occurred from SC3c to P3c.
November 30, 1941	USS *Suwanee* (CVE-27) Launched March 4, 1939. U.S. Navy acquired escort carrier on June 26, 1941, and commissioned July 16, 1941. February 14, 1942 became *Sangamon-class* escort carrier, then re-designated an auxiliary carrier.	P3c	Received from USS *Pokomoke* for further transport (FFT) to Naval Air Station, Pensacola, Florida. November 19, 1941. He was a passenger, not a crewmember. USS *Suwanee* FFT to east coast port FFT to NAS Pensacola, Florida. For course of instruction Photographers' School. Auth: BuNav ltr Nav-632-MJC 328 38 38 (Al's serial #) November 8, 1941
December 7, 1941	Imperial Japanese Navy attacked Pearl Harbor, Territory of Hawaii.		Transferred to NAS Pensacola Photographic School. USS *Arizona* (BB-39), *Pennsylvania*-class battle ship, sunk.
December 8, 1941			United States declares war: Japan.
December 11, 1941			United States declares war: Germany.
November 28, 1941 to March 31, 1942	NAS Pensacola, Florida	P3c	Photographic School – 16 weeks. World War II began for the U.S. just after Al started his training.
April 6 1942 to May 30, 1942	US NAS New York, New York	P3c	Enrolled for instruction at Fox MovieTone News – 6 weeks. Completed course on May 30, 1942.
1942	Anacostia, DC NAS	P3c	Temporary Duty – School of Photographic Interpretation

1942	Anacostia, DC NAS	P2c	**CR occurred – School of Photographic Interpretation
1942	Anacostia, DC NAS	PhoM2c	**CR occurred – School of Photographic Interpretation
February 1943	Anacostia, DC PSL	PhoM2c	Transferred to Naval Photographic Science Laboratory for Duty. Lab established February 24, 1943.
1943	Newport News, Virginia Receiving Station	PhoM2c	*Yorktown* Detail (USS *Yorktown*)
April 15, 1943	USS *Yorktown* (CV-10) *Essex*-class aircraft carrier. She carried F4U *Corsairs*, fighter aircraft. Al was a "Plankowner" or "Plank Holder" – a crew member of a U.S. Navy ship when the ship was commissioned.	PhoM2c	"Upon commissioning" data recorded as of April 30, 1943. Ship commissioned out of NAS Norfolk, Virginia. **CR occurred to Photographers Mate 2nd Class
May 21, 1943			Ship on its "shake down" cruise in the Caribbean.
May 21, 1943	Erie Proving Ground, Port Clinton, Ohio	PHoM2c	Believed to be assigned by Movietone News to film Erie Proving Ground's 25th Anniversary with a focus on female workers.
July 6, to July 24, 1943	USS *Yorktown* 2626 men on board; ship Sailed from Chesapeake Bay to Pearl Harbor, transiting through the Panama Canal.	PhoM1c	**CR occurred to Photographers Mate 1st Class
August 24, to December 31, 1943 movements:			Listed in the left columns are at least 6 battles that Al Payton may have been tasked to photograph.
August 31, 1943	Marcus Island (battle)		
September 7-19, 1943	Pearl Harbor/ supply runs to San Francisco		
September 29, 1943	Put to sea.		

October 5-6, 1943	Wake Island (battle)		
October 6-11, 1943	Return to Pearl Harbor		
October 11 to November 11, 1943	Training exercises (30 days)		
November 19, 1943	Gilbert Islands (battle)		
December 5, 1943	Passing raids on Wotje and Kwajalein Atoll		
December 9, 1943	Pearl Harbor (30 days training)		
January 16, 1943	Left Pearl Harbor – *Operation Flintlock*		The USS *Yorktown* went on to participate in 26 more military actions. She occupied Japan August 15, 1945 to October 1, 1945.
January 29 to February 23, 1944	Marshall Islands, Truk & Mariana Islands		
March 29 to April 30, 1944	Palau, Hollandia, & Truk		
February 25 to March 31, 1944	Pearl Harbor NYD Photographic Reconnaissance & Interpretation Section, Intelligence Center, Pacific Ocean Areas	PhoM1c	Assigned aboard the USS *Yorktown*.
		CPhoM AA or Ch-PhoM	**CR occurred to Chief Photographers Mate. Al took his examination aboard the USS *Yorktown*.
June 1 to June 11, 1944	U.S. Navy Yard, Pearl Harbor, Hawaii AIEA, T.H. – RS	CPhoM	Territory of Hawaii, Receiving Station.
June 12 to December 1, 1944	*Yorktown* to Pearl harbor, then Puget Sound for repairs	CPhoM	Record unclear. Believed to be in Hawaii. Unclear if he was aboard the USS *Yorktown* during battles in the in the Philippines (Leyte).
December 1 to December 11, 1944	USS *Sanborn* (APA-193) Haskell-class attack transport; moved troops to and from combat areas.	CPhoM (AA)	FA Amphibious Group 2. Temporary Duty. The ship was launched August 19, 1944, by Kaiser Shipbuilding Corporation, Vancouver, Washington. It was commissioned October 3. 1944.It left for Pacific Ocean duty on December 16, 1944.

December 15, 1944 to mid-January 1945	A.I.E.A., Territory of Hawaii, RS	CPhoM	Unknown duties. Record unclear.
1945 (months unclear)	USS *Auburn* (AGC-10) *Mount McKinley*-class amphibious force command ship.		FA Amphibious Group 2 Temporary Duty. Launched August 14, 1943, by the North Carolina Shipbuilding Company, Wilmington, North Carolina. Ship acquired by the U.S. Navy January 31, 1944 and commissioned July 20, 1944. Earned two battle stars in WWII.
1945 (months unclear)	CINCPAC Adv HDQRS DET Commander in Chief, Pacific Command Pearl Harbor, T.H.	CPhoM	For Duty.
Early June 1945	San Francisco, California RS	CPhoM	FFT Al is headed stateside to Ohio.
June 15, 1945	Port Clinton, Ohio	CPhoM	Marriage to Manuella Joyce Palmatier.
July 24, 1945	Minneapolis, Minnesota RS - HEDRON, Fleet Air Wing Eight (FAW-8), USNAS	CPhoM	FFT
September 5, 1945	Alameda, California NAS Personnel Separation Center.	CPhoM	Honorable Discharge.
September 8, 1945			Date of Release from U.S. Navy.
September 17, 1945	Moorhead, Minnesota		Registered for the Draft.

U.S. Navy Tour of Duty: Naval Air Reserve Training Program

1947 - 1955	U.S. Navy Reserve		Honorable Discharge from U.S. Navy Reserve on January 14, 1955.
October 22, 1948	U.S. Naval Air Station Minneapolis, Minnesota		"Net Service" computed back to February 23, 1947.

1952	FAW-81 Minneapolis, Minnesota Fleet Wing		Received Noel Davis Trophy. Awarded by Secretary of the Navy to air wing staff. Part of each man's permanent record.
1957 - 1960	U.S. Navy Reserve		Other records state he was in the Ready Reserve until March 17, 1960.
December 12, 1957	U.S. Navy Reserve Phoenix, Arizona	PHAC	Date of transfer requested "for further assignment."
March 17, 1958			Date paperwork received: Ready Reserve Transfer/Agreement Request from Minnesota to Arizona. Al agreed to remain in the Reserves.

Data excerpts: National Archives and Records Administration, St. Louis, Missouri; Fold 3 by Ancestry; Joseph Janney Steinmetz Collection/ Florida Memory Project; National Naval Aviation Museum, Pensacola, Florida; National Park Service; Campbell, 2014, *Flight, Camera, Action!*; Patriot's Point Naval and Maritime Museum; and on-line naval history resources. Dates for individual tasks assigned to Al Payton were determined by the best available data.

5. Table of Contents, Photography Class Training Manual, World War II, Pensacola, Florida

Chapter I
    Aerial Oblique Photography, General
    Service Oblique Cameras
    Taking Aerial Oblique Photographs
    Useful Information
    The Smith Aero Film Developing Outfit
    The Smith Automatic Film Dryer
    The Portable Flight Laboratory
Chapter II
    Aerial Photographic Mapping
    The Vertical Aerial Photograph
    Calculations Required for Vertical Photographs
    Aerial Photography Mapping, General
    The Single Lens Mapping Camera
        The K-3-A Camera
        The K-3-B Camera
        The F-14 and F-25 Cameras

    Calculations for a Mapping Mission
    Preparation for the Mapping Flight
    Making the Mapping Flight
    Aircraft Crabbing and Drift
    Instrument Method Versus Contact Method of Flying For Aerial Photographic Mapping

Chapter III
    Laboratory Procedure for Making Unrectified Mosaic Maps
    Use of Vertical Aerial Photographs for Construction of Line Maps
    Limitations in Accuracy of Mosaic Maps
    Relief
    Tilt
    The Ratio Print Camera
    The Radial Line, Template, and Slotted Template Methods of Orienting Aerial Photographs
    Projecting Control Data on the Mountant

Chapter IV
    Multiple Lens Mapping Cameras
    The T-3-A Mapping Camera
    Mapping with the T-3-A
    Developing the Film
    The B-7 Type Transforming Printer
    Mounting the Composite Photographs
    Multiple Lens Mosaic Maps
    Stereoscopic Aerial Photographs and Their Interpretation

Note: The Complete Course in Photography is Covered in Four Manuals; P-4a, P-4b, P-4c and P-4d. Data Source: Library, Naval Aviation Museum, Pensacola, Florida. Personal communication.

6. U.S. Navy Abbreviations Relevant to Alfred Payton's Service

BuNAV = Bureau of Navigation	AS = Aviation Support Equipment Technician	CPhoM/ChPhoM = Chief Photographer's Mate
BuAer = Bureau of Aeronautics	Sea1c = Seaman 1st Class	T.H. = Territory of Hawaii
FFT = For Further Transfer	SC3c = Ship's Cook, 3rd Class	USN = United States Navy
FAW = Fleet Air Wing	P3c = Photographer, 3rd Class	USNR = United States Navy Reserve
HEDRON = HQ Squadron	P2c = Photographer, 2nd Class	USS = United States Ship
NAS = Naval Air Station	PhoM2c = Photographer's Mate,	SECNAV = Secretary of the Navy
RS = Receiving Station	PhoM1c = Photographer's Mate, 1st Class	Pacific Ocean Theater = area including most of the Pacific Ocean and its islands

Research Resources

    I chose not to be strictly academic in citing my sources within the body of the book. Readers should know that I triangulated discrete pieces of data by using the following materials: on-line and hard copy data, primary and secondary resources, or by personally consulting with professional curators, archivists, librarians, and genealogists to locate and verify information. I have included the resources I used, whether or not the resource provided any data; "no information" is useful in research.

Primary Resources

Arizona
    Arizona Department of Health Services, Bureau of Vital Statistics, Death Certificate
    Memorial Lawn Cemetery, Phoenix, Arizona

Associations
    Camp Fire Minnesota, Minneapolis, Minnesota. https://campfiremn.org
    Camp Fire USA, Kansas City, Kansas. https://campfire.org
    Civilian Conservation Corps Legacy, Topeka, Kansas. www.ccclegacy.org
    National Association of the Deaf, Washington, D.C. nad.infor@nad.org
    Rosie the Riveter Association, Rosie, Alabama. https://rosietheriveter.net
    Stars and Stripes Central Office, Washington, DC. www.stripes.com

Documentaries
    American Experience: 1930s The Civilian Conservation Corps. Part 1 - 1929 and The Great Depression; Part 4 - The Great Depression - We Have a Plan. YouTube videos. https://www.bing.com/videos/search?q=FDR+Civilian+Conservation+Corps
    Arcadia Publishing: *World War II Prison Camps in Ohio.* Presentation, James Van Keuran, October 1, 2019. www.arcadiapublishing.com
    Fox Movietone News: *Testing Guns on Erie Proving Ground.* V25 #77, Tuesday, June 1, 1943 - http://library.sc.edu/digital/collections/mvtnwarfilms.html
    History Channel: *The Food That Built America.* https://www.tvinsider.com/798240/the-food-that-built-america-history-channel
    Northwest Television Network: *The History of Northwest Airlines.* https://www.youtube.com
    Periscope Film LLC Archive: *Bell Aircraft.* www.zenoswarbirdvideo.com
    Periscope Film LLC Archive: *Rationing In the United States during World War II.* www.periscopefilm.com
    Periscope Film LLC Archive: *The Fighting Lady USS Yorktown,* Part 1 through Part 7. www.periscopefilm.com
    Periscope Film LLC Archive: *The Women War Workers.* www.periscopfilm.com
    Periscope Film LLC Archive: *The Story of the Goodyear Aircraft Company, World War II Airplanes and Blimps, Women War Workers 844.* www.periscopfilm.com
    Public Broadcasting Station: *Desegregating Blood.* February 4, 2018. https://www.pbs.org/newshour/science/desegretatingblood.

Educational Institutions
- Dunwoody College of Technology, Minneapolis, Minnesota.
- Gallaudet University, Washington, DC.
- Osakis School District, Osakis, Minnesota.

Genealogy Resources
- www.Ancestry.com
- www.FindaGrave.com
- www.Fold3.com
  - Alfred James Payton
  - Claude J. Palmatier
  - Winston Erret Palmatier
  - Roy William Nordell

State of Georgia during World War II
- New Georgia Encyclopedia. https://www.georgiaencyclopedia.org
- Today In Georgia History, *Bell Bomber Plant*. https://www.todayingeorgiahistory.org

Historical and Genealogical Societies
- Cobb County Genealogical Society, Cobb County, Georgia. https://www.cobbgagensoc.org
- Cobb Landmarks and Historical Society, Inc., Marietta, Georgia. https://www.cobblandmarks.com
- Douglas County Historical Society, Alexandria, Minnesota. https://www.dchsmn.org
- Gilder Lehrman Institute of American History, New York, New York. https://www.gilderlehrman.org
- Minnesota Historical Society, St. Paul, Minnesota. www.mnhs.org
- MNOpedia, Minnesota Historical Society. https://www.mnopedia.org
- New Brighton Area Historical Society. http://newbrightonhistory.org
- Osakis Area Heritage Center, Osakis, Minnesota. https://osakis-area-heritage-information-center.hub.biz
- Ottawa County Historical Society, Port Clinton, Ohio. http://ottawacountyhistory.org
- Twin Ports Genealogical Society, Duluth, Minnesota. https://www.facebook.com/tpgs55802
- U.S. Army Historical Foundation, Arlington, Virginia. https://armyhistory.org

Libraries
- Akron-Summit County Public Library, Akron, Ohio. www.summitmemory.org
- Cline Library, Northern Arizona University, Flagstaff, Arizona. https://nau.edu/library
- Cobb County Public Library System, Marietta, Georgia. http://www.cobbcat.org
- Duluth Public Library, Duluth, Minnesota. http://www.duluthpubliclibrary.org
- Flagstaff City-Coconino County Public Library, Flagstaff, Arizona. https://www.flagstaffpubliclibrary.org
- Gayle Family Library, Minnesota Historical Society, St. Paul, Minnesota. http://sites.mnhs.org/library
- Harry S. Truman Library / Museum, Independence, Missouri. https://www.trumanlibrary.gov
- Ida Rupp Public Library, Port Clinton, Ohio. https://www.idarupp.org/genealogy
- Minnesota Digital Library, Minnesota Reflections. https://mndigital.org
- Moving Images Research Center, University of South Carolina, Columbia, South Carolina. https://www.sc.edu
- National Archives & Records Administration, St. Louis, Missouri. https://www.archives.gov

Rodney A. Briggs Library, University of Minnesota, Morris, Digital Collection, Archives and Special Collections, Morris, Minnesota. https://library.morris.umn.edu

State Library and Archives of Florida. https://www.floridamemory.com

Stewart A. Rose Manuscript, Archives and Rare Books Library, James Vinson Carmichael Collection, Emory University, Atlanta, Georgia. rose.library@emory.edu

University of Akron Archival Services Digital Collection, University Libraries, Akron, Ohio. https://www.uakron.edu/libraries/archives

Wayne Public Library: Your Library Off the Shelf. World War II Prison Camps in Ohio. www.arcadiapublishing.com

Wilson Library, University of Minnesota, Minneapolis, Minnesota. https://www.lib.umn.edu/wilson

Minnesota On-Line Resources

Cargill, Incorporated. 150.cargill.com/150/en/PORT-CARGILL-EST.jsp

Gopher Ordnance Works. www.gopherordnanceworks.com

Honeywell International. dl-corphoneywell@honeywell.com

Minneapolis-Honeywell Regulator Company. Charles Babbage Institute. gallery.lib.umn.edu

Minnesota Public Radio (MPR). www.mprnews.org

Minnesota

Douglas County Death Index

Minnesota Office of Higher Education

Minnesota Vital Records, Birth Certificates

Todd County Health and Human Services

Museums

American Air Museum in Britain, Duxford, England. http://www.americanairmuseum.com

Civilian Conservation Corps History Center, Chisholm, Minnesota. https://www.mndiscoverycenter.com

Friends of Historic NAS Alameda, Alameda, California. https://fohnasa.blogspot

Greyhound Bus Museum, Hibbing, Minnesota. http://www.greyhoundbusmuseum.org

Hennepin History Museum. https://www.hennepinhistory.org

Lawrence D. Bell Aircraft Museum, Mentone, Indiana. https://www.bellaircraftmuseum.org

Minnesota Discovery Center, Chisholm, Minnesota. info@mndiscoverycenter.com

Minnesota Military Museum, Little Falls, Minnesota. www.mnmilitarymuseum.org

Museum of Flight, Seattle, Washington. www.museumofflight.org

National Afro-American Museum & Cultural Center, Wilberforce, Ohio. https://www.ohiohistory.org

National Museum of the United States Army, Arlington, Virginia. https://armyhistory.org

National Naval Aviation Museum, Department of the Navy, Pensacola, Florida. https://www.navalaviationmuseum.org

National Women's History Museum, Washington, D.C. https://www.womenshistory.org

Ottawa County Museum, Port Clinton, Ohio. www://ottawacountymuseum.org

Patriots Point Naval & Maritime Museum, Mt. Pleasant, South Carolina. https://www.patriotspoint.org

The National World War II Museum, New Orleans, Louisiana. nationalworldwar2museum.org

U.S. Quartermaster Museum. http://www.qmmuseum.lee.army.mil

National Archives & Records Administration (NARA), National Personnel Records Center, St. Louis, Missouri. https://www.archives.gov

    National Archives Official Personnel Folder (OPF)
- Manuella Joyce Palmatier

    National Archives Military Records
- Alfred James Payton
- Winston Erret Palmatier

    Civilian Conservation Corps (CCC) Personnel Records
- Alfred James Payton
- Wharton Horace Palmatier

Newsletters

Bell Aircraft: *Bell Aircraft News* (hard copy) May 21, 1943 through May 13, 1944, and June 3, 1944 through August 24, 1945.

Civilian Conservation Corps, U.S. Company 1721, Ely, Minnesota. *Isabella Trail-Blazer*; January, April, July, August, September, October, November, December, 1935. Minnesota Discovery Center, Chisholm, Minnesota.

Civilian Conservation Corps, U. S. Company 1721, Ely, Minnesota. *Isabella Trail-Blazer*; June 21, 1935. 1935-06-21. Minnesota Historical Society. Accessed 24 Jan 2020. reflections.mndigital.org/catalog/mnhs3312

Erie Proving Ground: *EPG Echo* (hard copy, v1, Issues 3 through 8, May 20 through July 29, 1943).

Goodyear Aircraft: *The Wingfoot Clan* - Aircraft Edition (online June 4, 1941-August 22, 1945). www.summitmemory.org

Goodyear Aircraft: *The Wingfoot Clan* - Akron Edition (online January.11.1939 – December, 31.1945). www.summitmemory.org

National Park Service: USS *Arizona: At 'Em Arizona* (online April 1921 to August 1941, intermittent issues); August.17.1935, p. 2; September .07.1935, p. 2. www.nps.gov

Northwest Airlines History Center: *Reflections*, Fall 2011; and *Field & Hangar*, May 1945. http://northwestairlineshistory.org

Newspapers

Brainerd Daily Dispatch, Brainerd, Minnesota. 1907.

Duluth News Tribune, Duluth, Minnesota. March 28, 2020, p. B5.

Mason City Globe Gazette, Mason City, Iowa. June 1943.

Osakis Review, Osakis, Minnesota. 1933-1945, 1952, 1990.

Staples World, Staples, Minnesota. 1891, 1908.

The Coshocton Tribune, Coshocton, Ohio. 1938-1944, 1948, 1951, 1954, 1969, 1974, 1976, 1986.

The Iowa Recorder, Greene, Iowa. V.63, No. 45. Wednesday, June 9, 1943.

The Logan Daily News, Logan, Ohio. 1976.

The New York Times, New York, New York. March 27, 2020, p. A13.

The Sun, Flagstaff, Arizona. 1961.

The Times Reporter (also called *Dover Times Reporter*, and *Dover New Philadelphia Times Reporter*), New Philadelphia, Ohio. April 2007.

Ohio On-Line Resources
- Goodyear Aircraft Corporation. ohiohistorycentral.org
- Ohio History. http://www.ohiohistorycentral.org
- Ohio Memory Project. www.ohiomemory.org

Ohio
- Marriage Licenses

United States Official Documents On-Line
- US City Directories
- US Census 1900-1940
- US State Census 1905-1935

War History/ History of War On-line Resources
- America in World War II. http://www.americainwwii.com
- America's Navy: Forged By The Sea. https://www.navy.mil or https://www.history.navy.mil
- Battle of Attu. www.nps.gov
- Navy Cruise Books. https://www.navysite.de/cruisebooks/CV10-45
- New Georgia Encyclopedia. *How Marietta Won the Bell Plant.* https://www.georgiaencyclopedia.org
- The Short Snorter Project. shortsnorter.org
- Thomas K. Vincent, Brigadier General (biography). https://goordnance.army.mil/hof/2000/2001/vincent.html
- United States Army Ordnance Corps/The History of Ordnance in America. https://goordnance.army.mil/history/ORDhistory.html
- U.S. War Bonds. https://www.u-s-history.com/pages/h1682.html
- USS *Yorktown*. www.scharch.org
- Victory Gardens. https://www.history.com/news/americas-patriotic-victory-gardens
- Women Ordnance Workers (WOW) (accessed by state)
- World War II History. Worldwar2@historynet.com
- World War II War Bonds. www.sarahsundin.com/world-war-ii-bonds

Other Works Consulted

Books

Birdsall, Steve. *Saga of The Superfortress: The Dramatic Story of The B-29 and The Twentieth Air Force*. 1980. Doubleday and Company, Inc.: Garden City, New York.

Bishop, Chris (Ed.). *The Encyclopedia of 20th Century Air Warfare*. 2004. Amber Books, Ltd.: London, United Kingdom.

Blake, Sarah. *The Postmistress*. 2010. G.P. Putnam: New York.

Blum, Howard. *The Last Goodnight: A World War II Story of Espionage, Adventure, and Betrayal*. 2016. Harper Collins: New York.

Broehl, Wayne, Jr. *Cargill: Trading the World's Grain*. 1992. University Press of New England: Hanover, New Hampshire.

Brokaw, Tom. *The Greatest Generation*. 1998. Random House: New York.

Caldwell, Donald L. *Thunder on Bataan: The First American Tank Battle of World War II.* 2019. Stackpole Books: Lanham, Maryland.

Campbell, Douglas E. *Flight, Camera, Action! The History of U.S. Naval Aviation Photography and Photo-Reconnaissance.* 2014. Syneca Research Group, Inc.: Washington, D.C.

Clayton, Meg Waite. *The Race for Paris.* 2015. Harper Collins: New York.

Cooke, Alistair. *The American Home Front 1941-1942.* 2006. Grove Press: New York.

Fagone, Jason. *The Woman Who Smashed Codes.* 2017. Harper Collins: New York.

Henry, Chris and Hal Bryan. *The Final Mission.* 2020. Experimental Aircraft Association: Oshkosh, Wisconsin.

Henry, Mark. *The U.S. Army in World War II.* 2001. Osprey Publishing Ltd.: Essex: United Kingdom.

Horikoshi, Jiro. *Eagles of Mitsubishi: The Story of the Zero Fighter.* 1981 (English translation). University of Washington Press: Seattle, Washington.

Joukowsky, Artemis. *Defying the Nazis: The Sharps' War.* 2016. Beacon Press: Boston.

Kiernan, Denise. *The Girls of Atomic City: The Untold Story of the Women Who Helped Win World War II.* 2013. Touchstone Simon and Schuster, Inc.: New York.

Lomax, Judy. *Women of the Air.* 1986. Dodd, Mead & Company: New York.

McClure, Rhonda and Julie Tarr. *Researching American Newspaper Records: An Introductory Overview of Newspapers and the History of American Newspapers.* 2017. Heritage Productions, National Institute for Genealogical Studies. On-line.

McIntosh, Elizabeth P. *Women of the OSS: Sisterhood of Spies.* 1998. Naval Institute Press: Annapolis, Maryland.

McNaughton, James C. *Nisei Linguists: Japanese Americans in the Military Intelligence Service during World War II.* 2006. Department of the Army: Washington, D.C. https://history.army.mil/html/books/nesie_linguists.

Moore, Kate. *The Radium Girls: The Dark Story of America's Shining Women.* 2018. Sourcebooks, Inc.: Naperville, Illinois.

Mundy, Liza. *Code Girls: The Untold Story of the American Women Code Breakers of World War II.* 2017. Hachette Books: New York/ Boston.

Purnell, Sonia. *A Woman of No Importance: The Untold Story of The American Spy Who Helped Win World War II.* 2019. Viking Press: New York.

Resley, Shirley and Elva Tonn. *Our Osakis Heritage.* 1940 (reprinted 1992). Osakis Area Heritage Center: Osakis, Minnesota.

Rickman, Sarah Byrn. *Nancy Love and the WASP Ferry Pilots of World War II.* 2008. University of North Texas Press: Denton, Texas.

Sandvick, Gerald. *World War II Shipbuilding in Duluth and Superior.* 2017. Arcadia Publishing: Charleston, South Carolina.

Schultz, Duane. *Into The Fire; Ploesti The Most Fateful Mission of World War II.* 2008. Westholme Publishing: Yardley, Pennsylvania.

Simbeck, Rob. *Daughter of the Air: The Brief Soaring Life of Cornelia Fort.* 1999. Grove Press: New York.

Sommer, Barbara W. *Hard Work and a Good Deal: The Civilian Conservation Corps in Minnesota.* 2008. Minnesota Historical Society Press: St. Paul, Minnesota.

Sutton, Matthew Avery. *Double Crossed: The Missionaries Who Spied for the United States During the Second World War.* 2019. Hatchette Book Group, Inc.: New York.

Tibets, Paul W. *Return of the Enola Gay.* 1998. Mid-Coast Marketing: Columbus, Ohio.

Van Keuren, James. *World War II POW Camps in Ohio.* 2018. Arcadia Publishing: Mount Pleasant, South Carolina.

Wright-Peterson, Virginia M. *A Woman's War, Too.* 2020. Minnesota Historical Society Press: St. Paul, Minnesota.

Articles

Anonymous. *College Students Turning Away From Classic Studies: Trend Is Toward Professional and Technical Fields, Survey Shows. The Minneapolis Sunday Tribune*, December 14, 1930, p. 7.

Baldwin, Paul. *Military History of the Upper Great Lakes.* October 11, 2015. Michigan Technolocal University Student Project. http://ss.sites.mtu.edu/mhugl/2015/10/11/mesabi -range -mines-minnesota 1939-1945

Blondia, Amarilla. *Cigarettes and Their Impact in World War II.* In: *Perspectives: A Journal of Historical Inquiry.* pp. 10-19. www.calstate.edu.

Brown, Curt. *Hormel's amazing (piggy) back story. Star Tribune,* Minneapolis, Minnesota. Sunday, January 26, 2020. p. B4.

Granger, Steven. *Historic Buildings of the West Central School of Agriculture Converted to Use by the University of Minnesota, Morris, in 1960.* 1998. Plant Services, University of Minnesota - Morris: Morris, Minnesota. http://2010.morris.edu/docs/Hist_Bldgs_of_WCSA.pdf

National Center for Education Statistics. *120 Years of American Education: A Statistical Portrait.* U. S. Department of Education, Office of Research and Improvement: Washington, D.C. https://nces.ed.gov/pubsearch/pubsinfo.asp?pubid=93442
    Fig. 14 Enrollment in institutions of higher education by sex: 1869-70 and 1990-91. p. 65.
    Table 19: High school graduates, by sex and control of institution: 1869-70 and 1990-91. p. 55.

Stewart, Phillip W. *A Reel Story of World War II: The United News Collection of Newsreels Documents the Battlefield and the Home Front.* Fall 2015, v. 47, no. 3. https://www.archives.gov.

U.S. Department of the Interior, Office of Education. Civilian Conservation Corps Vocational Series #12. *Photography Part I and Part II. Photography, Outlines of Instruction For Educational Advisors and Instructors in Civilian Conservation Corps Camps.* 1933. Government Printing Office: Washington, D.C. .

U.S. Navy F4Us, *Corsairs*, in flight over the South Pacific. c. 1944, Library of Congress photo.

Experience History
B-29 DOC TOUR

ST. PAUL, MN | JULY 13-14, 2019

There are only two B-29 flying aircraft left in the world: *FiFi* and *Doc*. *Doc* is a Walt Disney creation from *Snow White*. Both B-29s tour in air shows in the United States.

Acknowledgements

Research of a small-town Minnesota woman who served her country on the home front during World War II was aided by many organizations, historical societies, libraries, historians, and genealogists. The willingness of others to share their time and resources with me cannot go unappreciated. I truly thank you.

R. Michael "Mike" Busch, my husband, was an "Airdale" aboard the USS *Saratoga* during the Vietnam era. He was an Avionics Technician and Aircraft Electrician and Aircrew. He is now a general aviation pilot with multiple aviation-related credentials. He was Director of Air Safety for Cirrus Aircraft, Duluth, for fourteen years. A long-time member of the Experimental Aircraft Association (EAA), he has been the president of EAA Chapter 1128 Two Harbors, Minnesota, for nearly a decade. He currently works with the Federal Aviation Administration (FAA) as a Designated Airworthiness Representative (DAR) inspecting the flight worthiness of amateur-built aircraft. Mike is an incisive source of information about the design, construction, assembly, and specific operational parameters regarding military and civilian aircraft, and about the history of aviation during World War II. Thanks, honey.

Sharon and Steve Frederickson, Oaskis Area Heritage Center, Minnesota, provided photographs of Palmatier family headstones. They spent hours searching through the *Osakis Review*, the town's newspaper, to find and photocopy newsworthy articles about the Palmatier family. Thank you for loving to do research about the people of Osakis! Thank you to the Douglas County Historical Society, Alexandria, Minnesota, for its summary of public data on the Horace Palmatier family. Thanks to Jay Hagen, Veterans Memorial Hall Program Assistant, St. Louis County Historical Society, for formatting the kinship diagram, a tedious process.

Librarians are a gift to researchers, and many assisted me. The reference librarians at Duluth Public Library, Duluth, Minnesota, obtained materials through interlibrary loan. They were encouraging as my eyes crossed reading microfilm for hours. Thanks to the librarians of the Wilson Library, University of Minnesota. The staff from the Thomas Cooper Library at the University of South Carolina, and their Moving Images Collection provided much needed information. Thanks to JoyEllen Williams, curator, Kennesaw State Special Collections Museum, Archives and Rare Books, for linking me with digitized oral histories of women who worked at Bell Aircraft, along with photographs, and a link to the *Bellringer* magazine.

The librarians at the Woodruff Library, Emory University, filled in many holes in my research by providing missing issues of *Bell Aircraft News* from the James Vinson Carmichael Collection. Thanks to Professor Kira Jones for locating and copying issues of *Bell Aircraft News* from mid-1944 to mid-1945. At the University of Georgia Libraries, I was pleased to connect with Katherine Sarah Norman Dahlstrand, a history doctoral student, who forwarded printed copies of the *Bell Aircraft News* from 1943 to mid 1944.

Thank you to U. S. Navy Captain Margaret "Peggy" Debien (Ret.), Ottawa County Museum, who forwarded copies of the *EPG Echo,* and who enthusiastically talked about the roles played by Erie Proving Ground and Port Clinton during World War II.

The staff from the National Archives and Records Administration (NARA), St. Louis, Missouri, provided excellent, detailed data which formed much of the military and civilian personnel information. NARA is truly a national treasure.

The Army Historical Foundation, Arlington, Virginia, interpreted information from U.S. Army World War II discharge papers.

Marlene Wisuri, Editor, Dovetailed Press, Duluth, Minnesota, with her calm demeanor, took my detailed manuscript and transformed it into a readable book. Her eye for design and content made the production just wonderful. Many thanks, Marlene.

Thank you to the staff of First Photo, Duluth, for processing personal family photographs. Their professional reproductions are much appreciated.

My cousins shared stories of our aunt and uncle, and were an excellent source for photographs: Carol Payton Spaulding, Genie St. John Jensen, and Sally Seward Pesta. Thanks to Katie Waughtel Jensen, Jane Waughtel Seez, and Ruth Waughtel Hollister for an update on Camp Fire Girls.

Once again, my friend Cora Knutson, Vice Regent, Greysolon Daughters of Liberty Chapter, Duluth, Minnesota, Daughters of the American Revolution, talked me off the ledge when my computer decided to rebel.

About the Author

Kathleen M. Cargill is a cultural anthropologist with Bachelor's Degree from the University of Michigan, Ann Arbor. She completed her Master's Degree in Anthropology and doctoral research at the University of Florida, Gainesville. Her master's work concerned the structure and function of a rural health clinic that served migrant agricultural workers, and her dissertation researched the structure and function of a group of rural fire fighters/ first responders before it was integrated by gender or ethnicity. These research experiences allowed her to move into her own family genealogy after her retirement from The College of St. Scholastica, Duluth, Minnesota, where she taught anthropology and served as the first Director of the Ronald E. McNair Post-Baccalaureate Scholars Program. She is the recipient of *The Woman Today*, Mentor Award, 2020 Rosie Award.

Kathleen is a member of the following: Twin Ports Genealogical Society, Minnesota Historical Society, Archaeological Conservancy, Wayzata Historical Society, St. Louis County Historical Society, Carlton County Historical Society, and the Minnesota Genealogical Society. In addition to her passion for anthropology, genealogy, and history, Kathleen is an avid gardener and sole owner of Beekeepers Press.

Other books by the author

Letters From Lucia: A Young Woman's Travels as World War II Looms

Waiting For The Big One: An Ethnography of Rural Southern Fire Fighters